Education and Dramatic Art

David Hornbrook

Blackwell Education

First published 1989

© David Hornbrook 1989

Published by Basil Blackwell Ltd
108 Cowley Road
Oxford OX4 1JF
England

British Library Cataloguing in Publication Data
Mornbrook, David
 Education and dramatic art
 1. Great Britain. Education. Curriculum subjects: Creative arts
 I. Title
 700'.7'1041

 ISBN 0–631 16263–1
 ISBN 0–631–16264–X pbk

Typeset by Graphicraft Typesetters Ltd, Hong Kong.
Printed in Great Britain by T.J. Press (Padstow) Ltd, Padstow, Cornwall.

To Denys John

Science is meaningless because it gives no answer to our question, the only important question for us, 'What shall we do and how shall we live?'

Leo Tolstoy

Acknowledgements

The author and publisher would like to thank the following for permission to reproduce copyright materials:

B.T. Batsford Limited for an extract from *Drama and Education* by B. Watkins; Century Hutchinson Limited for extracts from the following books: *Dorothy Heathcote; Drama as a Learning Medium* by Betty Jane Wagner, and *Teaching Drama; A Mind of Many Wonders* by Norah Morgan and Juliana Saxton; David Clegg and Robin Pemberton-Billing for an extract from *Teaching Drama*, published by University of London Press, 1971; *Drama Broadsheet*, the journal of the National Association for the Teaching of Drama, for Figure 1 in Chapter 2;

H.M.S.O., for extracts from *English for ages 5–16* and *Drama 5–16* in the *Curriculum Matters* series; The London East Anglian Group and the Inner London Education Authority for extracts from a pilot scheme syllabus for GCSE Drama and Theatre Arts (Dramatic Art) – Mode II, Modular; New Theatre Quarterly for the English translation of the performance analysis questionnaire, translation by Susan Bassnett.

We would also like to thank Martine Franck and Magnum Photos for permission to use the photograph on the cover, from a performance by Le Theatre du Soleil of *1789: The French Revolution, Year one*.

Every effort has been made to trace and contact copyright holders but in a few instances without success. We apologize for any errors or omissions in the above list, and would be grateful for notification of any corrections that should be incorporated in any future edition of this volume.

Contents

Part Two
Drama-in-education: Interpreting the Text

Part Three
Towards Dramatic Art

Preface

Walking across the playground one day, I overheard a fragment of conversation. Two third-year pupils had obviously been discussing the relative merits of items on their curricular menu. As I passed, unobserved, one said to the other, 'What about drama?' Drama?', replied her friend, with the facial expression of someone coming across something unspeakable on the lettuce, 'drama's *boring*'.

Food for thought, after five years as head of the school's drama department. A raw nerve touched. Drama boring? Impossible. In what other subject could pupils play games and express themselves as they liked? Was not drama the very embodiment of an education that sought above all to captivate the interest of the child? More honest reflection served only to deepen my anxiety. Was I really as confident as I had learnt to appear about what I was doing in my lessons?

I had brought with me from training college the idea that once in a school I should forget plays, actors and theatres and see myself instead engaged in what might be descibed as maturation therapy.

Drama was a kind of educational fertiliser; spread liberally about, it would help children to grow better. 'It', in those days, was a *pot pourri* of improvisation, games and trust exercises whose potency until then I had never doubted. As someone who had come to drama teaching from the theatre, it certainly left me less than inspired, but it was a shock to realise that its recipients might be, too.

Fifteen teaching years later, I now have the privilege of being able to observed large numbers of drama lessons in all manner of schools. I recognise in the young teachers I watch at work the same enthusiasm for drama, the same commitment to the pupils I like to think I myself displayed at that Bristol comprehensive school. I also see the same exhaustion and frustration, although worse now, as the added pressures of a harsher educational climate take their toll of energy and morale. What is more disturbing is that I frequently see the same drama lessons too.

It is surely surprising that, for all the methodological developments of the intervening years and for all the selfless dedication of drama teachers to their practices, the landscape of school drama should look much the same as we enter the 1990s as it appeared to do when I began teaching in the 1960s. Many might disagree, and, of course, some features have changed. Certainly in London, and doubtless elsewhere, gender and anti-racist issues, for example, now appear prominently on many drama teacher's agendas. Discussion generally is more common in the drama lesson than it used to be. Nevertheless, predominantly, children get into groups, pile up chairs, make up improvisations and show them at the end of the lesson. Even the introduction of GCSE has on the whole failed to break this pattern. Indeed, some syllabuses have implicitly enshrined it. Meanwhile, despite a plethora of books and journal articles assuring us that the contrary is the case, the questions we asked ourselves then about content, about aims, about evaluation, about discipline, about progression, remain largely unanswered.

Now, suddenly, there is a new urgency. When the National Curriculum Consultation Document was published in July 1987, drama teachers were appalled to see that drama was missing from the list of prescribed core and foundation subjects. Later, as the Education Reform Bill made its way through parliament, it became apparent that while art and music were to retain their subject status, drama was to be included in the remit of the English working group. Despite considerable lobbying on behalf of the arts as a discrete area of the curriculum, the government's original proposals passed into law largely unscathed. Drama is not a foundation subject.

In its report, *English for Ages 5 to 16*, the English working group deals as generously with drama as could be expected. Charged by the Secretary of State to consider English as providing 'one appropriate context for the development of drama across the curriculum', Professor Cox and his colleagues conclude that drama is 'both a creative art form in its own right and also an instrument of learning'. Given their terms of reference, it is hardly surprising that they place the greater emphasis on the latter. For the working group, 'drama is one of the key ways in which children can gain an understanding of themselves and of others, can gain confidence in themselves as decision-makers and problem-solvers, can learn to function collaboratively, and can explore – within a supportive framework – only a range of human feelings, but also a whole spectrum of social situations and/or moral dilemmas'. The Speaking and Listening programmes of study seem tailor-made for drama teachers; there, drama is 'recommended specifically as a learning medium'.

At secondary level, in key stages 3 and 4, acknowledgement is given to the place of performance and the study of dramatic texts. The report's authors see the 'mounting of school productions and active involvement in community or touring theatre' as 'of immense value'. Nevertheless, for drama teachers like myself, who long ago fought for the independence of their subject from English, the working group's quite genuine enthusiasm for drama is tempered somewhat with a sense of *déjà vu*. We have been here before. Also, at a time when secondary headteachers are hurriedly reorganising their curriculum structures to bring art, music, drama and dance together in 'arts clusters' of one kind or another, GCSE boards are scrambling to satisfy the demand for creative arts syallabuses, and the new BTEC in Performing Arts is galloping like the Good News from Ghent to the country's FE colleges, the curricular re-coupling of drama to English does seem peculiarly inapposite.

Perhaps we are ill-advised to seek for too much consistency in the government's new curriculum. By all accounts, it was expeditiously cobbled together as very much a second order political matter. Most observers believe that local management will have a much more profound effect on the country's education than the national curriculum. Whatever the philosophy underlying the government's simple ten-subject prescription (I attempt to unearth some of it in this book), the grammar school ideal of Tory Party mythology will not be what emerges from the various working groups and committees of professional educators. Who would have thought that ex-*Black Paper* editor Brian Cox, for example, once scourge of the progressivists, would, twenty years later, find himself being praised by the National Association for the Teaching of English for his stand against the crudities of parsing and learning by rote?

Foremost among the professionals concerned to protect the best of current practice against the winds of political opportunism are HM Inspectors of Schools. Within weeks of the publication of *English for Ages 5 to 16*, in July 1989, HMI's, *Drama 5 to 16* appeared in their *Curriculum Matters* series. In the document's first introductory paragraph, HMI assure us that drama is 'a practical artistic subject', ranging 'from children's structured play, through classroom improvisations and performances of specially devised material to performances of Shakespeare'. While *Drama 5 to 16* embraces all the many manifestations of drama in schools, including the use of drama as a learning method in the context of English, the picture it paints is of an arts discipline with its own particular associated skills and ways of understanding. With careful, strategic reference to the national curriculum, HMI suggest that 'drama encompasses the art of the theatre and involves some of the technologies or the applications of the sciences, as in designing and making scenery or controlling sound and lighting'. The document highlights the 'public aspects' of drama, emphasising the way 'performing and sharing work with others, provide important links between schools, parents and their communities'.

All this is very positive. In the same month the NCC Arts in School Project came to its formal conclusion with a hugely over-subscribed conference at the University of Warwick. Chastened perhaps by the events of the previous two years, 90 per cent of the 600 arts delegates voted for attainment targets rather than the recommended guidelines for the arts. Early in 1989, the British Film Institute's *Primary Media Education* spelt out what attainment targets in media studies might be like; as I write, the Arts Council is convening a working group to do the same for drama.

Things are on the move, and there is much still to play for. In looking at some of the paradoxes of drama-in-education I shall try to make sense of them against the background of this wider and fast-changing historical scene. In proposing ways forward I shall be revealing no secret formula, no transforming educational medication. My modest aim is to offer drama teachers ways of recognising, legitimating and developing what is best in their practice, in all its rich variety, so that curricular objectives may be articulated with more confidence and clarity.

Although the form of this book is unapologetically theoretical, it is not a book which itself proposes a pedagogic theory. It aims to be descriptive and interpretative rather than prescriptive and definitive. In that over-worked aphorism, it starts where teachers are, in the everyday experience of their classes and out-of-school drama activities, and it attempts to bring to all that enthusiasm, integrity and expertise, a structure whereby we may better understand both what we have been doing and where we might go.

In proposing 'dramatic art' as a form which is both social and sociable I have been much influenced by the work of the late Raymond Williams. His straightforward commitment to active democracy and a good common culture together with his refusal to regard as anything but extremely difficult the processes of getting there have been a constant inspiration. Closer to home, I would like to thank Sian Ede, Sally Hodgson, Andy Kempe and Ken Robinson for their critical support and patient reading of early drafts. Above all, I am grateful to Fred Inglis, whose sharp eye exposed many intellectual blunders but whose generous offerings of roast lamb and agreeable conversation sustained me over a long period.

David Hornbrook, July 1989

Part One

Drama-in-education:
Telling the Story

1

The Plot: The Rise of
Drama-in-education

Noble savages in an English Arcadia

Theory, and the challenge it implicitly presents to empiricism and 'common sense', is viewed, like ideology, with some suspicion by a culture traditionally disposed to favour practical ways of doing things. For years the drama-in-education community has been conventionally instrumental in just this way, generally preferring to discuss and progress working methods rather than to worry too much about their theoretical or ideological implications. However, simply to ignore the existence of theory in the conduct of human affairs is to render ourselves powerless in the first instance to interpret events and then to influence them. Formulating theories is the way we make sense of our experience by giving ourselves meaningful structures within which it may be explained.

I would argue that the ways we have been encouraged to talk about drama-in-education and its characterising practices are in the grip of implicit theories of this kind. In the struggle over methodology, which has dominated the school drama debate for over thirty years, they have long since been buried in the assumptions which inform the debate itself. It is my intention in this book to bring some of these theories out into the open.

Immanent to this project will be my belief that for drama to legitimate itself within education it must be theorised within culture and history as a demonstrably *social* form. My developing critique of current practice will show the extent to which drama-in-education has been traditionally preoccupied with the privatisation of experience, a paradox nowhere better exemplified than in its self-imposed isolation from generally accepted ideas about theatre. I will argue that far from being a radicalising process, this privatisation has manacled school drama to narrow forms of individualism which have inhibited access to our dramatic culture.

The distinctive discourse of educational drama arises from a series of inter-connected assumptions associated with the progressive education movement. This movement, in turn, has its origins in the revolutionary spirit of late eighteenth-century Romanticism, so that in Jean-Jacques Rousseau's model of pre-civilised man [*sic*] free from the corrupting influence of city life, his noble savage imbued with natural goodness whose infallible guide was his feelings, we may recognise the ghostly prototype of the paradigmatic student of educational drama.[1]

The autonomy of consciousness advocated by Rousseau, with its extention into a universality of moral feeling, where the source of moral rectitude is seen to reside not in the hands of the gods and their earthly representatives, but in the authentic examination of the self, 'the true and uncorrupted conscience', lies at the heart of the challenge that was to be offered to conventional ethics by Romanticism.[2]

This idea of a subjective morality accessible through an awareness of our true feelings also permeates thinking about school drama. It has long been supposed that pupils engaged in the spontaneous improvisation and role-playing of the drama lesson can lose themselves just sufficiently for their 'deeply felt', and by implication, *genuine*, morality to reveal itself. Gavin Bolton puts it succinctly when he proposes that while 'in the unreality of the classroom' pupils 'may adopt an intellectual posture of accepting the notion of shades of opinion, what surfaces in drama is their real feelings'.[3]

Real feelings and personal values are thus concepts common to Romanticism and drama-in-education. In both, they indicate a commitment to a private world of sensation where cognitive endeavour is often confined to knowledge about what one truly feels.

Rousseau, of course, also had strong views about drama. His well-known polemic against Jean le Rond d'Alembert,[4] who had suggested that the city of Geneva might improve its amenities by building a theatre, reveals not so much a puritanical dislike of pleasure, but rather a perception of theatre art as leading to the falsification of the self. To be sure, the cramped, odorous playhouses of eighteenth-century France can hardly have been places of moral or spiritual self-enhancement. For Rousseau, committed as he was to the authentic voice of conscience, the actor on the stage deliberately distanced himself from the universality of moral feeling, thus diminishing his own authenticity by 'counterfeiting himself', by 'putting on another character than his own'.

Rousseau proposed instead the replacement of those 'exclusive entertainments which close up a small number of people in melancholy fashion in a gloomy cavern, which keeps them fearful and immobile in silence and inaction,' with open-air festivities of communal participation:

> Let the spectators become an entertainment to themselves; make them actors themselves; do it so that each one sees and loves himself in the others.[5]

We can see clearly reflected in drama-in-education both Rousseau's deep-seated suspicion of the entire apparatus of theatrical illusion, his distaste for 'counterfeiting', as well as his enthusiasm for the home-made authenticity of participatory drama.

Certainly, in the contemporary context, it might fairly be said that real feelings and personal values have no more a place on the stages of Shaftesbury Avenue or the South Bank than they did on those of eighteenth-century Paris. However, already there are problems here. We should be careful of making too easy a distinction between the 'false' world of the theatre and the 'genuine' world of human interaction. Also, although we often speak confidently of our *real* feelings, how is it possible for us to make a distinction between the feelings we have so that we may intelligibly say of some that they are true and of others that they are false? Furthermore, who is to mediate between your morality and mine when our 'true and uncorrupted consciences' lead us to different conclusions? These (peculiarly modern) dilemmas will be much my concern in the argument that follows, for they lie at the heart of educational drama.

If not in its playhouses, historically England did provide more fertile and stable ground for the seeding of these particular products of Romantic naturalism than the turbulent politics of nineteenth-century France were able to offer. Without the home-grown images of political despotism that inspired the cataclysmic, liberationist visions of their European counter-parts, English Romantic artists turned instead to attack the economic despotism of the Industrial Revolution. This they saw as callous and philistinic, fundamentally at odds with the arcadian individualism of Rousseau's 'uncorrupted conscience'. The expanding working-class ghettoes of the new cities were the antithesis of naturalism, their inhabitants as far from ideals of simple pastoral nobility that it was possible to imagine. Against the bleak, dehumanising townscapes of industry the English Romantics fielded, not a class-based politics of revolution, but the sensibility of the radical individual. Human liberation was to come about not as a result of class struggle, but through love, creation and self-expression. There was to be a revolution of feeling, a new self-awareness, leading to a nobler, more progressive, humanism.

It is perhaps ironic that the first English progressive schools, established to further this aesthetic, were patronised by members of a prosperous and comfortable new social class who, in their revulsion with the industrial squalor brought about by their forebears' indiscriminate wealth-making, sought to insulate their children from its less attractive consequences. Schools like Abbotsholme (1889) and Bedales (1893) provided idyllic pastoral environments, far removed from the material and moral pollution of Blake's 'chartered streets',[6] where the sons and daughters of the rentiers could happily indulge in pre-industrial pursuits. The education they received eschewed the institutionalised brutalities and regimentation of the English public school, and fostered instead the cultivation of individual sensitivity. Progressive school teachers aimed to liberate the spirit of their pupils, allowing them access to the uncorrupted conscience of Rousseau's moral and aesthetic universe. It this respect they saw themselves as educational facilitators rather than teachers in the conventional sense, offering opportunities for the growth of learning in place of the imposition of knowledge.

It is here that the radical spirit of drama-in-education has its source. Advocates of school drama have long been the champions of a humane, child-centred individualism in education, believing, often passionately, in the liberating powers of self-knowledge. Most drama teachers in schools would probably still consider themselves to be 'progressive', in the widest sense of that word, favourably comparing their open and 'empowering' practices with what they see as the stifling, conformist pedagogy of other areas of the curriculum. Like true Romantics they are likely to share a deep suspicion of society's institutions and of hierarchies of all kinds, and will regard themselves as the allies rather than the directors of those they teach. Nowadays their naturalism is more usually expressed in the language of developmental psychology rather than in the soul-searching metaphors of Romanticism, but, as we shall see, the (by no means ignoble) ideals of progressivism still inform their practices.

Art and the play of life

There were, of course, no theatres in Arcadia. Virgil's young shepherds and poets were in as little danger of being corrupted by the 'intemperate madness' that Rousseau perceived in Aristotelian catharsis as were the boys and girls of Abbotsholme and Bedales. However, it is important to remember that although theatre as an institution was disapproved of, art itself, defined pre-eminently as the expression of an inner creative process, had by the end of the nineteenth century assumed a predominant place in the education of the liberated consciousness. Indeed, the idea that personal autonomy is fostered by art is fundamental to all progressive education. Children put paint on paper or make shapes out of clay with no avowed intention of ever becoming painters or potters, but because the very practice of art is seen as a way of nurturing a child's imagination and creativity.

The experiments of the Austrian art teacher Franz Cizek, who opened free classes for children at the School of Applied Art in Vienna in 1898, provide a pertinent example of the way in which these new ideas about art in education began to take shape. Young people came to his studio to paint and draw as the mood took them, and Cizek, always encouraging, made a point of never interfering or attempting to correct their drawings. From time to time he would randomly select work for display. An archetypal early progressivist, Cizek aimed through his classes to awaken the unconscious art which he believed lay in everybody. The colourful walls of today's primary and infant classrooms are evidence of his continuing influence.

Drama's eventual guarantee of a place in this aesthetic owed no more to conventional theatre practice than Cizek's art classes did to the academies. Rather, there was an understanding among early progressivists that the innocent make-believe of children's play was a form of highly beneficial 'natural' education in itself. By fusing 'play' in this sense with the idea of the 'player' on the stage, Cambridge schoolmaster Henry Caldwell Cook was the first to describe a comprehensive programme for what we might now call drama-in-education.[7]

Caldwell Cook saw play as an intrinsic human activity, 'the only work worth doing,' and believed intuitively in what the child psychologists were later to formalise into an influential theory of learning. As Head of English at the Perse School, he encouraged the performance of plays, both in the classroom and later in what must have been the first purpose-built drama room, which he called 'The Mummery'. He considered that 'acting out' motivated the boys to a more profound understanding of dramatic literature than could be achieved by formal teaching. While Shakespeare figured predominantly in what would now be considered rather formal exercises (fourth form pupils were expected to learn a minimum of twenty lines a week), groups of boys were also encouraged to write material of their own for performance. His book, The Play Way, published in 1917, its heady progressivism expressed in the author's idiosyncratic Boys' Own Paper style, completely reflects the reformist spirit of ideas about art and education abroad at this time.[8] Caldwell Cook's ideal school, his 'Play School' of the future, was, characteristically, to be situated in the country, away from the detrimental influences of city life, and would be governed by a kind of Athenian Assembly of all its members. Singing, Drawing, Acting and the

writing of Poetry would dominate the timetable alongside crafts like Car-
pentry, Weaving, Printing, Bookbinding and Gardening. Discipline was to
be founded on mutual trust and understanding, based on the observance of
'right conduct':

> We must let ourselves live fully, by doing thoroughly those things we
> have a natural desire to do; the sole restrictions being that we so order
> the course of our life as not to impair those energies by which we live,
> nor hinder other men so long as they seem also to be living well. Right
> and wrong in the play of life are not different from the right and
> wrong of the playing field.[9]

It is worth noting here, that by superimposing the morality of English team
games onto the free spirit of Romanticism, Caldwell Cook was unwittingly
rehearsing an ethical conundrum which continues to haunt drama-in-
education. At what point does our right to do 'those things we have a
natural desire to do' give way to the demands of 'right conduct'? In a world
where the values of the public school playing field are by no means
universally accepted, who is to adjudicate?[10] These are important questions, and I shall return to them later.

It was the advent of psychoanalysis, and in particular the attention given
by post-Freudians to the significance of children's play, that finally legitimated drama within the 'inner-world' concept of creativity favoured by
educational progressivists. The plausibly scientific recognition of play as a
form of instinctive learning, with its accepted 'naturalness' and powerful
'let's pretend' element, enabled the teleological gap between self-
authentication and acting to be convincingly bridged. By the dawn of the
new century, Karl Groos had already published the influential book in
which he identified play as practice for adult life,[11] and it was not long
before a succession of post-Freudian psychologists had elevated the play of
young children to a dominating position in theories of early learning. By
1952 Susan Isaacs was able to assert confidently that:

> The child's make-believe play is thus significant not only for the
> adaptive and creative intentions which when fully developed mark out
> the artist, the novelist and the poet, but also for the sense of reality,
> the scientific attitude and the growth of hypothetical reasoning.[12]

While theatrical performance, even in 'The Mummery', might still be
considered as the antithesis of naturalness, the fantasies of an innocent
child, acted out in the playground or street, could be represented as a real
drama, rich both in creativity and learning. Furthermore, psychology had

now declared such spontaneous 'acting out' to be necessary for the child's adequate development. This kind of performance, flowing apparently from the unconscious inner world of the child, could thus not only claim a secure place among those arts processes already dedicated to the exploration of subjective feeling, but by virtue of its psychological imperative, could also claim to transcend them. From being an innocent diversion, drama, through the offices of psychology, had become a fundamental need.

> Drama both of the less and more formal kinds, for which children, owing to their happy lack of self-consciousness, display such remarkable gifts, offers further good opportunities of developing that power of expression in movement which, if the psychologists are right, is so closely correlated with the development of perception and feeling.[13]

Brought in from the cold by the child psychologists and psycho-therapists of the 1930s and 1940s, drama was now in a position to make its mark on the school curriculum. It was to present its credentials not, as first might be expected, in the form of a body of theatrical skills and practices, but as a psychological process, dedicated to the aesthetic and developmental 'needs' of the young. With their acceptance, drama in schools may be seen as the crowning achievement of English progressivism, embracing as it does all that movement's major precepts. The universality of moral feeling and the primacy of the subjective, the authentication of the self through the exercise of the creative faculty, the need to play; these are the cherished tropes of drama-in-education. They encapsulate its humanity as well as its naïvety, holding together a vision of a better world, but, as we shall see, lacking still the crucial political and social dimension through which such a vision might be realised.

Child drama and after

By the outbreak of the Second World War all the guiding principles of school drama were in circulation. The war itself gave new impetus to thinking about education, providing the will and circumstance for the structural changes necessary for the incorporation of drama in the post-war curriculum. This wartime debate proved to be the historical backdrop before which the disparate philosophical elements of school drama progressed from the educational fringes into legitimacy. In 1943 the Educational Drama Association was founded, and in the same year Peter Slade was appointed Drama Adviser for Staffordshire; by 1951 school drama was receiving all-important Ministry of Education recognition.

It is true that many schools still include little or no drama in any part
of their curriculum, but so many others do find room for it in one
form or another that drama can now be regarded as an established
and worthwhile part of school life.[14]

Despite his early struggles, Peter Slade was soon to find himself established within an increasingly fashionable new progressivism. By the time
his seminal book *Child Drama* was published in 1954,[15] the philosophy
which inspired it was gaining significant influence in the corridors of
educational policy-making. Slade's book (together with its popular pocket-
sized follow-up which appeared four years later[16]) came to inform the
practice of a newly created generation of drama teachers.

The post-war population bulge and the expanding teaching force of
the 1960s had created an urgent need for more teacher-trainers.[17] School-
teachers with drama backgrounds ranging from English and amateur
dramatics to licentiateships from the speech and drama academies suddenly
found themselves swept into the new or enlarged teacher-training colleges
on a wave of progressivist enthusiasm, and entrusted with the preparation
of students in Educational Drama. Well-intentioned and optimistic, but
themselves often desperately ill-prepared, they turned to the only theory
available, and that lay in the pages of *Child Drama*.

Like Cizek, Peter Slade believed that the creative activity of children
should not be measured by adult standards; he argued that Child Drama 'is
an Art in itself'. In the classroom he stressed the importance of non-
interference in the natural creative process, suggesting that the teacher
should instead become a 'loving ally', not criticising or directing but
perhaps drawing a group's attention 'to some little piece of beauty they
may have missed'. Conscious no doubt of the force of the child-psychology
argument, he emphasised the distinction between the spontaneous processes of classroom drama, 'drama in the widest sense', and the theatre 'as
understood by adults'.

> Theatre means an ordered occasion of entertainment and shared
> emotional experience; there are actors and audience – differentiated.
> But the child, if unspoiled, feels no such differentiation, particularly in
> the early years – each person is both actor and audience.[18]

By elevating classroom drama in a way which sought not only to distance
it from general theatre practice but also to invest it by implication with a
superior moral status, Slade inherited the aesthetic of Rousseau's romantic
naturalism and inscribed it irrevocably in contemporary theories of drama
in schools. Indeed, such was the depth of this ideological commitment that

drama teachers soon found themselves redefining the word 'drama' itself, corralling it and branding it into the exclusive service of their practice. To this day there are drama teachers who will happily subscribe to a semantic sleight of hand whereby 'drama' gathers to itself all the affirmative elements of the discourse, such as creativity, sincerity and need, while 'theatre' has to resign itself to a thoroughly non-progressive and disapprobatory residue of illusion, inauthenticity and irrelevance.

As well as a mistrust of adult theatre, the primacy of self-expression and the discovery of moral truth by inner reflection quickly became recognised as characterising features of the new Sladian aesthetic.

> ... in this drama, two important qualities are noticeable – *absorption* and *sincerity*. Absorption is being completely wrapped up in what is being done, or what one is doing, to the exclusion of all other thoughts ... Sincerity is a complete form of honesty in portraying a part, bringing with it an intense feeling of reality and experience ...[19]

This emphasis on the active and spontaneous participation of children in dramatic games and improvisations draws our attention to another of school drama's inherent dilemmas; that of evaluation. If the teacher's relationship with Child Drama was vitally non-critical then how was it possible to know to what extent its educational aims were actually being realised? Attempts to deal with this problem have led to children being assessed not on how much they know or by what skills they have acquired, or indeed by some measure of originality of response, but on their degree of complicity with the structure set up by the teacher. Those members of the class who are (or who at least seem to be) most sincerely absorbed in what the teacher has planned for them are, by this token, the most meritorious; those equally absorbed in rival activities, such as chattering or looking out of the window, the least so. What is surfacing here is the dilemma surrounding Caldwell Cook's belief in 'right conduct'. Despite his enthusiasm for spontaneity and his desire not to criticise, Slade himself was in little doubt about the rules of 'the play of life'.

> Pointing out the need for cleanliness and good manners will often help them (the lads in the school) to grow up and be more acceptable to the young women ... Girls do not take kindly to rather ragged, rough mannered clowns who spoil the drama period.[20]

In terms that Aristotle might have understood, honour is due to those with clean hands and good manners! This tendency to assess acquiescence in the absence of any other acceptable criteria is still much in evidence, as we shall see.

Despite these reservations, there is no doubt that the pioneer work of Peter Slade in those years following the war enthused huge numbers of young teachers and succeeded in establishing drama as a force in state education. The Newsom Report of 1963 which expressed its concern over the education system's apparent failure with the less able, gave much credence to the psycho-therapeutic role of drama in countering the 'social maladroitness and insensitivity' of 'less gifted' young people. Art, according to Newsom, and Educational Drama in particular, should be regarded not as a 'frill', but as a way of helping young people 'to come to terms with themselves'.

By playing out psychologically significant situations, they can work out their own personal problems.[21]

The idea that school drama has much to do with children's psychological adjustment to their social circumstances figured prominently in the rash of handbooks which followed the success of *Child Drama*. Probably the most notable of these was Brian Way's *Development Through Drama*. Published in 1967 in the wake of The Plowden Report's endorsement of progressivism, *Development Through Drama* provided just the right mix of theory and practical advice to stimulate and inspire a second wave of young drama teachers in the enormous, post B.Ed. expansion.[22] Way reinforced Slade's distinction between 'theatre' and 'drama', but largely abandoned his idea of Child Drama as Art in favour of a comprehensive theory of personal development. Believing, along with the child psychologists, that play is practice for adult life, and hypothesising that it is an instinctive need artificially suppressed after early childhood, Way saw school drama as a means of restoring the 'natural' developmental processes which play encourages:

Fully developed people will seldom make poor or uninteresting drama, even though it may not be brilliant ... drama, far from being new, is closely interwoven in the practical implementation of both the spirit and the sbstance of every Education Act that has ever been passed, especially the idea of the development of the whole person.[23]

On closer inspection, the 'whole person', the unique 'human essence' for whom Way's drama lessons have been a gradual nurturing process, turns out to be a decent, law-abiding liberal humanist, the heir surely of Rousseau's noble savage, sensitive, tolerant, imaginative and reflective, fitting in well to the social environment, yet managing to be creative and original (within acceptable limits).

Through the mid-1960s and early 1970s book after book professed to demonstrate how drama-in-education developed 'self-confidence', or encouraged 'personal awareness and an awareness of others', or taught children how to co-operate in groups, or fostered qualities of 'tolerance and understanding', or helped children to become more 'self-disciplined'.[24] Just about the only thing school drama made no claims to do, and by this time many teachers would have been puzzled to have it suggested, was to equip young people with an understanding of their dramatic culture.

Learning through drama

There was a tendency in the 1960s and 1970s for drama teachers to be content with the assumption that as long as their pupils were sufficiently 'absorbed' in their improvisations then they were 'developing' satisfactorily. Books offering catalogues of 'ideas for drama' proliferated, and teachers dipped liberally into menus of themes such as 'Conflict', or 'The Family' or 'A Fairground'. However, on the whole they felt no particular obligation to contextualise the drama nor to attempt to improve the performance skills of their classes; instead they tried hard not to interfere (unless discipline demanded it) with the 'natural creativity' of their groups. Often children were led through imaginative exercises of one kind or another, or more frequently encouraged to play energetic drama games before collapsing into small groups to make up plays to be performed (time permitting) at the end of the lesson. Such educational scepticism as there was about these practices could be dismissed as straightforwardly reactionary, with the confident assumption that more traditionally minded teachers who might express worries about the noise and apparent anarchy of the drama class would, given time, become aware of its assuredly self-evident value.

There were some dissenting voices. John Pick and David Clegg both raised fundamental questions about the theory and practice of drama in schools, but after brief defensive flurries and a general closing of ranks, their concerns receded into obscurity.[25]

One of the handful of practitioners who responded in print to Clegg's challenge was a lecturer at the University of Newcastle upon Tyne, Dorothy Heathcote. In a letter published in 1973, Heathcote agreed with Clegg that school drama was suffering from a tendency to create 'high priests', unthinking allegiance to whom was ossifying practice. She shared his worries about teacher training, and argued that it was necessary to prepare drama teachers 'who can stimulate commitment' and 'follow it through to meaningful learning'.[26]

The changes of approach indicated here were radical, and were perceived as so by those who had seen Heathcote at work. Observers could hardly have failed to be aware of her dominant, directorial relationship to the drama, or of her willingness on occasions to become a participant 'in role', joining in apparently on equal terms with the children. They would also have noted the extensive time allowed for debate, even for writing, amounting to a conscious challenging and shaping of the children's ideas. (For an example, see Appendix A.) All this must have been profoundly unsettling for drama teachers used to the non-interventionist strategies of Child Drama and drama for personal development.

For Heathcote, the teacher's aim was to use drama 'in the way in which it will most aid him in challenging the children to learn'.[27] By channelling the motivating energy of dramatic play into the curricular imperatives of the teacher, she slowly succeeded in diverting thinking about school drama from its more overtly therapeutic course and re-defining it as a learning process. Through the sensitive agency of the teacher, Heathcote argued, the imaginative world simulated by the drama would reveal to a class new insights and understandings. With a most significant shift of emphasis, knowledge (as opposed to art or personal development) was now to be the goal; from this time forward drama would be claiming a place on the epistemological curriculum. Furthermore, the knowledge achieved through drama of this kind was judged to be of a special kind. Inaccessible through empiricism or logic, it was instead to be induced through the examination of the 'subjective process'. 'Drama for understanding' or 'drama for knowing' became key concepts in a new language of 'authenticity', 'negotiation' and 'universals', whereby it was argued that by manipulating dramatic improvisation, children could be led to an 'authentic experience', a so-called 'deep knowing', of the essential truths of the human condition. Rather than being the subject of pedagogy, drama-in-education became a sophisticated form of pedagogy itself.

It should not be forgotten that these changes were being brought about against a background of educational contraction. By the early 1980s the number of specialist initial training courses in drama teaching had fallen from over fifty in the mid-1970s to only seven. While this to some extent reflects a more general cutback in teacher education, the relative drop in drama courses was particularly severe. There were many drama teachers at this time understandably willing to see Heathcote and her new methodology as the potential saviours of their discipline.

Thus it was that, despite Schools Council recommendations for a more eclectic approach,[28] the dissection and analysis of Heathcote's methodology came to mark out the parameters of acceptable drama in schools. Likewise, the charismatic qualities of her remarkable presence began to bewitch the increasing numbers of drama teachers who came to watch and participate in her workshops; two early converts described her work as 'breath-taking'.[29] By 1979, a comprehensive account of her techniques, *Dorothy Meathcote: Drama as a Learning Medium*, was on the shelves of English book-shops.

For ordinary teachers inspired by her innovative way of working, the old handbooks of themes for drama now seemed paltry. New collections of lesson ideas by drama specialists with ordinary school experience translated Heathcote's idiosyncratic skills, such as 'teacher-in-role', into manageable techniques for the classroom.[31] Less happily, as we shall see, a fierce sectarianism gripped drama-in-education as ranks closed around the new methodologies. A host of eulogies flowed from the pens of Heathcote devotees during the 1980s, ranging from the worthy to the unshamefacedly messianic, but all united in their devotion to the words and deeds of this remarkable figure. Even after her retirement from Newcastle in 1986, past accounts of Heathcote's drama workshops were still being dissected and analysed by her admirers for the wisdoms they might offer up.

Unfortunately, for some at least, the return from Damascus proved to be a sobering experience. The newly converted, not unnaturally, attempted to imitate Heathcote's techniques back in their classrooms, but confronted with the frustrations of their forty-minute lessons and the daily battles of the school many teachers saw themselves as failing to live up to her exacting standards (see Appendix A). For others, it has to be said, the Heathcote revolution simply passed them by. Despite its persuasive methodology and its very considerable claims on the curriculum, evidence suggests that this latest manifestation of drama-in-education was rather less successful in engaging with the day-to-day practice of drama teaching than might be thought from reading the literature.

While this chapter has been by way of a contextualised history of an educational movement, I have also attempted to set the scene for some of the agruments which follow. Thus, while tracing the development of drama-in-education from its ideological origins in late eighteenth-century Romanticism through to its emergence as an expressive form within progressive education and its acceptance onto the English school curriculum, certain key dilemmas have been identified. I wish now to look more closely at two principal players in our story and examine the strange but powerful fusion of practice and personality which sustained their hierarchical dominance over drama-in-education in the 1980s.

2

The Players: Dorothy, Gavin and the New Muggletonians

I will give power unto my two witnesses, and they shall prophesy one thousand and two hundred and threescore days . . .

(Revelation 11.)

Mystifications and dramatic midwifery

It is impossible to embark upon an examination of the complex texture of drama-in-education in the 1980s without acknowledging at an early stage the overarching presence of Dorothy Heathcote and Gavin Bolton. Although by this time both had long been members of university departments, their domination of thinking about practical, classroom drama during the 1980s was comprehensive, at least as influential as Peter Slade's had been for an earlier generation of drama teachers. They managed to inspire in their supporters a tenacious loyalty to the forms of dramatic pedagogy which they advocated, forms which by the mid-1980s seemed to many set to change irrevocably the agenda of drama-in-education.

In the event, as we shall see, history was not to deal kindly with their version of drama as cross-curricular pedagogy, and the impact of the new methods on actual classroom practice was in reality very much more modest than has often been claimed. Also, although the radical seriousness represented by techniques such as 'teacher-in-role' blew through the aimless games and improvisations of many drama classrooms of the 1970s with the promise of a new purposefulness, this alone is not enough to explain the way these two practitioners maintained a such a grip on the field for over a decade.

In 1954, Peter Slade had painted a vivid picture of the magical world of Child Drama, which he claimed should remain for the child a realm of mystic secrecy'.[1] Subsequent literature abounds with similar sentiments.

In creative drama work . . . we are helped enormously to soar into the world of magic and mystery – the world in which our most private and peculiar selves obtain that which enables the metamorphosis from 'existing' to 'being' to happen.[2]

By contrast, in her early writings, Dorothy Heathcote speaks of what she does with an appealing clarity. Here she is in the same year, 1967, defining 'dramatic improvisation':

> Very simply it means putting yourself into other people's shoes and, by using personal experience to help you to understand their point of view, you may discover more than you knew when you started.[3]

However, as the years passed, and forced perhaps by increasing demands to theorise her practice, this refreshing directness was replaced by a more convoluted, digressive style, where valuable insights into her dramatic practice became mixed up with excursions into her private and idiosyncratic bibliography. The result produced an effect hardly less mystifying than that which had so characterised the writing of her predecessors. This is all much in evidence in a published interview with David Davis twenty years later. Here is a section of that interview which its editor has seen fit to highlight:

> ... if theatre is anything to anybody, it is thick description, and if theatre is to be used for perception, perception will only come through thick description, this laid upon that, provided that slow incrementing of one experience on another is filled with – filled with joy.[4]

Later, Davis asks her about Brecht (editor's emphasis):

> I've always liked the notion of Brecht – I've never read him and I've never seen him, not in what I'd call a real Brechtian production – but always, even as a kid, I liked the notion of *'that which shall stand for this'* – not the book that looks like the book, but this that shall stand for it. I love that, I get great pleasure out of it, because I *play*, you know, I think that is *deep play* – that *I can see what I'm making it out of*. I love that.[5]

All true mystics and therapists demand of us that we suspend our rational disbelief and submit ourselves to their power before we can expect to reap the spiritual benefits. In such circumstances, as Ernest Gellner has pointed out, *'critical* considerations become assigned to the realm of symptoms, of the reducible, while *assent* is part of the endorsed authenticity.'[6] I would suggest that spiritual acquiescence came to characterise the discourse of drama-in-education in the 1980s and that the kind of dense, mystifying language illustrated above played a major part in Heathcote's ascension. It helped to envelop her with an aura of pedagogical magic which served both to deflect criticism and to reinforce her mystical status. Time and time again, the strident assentiveness of the language used to describe Heathcote and her work transforms potential analysis and explanation into simple expressions of allegiance.

> Heathcot-ites often sound like a nauseous, self-congratulatory group, but if affirmation is genuine it breeds that 'we-feeling' which our reductionist, mechanistic, techne-orientated society will slowly and inevitably destroy if it is not co-operatively challenged ... Dorothy Heathcote teaches people to dance with butterflies not fossilize them.[7]

> By heroic ... Dorothy refers to that level of experience wherein a person finds himself at one with the universal elements of existence, seeing himself suddenly not as an individual with private 'worldly' preoccupations, but as part of the mystery and magic of creation ...[8]

> When the moment of knowing is born, Dorothy weighs and measures it, pronounces it fit, and then, most difficult and important of all, gives it back to the person who made and fought for it.[9]

This last example, which is taken from an extended midwifery metaphor, is particularly revealing, for it combines the image of the plain woman rolling up her sleeves to do the job, with that of the officiating priestess. As Ann Seeley points out, with respect to this same passage, 'there was a time, after all, when "witch" and "midwife" referred to the same person'.[10] Seeley is understandably disquieted by the sexual politics of the analogy. However, this synthesis is likely to remain attractive to a discipline which has historically seen itself as uniquely equipped to lead children from the ordinary to the transcendent, from the 'real world' of the classroom to an 'awesome awareness of universal truths'.[11] With the subsequent need both to substantiate and advertise its metaphysic, the canonisation of a practitioner seemingly so specially able to conjure such transfigurations is then but a small step. What follows is that casual utterance becomes inscribed as text, texts become sacred, and dissent is reducible to heresy.

> Wherever Heathcote goes, she generates excitement and even adulation. She emanates power. Her power is like that of a *medium*, bringing into the present the distant in time or space, making it come alive in our consciousness through imagined group experience ... A spell has to be cast; rituals must be followed; conditions have to be right; the universal inherent in this moment must be realized, and she's witch-like in her control leading to this effect.[12]

Keeping it in the family

Gavin Bolton's rise to prominence in the shadow of Heathcote allowed him to complement his mentor in significant ways, not least by his attempts to give Heathcote's highly intuitive methodology respectable intellectual form. As Seeley comments, Heathcote's own explanations of her work 'depend upon a use of language which is idiosyncratic and not accessible to the traditional tools of academic criticism'.[13] Bolton, on the other hand, apparently able to 'play the academic game', was rapidly cast as drama-in-education's resident theoretician.

Seeley also reveals how Heathcote was invariably constructed by the school drama movement in conventionally feminine terms ('the midwife of creative knowing'), while Bolton ('the cool evaluator') was allowed to fulfil the expectations of the conventionally masculine. Certainly, in the archives of drama-in-education the names of Heathcote and Bolton will remain difficult to separate, if for no other reason than that they will be remembered for having 'mothered and fathered' the pedagogy upon which the reputation of school drama was once staked. For those who became committed to that pedagogy, however, these two eminent practitioners are more likely to be remembered familiarly as 'Dorothy and Gavin'.

We (Gavin and I) were discussing how we realise our own knowledge, and I said that I felt that I 'burrowed along like a mole in the dark', occasionally coming up to look around for a brief spell, whereas I felt Gavin flew over the terrain like an eagle seeing a large landscape and the patterns of it ...[14]

This extract from a piece by Heathcote was subsequently much used to differentiate between what were seen as the complementary attributes of the two progenitors. Its cosy 'Wind in the Willows' quality delivers a reassuring message to the offspring, who need little persuasion to respond in like manner – 'please, Eagle and Mole, don't apologise, don't feel threatened'. In the manner of families, Dorothy's and Gavin's deflects external criticism and quickly closes up against attack.

There is another less happy theme in Gavin's talk which is concerned with ideological conflicts between Gavin, Malcolm Ross and John Fines. My own feeling is that this conflict (made ugly by the fulminatory attacks on Gavin from Ross) arises from the nature of the academic roles shared by all three.[15]

Here, the disapprobatory use of Malcolm Ross's surname heightens the sense of exclusion while at the same time reinforcing the collective solidarity of the family itself. As for John Fines, his loyalties are quite clear:

> Now when you have had your hand slapped by someone as good and wise and noble as Gavin the best course of action is to stuff it into your armpit and grimace a little, but quietly in a corner . . . Surely we should all reverence what he has done and wait calmly but eagerly for the next episode?[16]

The trouble with this mode of discourse is that it obscures the vital distinction we must always make between utterance and utterer if we are to attempt a constructive evaluation of what is being said. The employment of first names, the avuncular familiarity, the selective use of critical judgement, make it almost impossible to prise the text from the personality. In a blur of disciplinary defensiveness, Gavin becomes inseparable from Gavin's theories; to challenge the idea is to threaten the person.

This tendency to conflate personality and agency is not, of course, confined to the world of school drama, but is a much more general feature of the twentieth-century consciousness, as many commentators have noted. Richard Sennett, for instance, makes the point that, as we are now prone to accept public exhibitions of authenticity for guarantees of political competence or incorruptibility, a charismatic political leader has no need to resort to demagogy to retain power.

> He can be warm, homey, and sweet; he can be sophisticated and debonair. But he will bind and blind people as surely as a demonic figure if he can focus them upon his tastes, what his wife is wearing in public, his love of dogs . . . What has grown out of the politics of personality begun in the last century is charisma as a force for stabilizing ordinary political life.[17]

Thus, the charismatic leader is free to display political or intellectual incompetence, or to admit to ignorance in areas which must seriously challenge his or her credentials to be a leader, just so long as the heart is worn on the sleeve (how often did we hear Ronald Reagan definitively described as 'a nice guy'?). The cult of personality which is ready to endorse all manner of actions and pronouncements on the grounds that they are 'authentically' felt by the protagonist, infuses drama-in-education, and has helped to hold its familial structure together.

Assaulting the ivory towers

Ever since drama teachers first moved away the desks and chairs and asked the children to 'find a space', educational drama has had 'doing' at the top of its methodological agenda. There has long been an assumption that, if drama in school achieved nothing else, at least it released pupils from the conventional structures of teaching and learning for which the traditional classroom layout was such a stark metaphor, and allowed a new physical freedom within which the expression of ideas and feelings might take place. In the early days 'doing' in this physical sense dominated the drama lesson to the exclusion of anything much else.

> Pupils who enter a drama lesson do not want to spend long periods of time locked in discussion. At first the class should consider suggestions quickly, begin rehearsal and then discuss and rehearse simultaneously, otherwise a conflict of ideas and personalities develops within the groups and nothing is created.[18]

For Fairclough here, and for drama teachers like him in the 1960s and early 1970s, so long as pupils were purposefully engaged in the prescribed activities, the criteria of Child Drama were considered to be satisfactorily fulfilled. While the 1980s brought the legitimation of 'discussion' as a valid constituent of the new 'learning through drama process', the legacy of 'doing' is still very evident among drama teachers. Physical activity is considered by many to be a supremely better way of resolving difficulties than mere intellection.

This emphasis on 'doing' has allowed drama to be increasingly identified with those pupils less likely to reach high levels of academic attainment. Drama teachers have thus become institutionally as well as temperamentally associated with the lower ability range. This allegiance has, in turn, led to a fiercely reductionist view of all forms of 'academic elitism'. Writers misguided enough to argue for a more intellectually rigorous approach to the teaching of drama are peremptorily dismissed as those who 'would lead drama in education away from the classroom where it belongs and towards the slowly stagnating swamps of academia'.[19] Jonothan Neeland's championing of 'Eagle and Mole', whom he exhorts to 'write for the *real audience* – classroom teachers, not obscure academics with axes to grind',[20] reflects this same antagonism, as does this teacher's spirited defence of Heathcote:

> D. H. [Dorothy Heathcote] constantly apologises for not having the answers or the right words. She should not *have* to apologise ... Art is

process. Creative struggle is infinite. Dead lines for dissertations . . .
create exactly that: *'dead-lines'* . . . Don't let these 'dead lines' rot on
these pages – resurrect them. Write or speak to me. Write or speak to
each other. Write and speak to yourself, but above all, do it affirma-
tively and trust your own intuition . . .[21]

It is worth noting that enthusiasm for simple subjective experience has
not prevented students of theories of dramatic pedagogy from arguing their
case in the most convoluted 'academic' ways. Thus, many writers who had
sprung to the defence of the idea that one can somehow subjectively *know
what should be done* have themselves engaged in objectifying projects of one
kind or another in defence of this same subjectivity. Examples are plentiful;
Figure 1 is an extract from a piece entitled 'Three Layers of Meaning in
Drama' by an ex-student of Heathcote's:

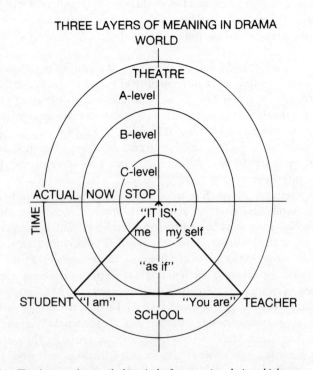

THREE LAYERS OF MEANING IN DRAMA

Figure 1   *Teacher, student and object/role form a triangle in which every person as
an 'I' is related to the object/role, the 'it'. The diagram shows the prime elements of
drama: two persons interrelated to each other by their mutual interest in an object or a
role which is embodying the theme or aspects of it . . .*[22]

Such an approach illustrates the highly selective nature of drama-in-education's attacks on theoretical discourse. Writing about school drama notoriously swings between extremes of obfuscation and honest naïvety, so that a simple statement of innocent incomprehension can be held to be a quite legitimate response when the intellectual going gets tough.[23] Within the family, such candid declarations serve only to reinforce the authenticity of its favoured members. After all, as Johnson and O'Neill point out, did not Dorothy herself benefit from her lack of contact with contagious academe?

> She never trained as a teacher or taught as a full-time member of staff in a school, and accounts for what she calls her 'innocence' of vision and expression by the lack of early exposure to intellectual and academic models. It is partly this which gives her work its unique flavour . . .[24]

Once again, by demonstrating, however briefly, their homely lack of academic 'pretension', their 'genuineness' as ordinary, common-sense kinds of people, while implying at the same time that their practices could be 'scientifically' validated if necessary, messengers and messages are jointly endorsed in the terms of the conceptual structures they themselves have helped to build. In the chumminess of the conference, theoretical discourse is not so much understood as measured by its author's family status. If 'Dorothy' chooses to use a language all of her own to describe her practice, that is an indication of her unique powers and our feeble comprehension. For Neelands, 'Dorothy's statements are not mystical – it's just that the academic, rigorous, objective, technical jargon . . . doesn't always exactly express her intentions as an artist'.[25]

The dilemma of appraisal

This perception has not helped the development of coherent assessment procedures for drama in schools, particularly as the major theorists of drama-in-education have themselves paid very little attention to how achievement in drama might be measured. At one time, of course, such matters were thought not to be the concern of educational practices which dealt with the intangible qualities of natural creativity and self-expression. However, in recent years the requirement for suitable evaluative criteria has become increasingly recognised; this has been no less the case in the arts than in other areas of the curriculum. Efforts that have been made to

formulate evaluative schemes for educational drama strikingly reveal the
field's contradictions and paradoxes. As Derek Rowntree explains:

> If we wish to discover the truth about an educational system, we must
> look into its assessment procedures ... How are its purposes and
> intentions realized? To what extent are the hopes and ideals, aims and
> objectives professed by the system ever truly perceived, valued and
> striven for by those who make their way within it? The answers to
> such questions are to be found in what the system requires children to
> do in order to survive and prosper. The spirit and style of student
> assessment defines the *de facto* curriculum.[26]

We have seen how Slade's conception of Child Drama, with its criteria of
'sincerity and absorption', raised difficult questions about appraisal. These
kinds of problems have continued to beset drama-in-education as it has
resolutely set its face away from theatrical practice and critical aesthetics.
In the early days, this dilemma was sharply manifest in the arguments over
the drama syllabuses of the Certificate of Secondary Education (CSE).
Those teachers who had not rejected the whole idea of assessment in drama
out of hand tried agonisingly to evolve means of testing 'involvement', or
the 'authenticity of response', or even 'development'.

A brief look at the assessment criteria of the first General Certificate of
Secondary Education (GCSE) syllabuses in drama reveals similar confu-
sions, this time inspired by the redesignation of school drama as a 'learning
process'. The *Leicestershire Mode III Drama*, for example, redefines drama as
'a problem solving activity', and aims, 'to foster confidence in adopting a
view to human problems, ideas and attitudes', and 'to develop competen-
cies met within socially interactive processes'.[27]

The lengths to which drama-in-education will sometimes go to exclude
discussion of the theatre from its assessment criteria and the evaluative
incoherence that arises as a consequence are well exemplified in Bolton's
post-mortem on a well-documented workshop at the Riverside Studios in
1978. After a series of three one-and-a-quarter-hour demonstration lessons
Bolton reflects with some satisfaction on what had been achieved with the
group of children:

> What do I think they had learnt? ... trust; protecting; negotiating
> meaning; and containing. I claim that each of these is a worthwhile
> experience for me and the class to share. But more than that I would
> be satisfied if I could guarantee that they have learned three vitally
> important things:
>
> 1) a new sensing of dramatic form and a glimmer of what works in
>   the dramatic process

2) at least a tentative grasp that drama is for understanding-this is its purpose

3) that this understanding is reached through finding an integrity of feeling.

I would not expect that the children themselves could articulate these points. If indeed I have planted these seeds then that class and I are ready to move forward with leaps and bounds. I may have achieved in three lessons (three long consecutive lessons) what it takes teachers with their one hour a week six months to achieve – and what those confined to thirty-five minutes periods have little chance of achieving.[28]

It is not necessary to pick over the bones of this workshop to have very substantial reservations about this piece of appraisal. For one thing, while it might reasonably be said that the children had learnt to trust a specific person, or set of purported facts, I am unclear how 'trust', or for that matter 'containing' or 'protecting', can ever be acquired in this *generalised* sense. Also, the three 'vitally important things' with which Bolton would express satisfaction seem to be excessively modest outcomes, particularly as there is no expectation 'that the children themselves could articulate these points'. An unarticulated, 'tentative grasp that drama is for understanding' must be very difficult indeed to spot. One is left with the impression that if this really is all that can come from such prolonged and concentrated educational drama work, then, as he rightly points out, what hope for the classroom teacher?

We should be profoundly concerned about the paucity of these outcomes and alarmed by the complacency with which they are offered. If drama teachers are being presented with these scarcely sustainable, minimal claims as a model of evaluation, it is no wonder that their own more formal assessment schemes are often such a muddle. A recent book by Norah Morgan and Juliana Saxton, in which the authors have attempted to construct a comprehensive system for teaching drama based on the ideas of Heathcote and Bolton, unwittingly but vividly illustrates my point. The book concludes with a labyrinthine grading scheme, part of which is reproduced in Figure 2.

If we analyse the substance of what is being appraised here, from the first section, 'What is to be evaluated', there emerges a form of Caldwell Cook's 'right conduct', concerning itself with the degree of compliance of the child with the structure imposed by the teacher. The second section, 'What is to be assessed', incorporates this hidden agenda of acquiescence (a higher score is awarded to the boy who has submitted himself to the activity

Drama as a subject
Improvisation: Sitting-down drama Day 2

What is to be evaluated		Lance	Comments	Martyn	Comments
Attendance:	(10)	9	Grudging	10	
Punctuality:	(10)	10		7	Late again!
Respect for space and equipment:	(5)	2 $2\frac{1}{2}$	Belongings spread around	5	
Rules of the game/ following instructions:	(5)	4	Chatting	5	
Homework:	(5)	2	Messy journal	5	Impeccable
Total marks	(35)	$27\frac{1}{2}$		31	

What is to be assessed				
Level of personal engagement:	C→B+	Barely engaged to Committing	B+	Committed
Expression of feeling:	A	A way with words	B+	Real concern
Work as process:	B	Product-oriented	B+	
Maintaining role:	C→A−	From the superficial to the real, even when we are not watching!	B	Likes to feel safe
Energy applied appropriately:	C	When it suits him	A+	
Expressing in another mediium:	C	Thin! Does not see this as a way of being 'seen',	B+	Thoughtful but dull

Figure 2   *Teacher's thinking about her evaluation/assessment of Lance and Martyn*[29]

sufficiently energetically) and attempts, once again, to grapple with drama-in-education's longstanding preoccupation with the expression of 'true feelings'. However, while the authors are anxious to grade the genuineness of the feelings expressed, it is never made clear how this can be reliably ascertained, particularly if a pupil's high score in 'Maintaining role' suggest more than fair competence in the skills of deception.

The problem is, and it is a most serious one, that given the progressivist legacy of drama-in-education together with its recent transmutation into pedagogy, it is difficult to see how the jumble of associated but too often contradictory teleological explanations can ever produce schemes with much more coherence than this. As was quickly discovered by the old CSE Boards, in allocating marks to children's drama, you can grade the level of a child's co-operation with the creative enterprise, and you can grade their creative ability and their acting skills. Beyond that you are in the realm of metaphysical speculation. How Bolton evaluates 'containing', for example, is difficult to imagine.

None of this should be mistaken as an argument for a set of practices prescribed by the exigencies of formal assessment. I have simply applied Rowntree's proposal about finding the truth of an educational system through its appraisal structures, and concluded that in its efforts to formulate evaluative schemes of one kind or another, drama-in-education has nowhere more completely exposed the serious weaknesses in its own conceptual apparatus. It would not be an over-simplification, for example, to say that the child who is 'good at drama' in the scheme quoted here, would be one who toes the line and appears to be sincere. He or she, in other words, who can *successfully take us in*. Paradoxically, we have a prgramme which has abandoned the cultivation of Rousseau's natural nobility in favour of the encouragement of the street-wise cut-and-thrust of effectiveness and appearance.

The two witnesses

Unlike earlier manifestations of drama-in-education, the new orthodoxy cast in Heathcote's Newcastle workshops was absorbed into the thinking and practice of school drama with an especial vigour. Heathcote and Bolton between them seemed able to inspire an astonishingly uncritical loyalty which invested in them a unique, apparently indisputable, authority. Rather like the seventeenth-century Muggletonians, who put their salvation in the hands of John Reeve and Lodowick Muggleton, believing them to be the 'two witnesses' of *The Revelation*, substantial numbers of drama teachers in the 1980s seemed happy to forsake the discourse of the wider educational community in favour of the witness of 'Dorothy and Gavin'.

The concluding passage of Wagner's account of Heathcote's teaching well illustrates that strange mixture of awe and whimsy which came to surround her performances:

> Learning to teach from Dorothy Heathcote is like dancing with a whirlwind. The symphony she hears sweeps you along with a sense of its rhythm; still you have very little understanding of the steps your

feet must take when her leadership is gone and you are left to dance alone. My hope is that this book will spell out some of the steps so that you can start the dance; but the music you hear must be in your own soul.[30]

Frequent use of this kind of semi-magical imagery reinforced the evangelical thrust of the new orthodoxy, wrapping Heathcote's already powerful physical presence in a cloak of spirituality around which an increasingly beleaguered discipline could rally. As Christopher Hill writes of the disillusionment which followed the collapse of the radical programmes of the English Revolution:

> If anything was to be salvaged from the wreckage of radical hopes, some legitimating force was required. The Muggletonians had the indisputable authority of the Two Witnesses. What could not be won by political means might be secured by divine assistance.[31]

Undoubtedly, Heathcote and Bolton succeeded in providing far more than a new methodology for the teaching of drama. Like Reeve and Muggleton, they offered a wisdom that claimed its origins in a deep spiritual truth and a unifying vision of humanity which absolved their followers from further moral or ideological speculation.

However, the dangers of the self-approving system which drama-in-education engendered for itself during the 1980s, and of which Heathcote and Bolton were the unchallenged ambassadors are, I hope, obvious. The intense personalisation of practice, combined with a mistrust of disinterested analysis, meant that it became almost impossible to challenge the premises upon which the practice was built. Meanwhile, without the checks and reassessments that genuine debate brings with it, the elders became more self-assured and less in touch with reality, gathering their disciples around them as a shield against an increasingly unsympathetic educational world. Like the disappointed Muggletonians, and Fifth Monarchists, and Ranters and Diggers of the seventeenth-century, 'when the kingdom of Christ failed to arrive, the faithful could retreat into their own communities and enjoy there much of the equality, comradeship and fraternity that the outside world denied them'.[32] Sadly, as the 1980s came to an end the promised kingdom of drama-in-education must have seemed as far off as ever, paradise indefinitely postponed. The 1988 Education Reform Act heralded a very different educational environment from that marked by its predecessor in 1944. After a decade of dramatic hagiocracy too many ordinary drama teachers were to find themselves dangerously ill-prepared for the demands it would make upon them.

3

The Setting: Events on the Public Stage

The 1960s settlement

The single-minded pursuit of classroom strategies, the struggle for a *methodology* of drama teaching, which marks the past ten or fifteen years of developments in educational drama, was based upon the belief that if 'drama as a learning medium'[1] could be shown to be pedagogically effective, then drama-in-education recast in this way would be able to justify a place for itself (and its practitioners) at the very core of the school curriculum. I shall suggest here, and in the following chapter, that the exclusive attention consequently paid to theories of dramatic learning had in fact quite the reverse effect, playing a significant part in drama's relegation in the national curriculum of the 1988 Education Reform Act.[2]

The wider origins of this paradox lie in the shifting of the post-war ideological balance of political life in England, well under way by the mid-1970s, but largely ignored by those in positions of influence in the drama-in-education movement. The latter, with their heads down amongst their methodologies, rarely looked up to consider the serious implications of these changes for a subject discipline still with only a tenuous hold on the timetable.

As far as education is concerned, the 1960s can be recognised with hindsight as years marked by consensus politics. The Centre for Contemporary Cultural Studies has called this general agreement over educational aims 'the 1960s settlement', seeing it as 'the product of a distinctive alliance of three groups of forces: leading sections of the Labour Party, the organized teaching profession, and certain key intellectuals in the new education-related academic disciplines'.[3]

In fact, this 'progressive' alliance spread more widely still, resting not only on the pragmatic socialism of Anthony Crosland, but also on the non-conformity of his Tory opposite number, Edward Boyle.[4] Both men presided over a period of educational expansion fuelled by popular demand. During the 1960s education grew at a greater rate than any national enterprise except gas and electricity. Each year successively greater numbers of children gained GCE O and A levels. By 1963 The Robbins Report was warning of 'an educational emergency' in higher education because of the effects of the post-war 'baby boom'.[5] Education spending as a proportion of gross national product rose from 3.2 per cent in 1955 to 6 per cent in 1969 (a period covered by both Conservative and Labour governments), partly because of public demand and partly through a conviction that Britain had to modernise its social and economic infrastructure in order to compete successfully in world markets.

Greater access to education at all levels of society was a key element in this strategy. There was an expansion of further and higher education and a new commitment to the comprehensive school. Ways were sought to reduce barriers to opportunity for working-class children, traditionally inhibited by the élitism of the universities and contained within the low expectations of the secondary-modern school. There was a perception by government, endorsed by Newsom[6] and other reports from within the education establishment, that the young of the nation represented a key resource in a new technological age, and that Britain's economic future depended to a large extent upon that growing population's ability to live within and manage that new age. This ability could only be achieved, and later sustained, it was thought, by opening up educational opportunities right across the social spectrum.

This, then, was the tide upon which drama-in-education found a secure anchorage. Concerned more with the processes of delivery than with the politics of provision, the non-politicians in the settlement alliance (the teachers and their allies in the universities) saw the child-centred, developmental premises of the progressive movement, of which school drama stood as such a prominent representative, as ideally placed to serve the new egalitarianism. Among the state agencies, too, there was perceived to be a need for children of different social classes to understand each other better, or, as a Schools Council document argued in 1967, a requirement that education should aim 'to help students find within themselves the resources that alone can help them live at ease in the changing world'.[7] The dismantling of these cultural barriers would come, it was assumed, not as a result of political revolution and reconstruction, but through the increase of awareness and understanding brought about by the exercise of the socio-psychological principles of progressive teaching methods. Child-centred models of classroom practice, it was thought, would help this process of adjustment, particularly for that large group of pupils whom Newsom had identified as having abilities 'artificially depressed by environmental and linguistic handicaps'.[8] Brian Way is thus perfectly in tune with his time when, in the first chapter of *Development through Drama*, he declares that,

> So far as is humanly possible, this book is concerned with the develop-
> ment of people, not with the development of drama ... Education is
> concerned with individuals; drama is concerned with the individuality
> of individuals, with the uniqueness of each human essence ... drama
> encourages originality and helps towards some fulfilment of personal
> aspiration.[9]

This emphasis on autonomous fulfilment was given added impetus in the secondary sector because of the undoubtedly beneficial effect the new child-centred methods had on the daily guerilla warfare of the school. By allowing particularly 'difficult' pupils informal space to express opinions and debate their concerns, teachers often found the task of pedagogic intervention considerably eased.[10] The exceedingly flimsy content bound-aries of the drama lesson made drama-in-education a particularly suitable vehicle for this kind of approach. Drama teachers found themselves in-creasingly called to service courses directed towards the lower end of the ability range, with repertoires of trust exercises, group therapeutics and games.[11]

While for many teachers who can look back on this time it was indeed a kind of 'golden age', the 1960s settlement and the progressivist ideas which flourished under its protection were the result more of a series of fortunate economic and political coincidences than of a sustainable ideological momentum. A period rich with curriculum initiatives and methodological advances, it was also one marked by political compromise and educational pragmatism. Opportunities to alter radically the structure of the education system, by removing the anomaly of a parallel private service, for example, or even by simply legislating away the lingering tri-partite system of gram-mar, technical and secondary-modern schools set up by the 1944 Act, were either not taken by the 1964–70 Labour Government (which after 1966 had a ninety-seven seat majority), or only tardily embarked upon. The Labour Party in power asked for no report on comprehensive education, for exam-ple, and seemed content to leave the problems of the new schools to the experts.

Similar caution characterised the introduction of the new Certificate of Secondary Education (CSE) in 1965. While the new syllabuses gave teachers control over public examinations for the first time, and introduced continuous assessment on a wide basis, the examination system itself, with GCE O levels remaining for the more able, reinforced the old grammar/ secondary-modern divisions and gave them an anomalous structural home within the comprehensive system. Many curriculum initiatives (such as European Studies, for example) perished as they tried to make headway within the tangle of historical compromises and vested interests which for so long had plagued English education, and which no real efforts were made to displace.

Meanwhile, the tendency of the teaching profession itself to overlook the material ambitions of parents for their children, and governmental reluctance to become involved with what David Eccles once called 'the secret garden of the curriculum', served to distance and even alienate the general public from educational affairs. The alienation was soon to be recognised and exploited, as a loose alliance of the political right sought to fill the policy vacuum and mobilise public concern.

New ideologues

Before the decade was over, the first of a series of polemical literary essays, the notorious Black Papers on education, had been published.[12] Viewed by many teachers at the time as little more than an aberrant outburst from the extreme right, the writers who contributed to these documents nevertheless set out to challenge the premises upon which the educationalists of the 1960s had founded their strategies for egalitarian reform.

By attempting to appeal, over the heads of the educational establishment and the political consensus which supported it, to the 'common sense' of the man or woman in the street, contributors found that they could exploit widespread popular uncertainties. It was in the overt populism of this project (and the model it was later to provide for the *poujadiste* ascendancy of the 1980s), rather than in the presentation of a coherent alternative programme, that its success lay. Also, it has to be said that the association in the minds of the press and the public of key elements of the 1960s settlement, such as the comprehensive school, mixed-ability classes, and progressive teaching methods, with an intellectual 'liberal' élite out of touch with the aspirations of ordinary people, was by no means an entirely mistaken one.[13]

The Black Paper writers mustered discontent around three distinct themes, namely standards, parents, and teaching methods. Cyril Burt, for example, claimed that 'attainment in the basic subjects' had actually declined since the First World War, and that judged by 'tests applied and standardized in 1913–14, the average attainments in reading, spelling, mechanical and problem arithmetic are now appreciably lower than they were 55 years ago'.[14] Burt's later (subsequently discredited) findings, relating to inherited intelligence, proved another popular theme among Black Paper contributors, many of whom were convinced that working-class children were, on average, innately less intelligent than their middle-class peers. By this account, devices such as comprehensive schools and mixed-ability teaching were an egalitarian illusion, doomed from the start in the face of genetic reality. At the root of this proposition lay a form of social Darwinism similar to the competitive survivalism favoured by right-wing economists. According to this view, it was natural, indeed desirable, that the intellectually able should climb on the backs of the weak. This vigorous, healthy process, it was argued, was being blocked by the cranky permissiveness of 'progressive' teaching.

Parents were central to the Black Paper project, and were to be enlisted in support of it once the amorphous sense of concern already identified had been amplified sufficiently into 'the crisis of education'. The 'common sense' of the 'ordinary parent' was contrasted favourably with the 'woolly-thinking progressivism' of the intellectual left. Here is Rhodes Boyson (then head of Highbury Grove School) arguing that parents wanted nothing more from the secondary-modern school than that it should emulate the grammar school with 'an attractive uniform, some exclusiveness of intake, and the creation of tradition':

> ... parents see schools largely as places which train their sons and daughters for better jobs ... secondary modern schools with progressive methods, rural science, much art and music and freedom of development endeared themselves to no-one other than the vaguely idealistic, unworldly and levitating types so well represented and influential amongst education officials and advisors.[15]

Public reservations about the unfamiliar teaching methods of progressivism were easy to exploit. Concrete evidence played only a small part in this attack, which instead leant heavily on fears about discipline and control. The comprehensive school was deemed to have made a significant contribution to the 'pop and drug' youth culture of the 1960s and 1970s, while attempts on the part of teachers in the same schools to devise new strategies for the delivery of education were ridiculed as absurd and irresponsible.

> ... I know that the best comprehensive school heads ... will have no truck with libertarian absurdities ('child centred' education, free activity, no rules, no streaming, no examinations, no teaching [and therefore no learning]) but there is enough evidence to show that the comprehensive outlook only too often involves 'progressive' concomitants. Just as the Labour Party and the trades union movement have always acted as an umbrella to shelter crypto-communists and fellow-travellers of all kinds, so the comprehensive platform attracts the

educational crank, anarchist, permissivist, sentimentalist as well as some really hard-faced politicians.[16]

The frustrated rage of *petit-bourgeois* aspiration surfaces everywhere in the Black Papers relentlessly pitting itself against the evils of a utopian intellectualism. Resisting the 'anarchy and permissivism' of the comprehensive were the good old solid 'common sense' values of the grammar school, with its familiar (although by no means always accurate) images of discipline, formal teaching and academic achievement. There was no place here, it was argued, for the vague idealism of the 'hippie' teacher, or for the 'thick' who would hold the class back,[17] or for 'time-wasting pseudo-subjects' like social studies or drama. The populist appeal of the grammar school was that, unlike private education, its 'excellence' was available to all.

While the Black Papers and the associated responses were at the time on the whole ignored by teachers, the speech which Prime Minister James Callaghan delivered at Ruskin College in October 1976, at the launch of the Labour Government's 'Great Debate' on education, signalled to many that the 1960s settlement was already a matter for the history books. In fact, the speech marked the end of a long post-war period of educational expansion, and began a process of governmental reassessment and economic contraction, in which the teaching profession, and those academics most associated with it, were to become increasingly marginal to the creation and implementation of education policy. In his speech, Callaghan laid down the parameters of the debate in a series of questions relating to the 'real world' to which he was in no doubt the nation's education service must perforce adapt:

> Let me repeat some of the fields that need study because they cause concern. There are the methods and aims of informal instruction; the strong case for the so-called core curriculum of basic knowledge; next, what is the proper way of monitoring the use of resources in order to maintain a proper national standard of performance; then there is the role of the inspectorate in relation to national standards; and there is a need to improve relations between industry and education.[18]

From the mid-1970s onwards, advocates of progressive education were to find themselves increasingly on the defensive in educational policy-making at all levels. In this respect, it should be remembered that developments in drama-in-education after this time (and that includes all the major writings of Heathcote and Bolton) must be set against a background of a broken consensus, and within a political and economic climate fast changing to meet the concerns which had been so effectively articulated by Cox and Dyson and their fellow Black Paper contributors in 1969.

No longer can it be accepted that progressivism and comprehensive schemes are necessarily right, or that the future necessarily lies with them. The Black Paper has encouraged parents, teachers, M.P.s to speak out on the present day abuses in education. There are many signs that the trend is now back to more balanced and tried views . . .[19]

Anything you can do

These 'balanced and tried views' were much in evidence in the Labour Government's Green Paper, *Education in Schools*, published in July 1977. It contained, for example, the suggestion that there should be national agreement on curriculum content, with a core of essential subjects:

> . . . it is clear that the time has come to try to establish generally accepted principles for the composition of the secondary curriculum for all pupils . . . there is a need to investigate the part which might be played by a 'protected' or 'core' element of the curriculum common to all schools.[20]

Education in Schools also urged the Department of Education and Science to be less reticent about intervening in matters traditionally left to the 'professionals':

> It would not be compatible with the duties of the Secretaries of State . . . or with their accountability to Parliament, to abdicate from leadership on educational issues which have become a matter of lively public concern.[21]

There was to be a greater involvement of the commercial sector in policy committees; a core curriculum should be able to 'offer reassurances to employers' as well as to teachers and parents. Above all, schools were to be diverted from the egalitarian pursuit of that legacy of Renaissance humanism, the well-rounded citizen, to 'education for investment, education for efficiency',[22] or in other words, to the preparation of pupils for an effective place in the service of the economy.

Amidst all this concern for economic relevance, it should be remembered that the relationship between a nation's economic performance and its education system remains unproven; some economists have even argued that education policy has no appreciable effect whatever on the operation of the economy.[23] Nevertheless, from the mid-1970s, it was against predictions of economic demand that education policy was increasingly measured. This necessarily entailed attacks on the institutions within the service most identified with the old progressive ideal. In 1977, for example, the Schools Council was forced to change its constitution to reduce the representation of teachers. Even the Department of Education and Science itself was not considered sufficiently free from the taint of the 1960s settlement. From its creation in 1974, the Manpower Services Commission (MSC) (directly answerable to the Secretary of State for Employment) became an agency of growing importance in the delivery of education policy. The implications of the new utilitarianism for subjects like drama which had floated into the curriculum on a tide of progressive ideas were potentially very grave.

By the early 1980s there is evidence of attempts from within the field to reach an accommodation with the changing political climate. Indeed, it is possible that the growing advocacy of Heathcote's theories of dramatic pedagogy could be interpreted as a generalised, almost subliminal, acknowledgement of the changing political context. The reinstatement of the teacher as the key motivating figure in the lesson, for example, which was being widely advertised as the model for good practice by the 1980s, could be interpreted as an attempt to disassociate educational drama from what Cox and Dyson had called the 'excesses of *laissez-faire* permissivism' with which it had for long been identified. The coloured lights and noisy disorder of the 1960s drama lesson must surely have embodied all that the new idealogues most mistrusted and sought to eradicate.

Paradoxically, it was the influence of the MSC and its associated enterprises which was to offer educational drama a role within the new 'realism'. Through the MSC, the Government sought to by-pass the established structures of the old consensus and the teachers who still subscribed to its ideals. There was a concerted attempt not simply to adjust the balance of the post-sixteen curriculum, but to inculcate young people, particularly working-class young people, with the values, attitudes and disciplines appropriate for a shrinking labour market. Thus, taking a priority over training in specific trades, was the acquisition of general social dispositions suitable for members of the new 'flexible' work force, a menu of what came to be euphemistically known as 'life and social skills', or simply, 'life skills'.

Life skills mean problem-solving behaviours appropriately and responsibly used in the management of personal affairs. *Appropriate* use requires an individual to adapt the behaviours to time and place. *Responsible* use requires maturity, or accountability. And as behaviours used in the *management of personal affairs*, life skills apply to five areas of life responsibility identified as self, family, leisure, community and job.[24]

Among the drama-in-education community, favourable readings of this agenda were quick to interpret it as offering opportunities for the licensed maintenance of the child-centred premises of progressivism. For many drama teachers, the presence of words like 'appropriate', 'personal' and 'self' was enough to signify an identification with the values of individual development and awareness to which they could happily subscribe. By then they had at their disposal a set of dramatic practices sufficiently morally emasculated for questions about the *nature* of the individual development and awareness not to arise. As a consequence, the 'life skills' project had not been long in schools before aggrieved drama specialists were protesting that its tutors and organisers were poaching on their methodological territory, as this letter indicates:

Anyone *au-fait* with the aims and activities of Educational Drama will of course realise that this 'new' area (Life skills) is in fact based on these same aims and objectives eg. social awareness, confidence, ability to reason etc. using role-play, simulations and discussion groups . . . we as drama teachers have been 'teaching' these 'lifeskills' now for many years . . . I feel the ordinary drama teacher is now finding that his specialised field is in fact being 'taken over' by various members of the profession, who I presume feel qualified and confident enough to engage in these activities after one or two training weekends.[25]

Other practitioners began to declare themselves ready and able to participate in the 'life skills' movement. In 1983, for example, Kathy Joyce, contributing to a series of articles entitled 'Drama and the Lifeskills Trend' (which included a piece by the Director of Understanding British Industry) saw school drama techniques being used to look at 'different strategies for behaviour, coping, surviving or succeeding'.[26] In similar vein, David Morton, Adviser for Drama in Leeds, predicted that in future society would 'need an increasingly versatile workforce able to respond to rapidly changing needs', and that drama would have a significant part to play in developing the 'self-reliance and small-scale entrepreneurial skills that will allow young people to *create* work'.[27] The following year, the editor of *London Drama* was worried that more energy might be spent 'defending drama as a subject than in positively examining the aims and objectives of the new courses',[28] while a contributor to the same journal urged teachers to face up to the fact that 'not only youngsters but professional adults also must be prepared to adapt to the demands of the changed market place':

> ... if you want to survive in the new regime you will have to start teaching youngsters the self presentation skills involved in convincing an employer of their worth, of dealing with irate customers, or even how to sell encyclopedias.[29]

It is clear that having identified a place as a service agency in the less amenable post-Ruskin world of education, there were plenty of drama specialists who lost little sleep while taking what opportunities arose to market their practices across a whole range of training schemes and vocational initiatives. David Davis's was almost a lone voice warning against the indiscriminate embrace of 'life skills'. In a fiery article he castigated the 'deference' which he saw 'at the centre of MSC social and life skills courses', and which, in his view, characterised the 'hidden curriculum of society at large'.

> It aims to socialise young people in an 'acceptable' way, i.e. it programmes them to accept and deal with unemployment under the guise of preparing them for employment ... there is no place for drama on schemes which help prepare youth to survive under capitalism as unemployed individuals, who will not cause trouble ... I think educators should be opposed to all MSC courses, particularly YTS, and campaign against them through their union organisations and should not be involved with using 'drama' [role-play] for deference.[30]

However, as we shall see, the conceptual structures of drama-in-education had no means of taking this, or any other prognosis based on political or cultural premises, onboard. Progressivism itself lacked any political or historical dimension, and drama teachers schooled in that tradition were too used to limiting their methodological vision to the inner world of sensation and feeling to be able to grasp the implications of these new realities in significant numbers. And after all, had not 'Dorothy' herself involved her post-graduate students in industrial management training courses? Unfortunately, history was not to reward kindly the simple opportunism which turned a deaf ear to Davis's counsel and instead sought to locate drama-in-education in the programmes of the new educational ascendancy.

Drama and the struggle for the arts

The sad fact is that all the arts have been victims of this ascendancy, which, in a series of measures culminating in the 1988 Education Refrom Act, has systematically set out to make the fantasies of the Black Paper writers a reality. The historical association of the arts in schools with unregulated self-expression has not endeared them to their new political masters. However, while each art form has struggled in its own way with questions of legitimacy in the post-Ruskin world, visual art, poetry, music and dance in education have not abandoned their aesthetic function for generalised pedagogic ends to quite the same extent that drama has sought to do. Their fight has been instead to lay the ghosts of the 1960s and to establish a public consciousness of the intrinsic value of the arts in education.

It was in this context that in 1982 the Calouste Gulbenkian Foundation published a comprehensive and carefully argued case for the arts which openly addressed the scepticism of their detractors in a language marked by its clarity and accessibility, and by the absence of jargon.[31] Ever since its appearance, *The Arts in Schools* has provided an invaluable reference point for arts workers concerned with education and for teachers involved in the arts. Its usefulness lies not only in the arguments it proposes, but in the conceptual unity it provides across all sectors of arts provision, offering a language which Arts Council officers can share with professional educators, for instance. The establishment of this *commonality of discourse* has been a crucial first step in the struggle for arts education.

Early on in the book, its authors quote from an editorial in *The Times Educational Supplement* which succinctly expresses the underlying theme of the whole report:

> Art in all its forms has been since time immemorial the means by which humans keep up their collective spirits and make sense of each other and their world. A human and intelligently conceived arts education, shading off in a medley of other directions while retaining its own inalienable character, is something whose value only the bigoted or the very stupid could deny.[32]

It must be gratifying to the report's authors that subsequently no Local Education Authority or Department of Education and Science curriculum statement has failed in some measure to take account of the aesthetic field. In all major public reports on what should be taught in out schools, there has been a tacit but quite consistent acceptance of the view expressed in *The Arts in Schools* that the arts 'are absolutely worthwhile spending time on for the sake of satisfactions that are intrinsic to them'.[33]

But then, only a year after Callaghan's Ruskin appeal for industrial relevance, Her Majesty's Inspectors were recommending that 'the aesthetic and creative' should be considered as one of eight 'essential areas of experience' within the curriculum:

We see the curriculum to be concerned with introducing pupils during
the period of compulsory schooling to certain essential *areas of experience*. They are listed below in alphabetical order so that no order of
importance may be inferred: in our view they are equally important.

The aesthetic and the creative
The ethical
The linguistic
The mathematical
The physical
The scientiflc
The social and political
The spiritual.[34]

A similar commitment is well illustrated by the acceptance by the Inner
London Education Authority in 1984 of the Hargreaves Committee report,
Improving Secondary Schools. Hargreaves proposed six essential areas in
the fourth- and fifth-year core curriculum, of which the 'aesthetic' was one.

> ... the creative arts should be grouped together, either as a con-
> strained option from which every pupil must select at least one
> aesthetic subject, or as a combined/integrated course which contains
> at least two subjects ... this creative, aesthetic potential cannot be
> allowed to go untapped.[35]

All through this period the place of the arts continued to be officially
acknowledged. In the 1985 White Paper, *Better Schools*, along with eight
other areas the Secretary of State for Education recommended that 'the
content of the primary curriculum' should 'introduce pupils to a range of
activities in the arts'. He considered there to be 'wide agreement' that
'during the first three secondary years the curriculum should continue to be
largely common to all pupils', and that this principle should also apply 'to
aesthetic subjects, where all pupils should study over the three years,
music, art and drama on a worthwhile scale'.[36]

Even as the 1987 Conservative Government was preparing its education
legislation, Angela Rumbold, Minister of State for Education and Science,
repeated this commitment to aesthetic education:

> Education in the Arts is a fundamental part of our educational prop-
> osals for the curriculum. Without it we would be allowing our chil-
> dren to have missed a huge area of enrichment during their years in
> school, and an essential preparation for all that lies before them in
> their adult life.[37]

Despite all these encouraging noises, however, in reality the arts remained a low priority. Popular wisdom now favoured the technological and the vocational over the expressive and developmental when it came to the allocation of scarce resources. Above all, perhaps, even in schools where drama, music, dance and visual art all continued to flourish, it was the *idea* of the arts that was felt to be undervalued. There was an acute consciousness among arts teachers that they were living and working in a culture which was generally ill-disposed towards the kinds of sensitivities they were concerned to foster and sustain.

The 1988 Education Reform Bill appeared to confirm their worst fears. The exclusion of certain specific art forms – drama, dance, media studies and film – from the list of foundation subjects prescribed by the Bill led to extensive lobbying to replace the words 'art and music' simply with 'the arts'. It was widely assumed by the arts education community at the time that a combination of carelessness and ignorance, together with Conservative Party nostalgia for grammar schools, had dictated that Art and Music should stand as the sole representatives of the aesthetic field.[38]

While the failure of the 1988 National Curriculum to enshrine in legislation the recommendations of *Better Schools* (notwithstanding repeated reference to them) with respect to the arts was a serious blow to the development of a coherent aesthetic curriculum for schools, it has to be said that divisions within the arts community itself had played no small part in this hierarchical fragmentation. There is no doubt in my mind that drama-in-education's public reluctance to identify unambiguously with the arts curriculum contributed in no small measure to its exclusion from the list of prescribed subjects. To curious outsiders, the distinctions so forcibly made by some drama teachers between *their* drama and that going on in the theatre down the road, for instance, remained less than comprehensible.

The unhappy truth is that the internal logic of its own aims and practices conspired with history to exclude school drama from the very curriculum it once sought to colonise. The failure of its most public advocates to appreciate the implications of political change was parallelled by an opportunism on the part of many practitioners who preferred to embrace whatever new initiative seemed to offer the chance of short-term survival, rather than to face up to the challenge of uncomfortable but long overdue re-evaluations. The narrow sectarianism of its methodologies, together with a lack of curiosity concerning the intellectual or artistic world beyond its own very limited bibliography, led educational drama blindly yet remorselessly forward out of the subject-based curriculum and into the wilderness.

4

Dramatic Tension: Barricades and Bewilderment

The situation of our time
Surrounds us like a baffling crime.

(W. H. Auden, 1940.)[1]

Reaction and intervention in the 1980s

The relegation of the teaching profession to the margins of policy-making in the 1980s was a further manifestation of the pressure to integrate education with the management of the economy. School teachers, all too easily associated in the public mind with permissive, vaguely leftist thinking and indiscipline, were easy scapegoats when the rigorous imposition of a new enterprise culture began to reveal the country's industrial and commercial shortcomings. The perception that the teaching profession itself bore some of the blame for these shortcomings and that it had as a consequence disinherited itself from the processes of educational policy-making, seemed to bear out the arguments of the Black Paper contributors, and led to increasing direct governmental intervention in educational affairs.

During the 1980s, the Conservative administration sought to impose on teachers an unprecedented number of new and highly demanding initiatives. In 1984, the Secretary of State for Education, Sir Keith Joseph, announced the introduction of a single system of examinations at sixteen-plus, the General Certificate of Secondary Education (GCSE), to take effect from 1988. Despite industrial action in schools (against financial cut-backs) which resulted in a boycott by teachers of preparation for the new examinations, the government ignored nationwide teacher opposition to its time-table for the GCSE and pressed ahead. In the same year, the White Paper, *Training for Jobs*, announced that one-quarter of the Government's funding of non-advanced further education (NAFE) would in future be reallocated to the MSC. This would enable it 'to purchase a more significant proportion of work-related non-advanced further education provided by local education authorities'.[2] Meanwhile, the expanding Technical and Vocational Education Initiative (TVEI)[3] (funded with over £1 billion from the MSC) further reflected the Government's emphasis on skills training and its mistrust of local education authorities. Although for a time the TVEI released unprecedented volumes of cash to consortia institutions, its operation placed additional responsibilities for planning and delivery onto an already overstretched teaching force. As Reid and Holt remind us, this 'proliferation of new curricula' for the fourteen to eighteen age range led to segmentation, duplication and confusion:

> ... even if a common institution were proposed to house all these offerings, it would still be hard to raise questions about the aims of education for the age-group as a whole, while these sub-groups continued to follow distinctive curricula representing competing rather than complementary versions of what education should be about.[4]

However, the introduction of the 1988 Education Reform Bill into Parliament, with its proposals for a national curriculum, 'opting-out' schools and the abolition of the Inner London Education Authority, threatened to compound rather than alleviate these problems. Simultaneously, The Black Report on assessment and testing (TGAT) seemed set to make still further demands of teachers in terms of time and co-operation.[5] The indication contained in the Report of further major adjustments to the sixteen-plus assessment system at a time when the difficulties accompanying preparations for the GCSE had left teachers doubting the ability of the rapidly cobbled-up examination boards to cope, and while they themselves were sweating to complete unfamiliar grade sheets and profiles for the new examination, served to alienate the teaching profession still further from a major piece of education legislation about which it had never been seriously consulted. The Assistant Masters and Mistresses Association claimed at this time that staff were 'being pushed to breaking point' by government initiatives which were being introduced only 'at tremendous cost to individual teachers',[6] while a report in June 1988 from the High Stress Occupations Working Party of the Health Education Authority (the government's own 'health watchdog') disclosed that teachers were not only 'vulnerable to major shifts in philosophy and policy introduced by successive governments' but that they were 'sometimes accused of failing to do something in one circumstance and then attacked for doing the same thing in another'.[7] At the same time, cuts in expenditure on education, often effected through centrally imposed restrictions on local government spending in the areas of greatest deprivation, served further to demoralise the teaching force. By the end of the 1980s, many teachers, particularly in the inner cities, were facing larger classes yet could rely upon far less support.

Effective teacher response to all this proved extremely difficult to orga-nise. Partly, the lingering nostalgia for 'those good old days' of the popular imagination, when 'teachers really were teachers, well-loved, well-hated, stern, gentle, telling you what, not asking what you want, sticking to the 3Rs, and not getting mixed up in all this difficult stuff where there's no right answer',[8] made it almost impossible for teachers' organisations to mount a successful public defence of practices evolved in the 1960s and 1970s. Also, teachers were themselves politically deeply divided. While some unions took selective strike action in support of better pay and conditions, others campaigned for the retention of corporal punishment (it should not be forgotten that in the General Election of 1983, nearly half the teaching force had voted Conservative[9]).

This, then, was the battleground upon which drama-in-education had to make its stand. It was amidst the daily skirmishes of classroom and staff-meeting, rather than in the rarefied ambience of the demonstration lesson, that the real battle for school drama would have to be fought.

Bewilderment and acquiescence

In 1975, David Self had described giving a demonstration lesson in front of some students in a 'bad' comprehensive, where he had been completely unprepared for the 'shambles that ensued'.

> Halfway through the second week's lesson, in which there had been further chaos and in which every group improvisation had degener-ated into brawling *between* groups, I brought the class together and said a few quiet words about discipline ... On the bus back to college, one student was worried. 'With all respect' he asked, 'aren't you afraid you might have repressed their natural spontaneity?'.[10]

Twelve years later, a young drama teacher wrote this about his experiences as a probationer in an East London comprehensive school:

> Truancy was high (teachers as well as pupils) and the nervous break-downs among staff were many. The tension that a new teacher gets when he/she enters the classroom for the first time never goes away ... On my first day I was pelted with stones, told to 'fuck off' and the

nicest thing that was said to me was, 'You must be the new fucking poofter drama teacher'.[11]

No teacher would doubt that there are times when Peter Slade's confident assertion that school drama is 'a virile and exciting experience, in which the teacher's task is that of a loving ally'[12] offers us a less than adequate account of the realities of the drama classroom. The pastoral idyll of progressivism can sometimes seem a long way off from the battered corridors of the inner-city school where children are by no means always willing to suspend their disbelief. Part of the trouble is, that while dislike of most other subjects is generally accompanied by a grudging acceptance by pupils of their legitimacy, children who fail to get enjoyment from the drama lesson really do not see the point of it. Unlike colleagues in Science or History, the drama teacher has been divested of any reassuring body of 'important' knowledge to justify his or her presence in the timetable, and reference to the subject's expansive pedagogic claims can sound pompous and hollow amid the hubbub of the drama class. After all, a child might not unreasonably reply, if drama is such a profound embodiment of all that is desirable in education, why isn't it taught beyond the third year?

When faced with it, teachers have reacted in different ways to manifestations of this apparently intractable antipathy. Some so-called drama classes have become general discussion sessions, the teacher knowing that only by abandoning the 'threat' of having to *act* something, can any sense of focus be achieved. In others, and for similar reasons, teachers have fallen back upon popular menus of games and exercises in order to keep 'difficult' classes occupied until the life-saving bell.[13] However, while games can certainly be useful teaching aids, their unselective use simply serves to reinforce children's suspicions about drama's legitimacy as a subject, and to set up expectations of its practices as indistinguishable from play and demanding of the same forms of immediate gratification. At the same time, it has to be acknowledged that teaching in an institution is often wearisome and repetitive, that children can be fractious and unpleasant, and that the creative stimulation which they have continuously to inject into the successful drama lesson makes quite unique demands on drama teachers' imagination and energies (see, once more, Appendix A). As pressures on teachers build up, the temptation to accept and even defend the validity of discussions and games under the accommodating umbrella of drama becomes less easy to resist.

At the same time, of course, it has to be said that thousands of young people across the country look forward to their drama lessons and clearly find them stimulating and enjoyable; also, that most drama teachers work well beyond the call of duty to achieve this. Nevertheless, although some have certainly managed to incorporate elements of the new methodologies into their teaching, there does appear to be a disturbing gap between the received wisdom of the field as broadcast in the literature and the actual experience, favourable and unfavourable, of the average school drama class.

Even in the 1970s, Margaret Wootton recognised that many teachers 'found it almost impossible to reconcile abstract ideals with the practical restrictions of time, space and the school curriculum'.[14] Throughout the 1980s, for example, Bolton and Heathcote were notably silent on the fundamental matter of accommodating their dramatic pedagogy to the bi-weekly fifty-minute drama lesson. How was the much-vaunted 'moment of awe' to be achieved to the accompanying clatter of the school kitchen behind the partition? Similarly, they advanced no strategies for the development of GCSE syllabuses or for responding to the performing arts courses in the TVEI. The paradox lies not in the omission itself (we all draw up our own agendas) but in the fact that despite it, as we saw in Chapter 2, letters in the journals from the faithful continued to evince an unproblematic equation between the ideas of 'Gavin and Dorothy' and the experience of the 'ordinary teacher'. Contributors rarely paused to examine or question the fundamental tenets of the 'learning through drama process', either with respect to their intellectual coherence or to their suitability for the classrooms of the 1980s.

Instead, two ideologically opposed camps arose to champion the cause of dramatic pedagogy. One, as we have noted, saw it as a way of legitimating drama within the new vocationalism; the other, by contrast, sought to politicise the methodologies and press them into the service of revolutionary politics.

For those anxious to preserve their forms of practice by seeking an accommodation with the times, drama-in-educatin's problems were perceived to be largely those of marketing, to be resolved by more resolute demonstrations of educational drama's effectiveness to a new generation of curriculum managers. By and large they continued to base their case upon forms of dramatic pedagogy which could at best expect a place as a low-status servicing agency for the new curriculum. Even as the Education Reform Act became law in 1988, Geoff Readman in a piece entitled 'Drama in the Market Place?' was still arguing that drama's exclusion from the National Curriculum could be laid at the door of communication failure. After all, he pointed out, was not role-play widely recognised in the world outside the classroom?

It is used extensively in Industrial Management Training; it features regularly in counselling situations for professional care workers; it is recognised as an effective tool for people to explore their personal problems, and it serves a whole host of uses when used to simulate real-life situations and experiences. All of which seems to indicate that Drama should be a central part of the present Government's plans.[15]

The advocacy of programmes of this kind illustrates how far down the line towards utility status the commitment to dramatic pedagogy has led us. There has been a quiet disengagement from many of the proud dissenting values of progressivism and a corresponding shift towards forms of effectiveness which are untroubled by principle or position. In a sense, drama has cast itself as the 'Yosser' Hughes of the curriculum; no job is too difficult or inappropriate so long as it *is* a job.[16] Perhaps we need to ask if this is really how we want to see ourselves, or if there are not, after all, certain principles demanded of us as teachers of the art of drama which will not so easily and opportunistically succumb to the pressures of the market.

Calls to the barricades: Freire, Boal and the radical left

Deeply opposed to any idea of accommodation, on the other hand, was a loose, often highly factionalised, alliance of teachers on the political left. Grouped around concern over issues of class, gender and race, and a commitment to the idea of education as 'empowerment', its members expressed their opposition to government policies with a rare degree of analytical sophistication. Increasingly, during the 1980s, associated with the left radicalism of the Theatre-in-Education movement,[17] this alliance sought to press the dramatic pedagogy of Heathcote and Bolton into the service of revolutionary social change. In short, they believed that its revelatory processes enabled young people to see, understand and challenge the 'objective' structures of political oppression.

For the most committed, Heathcote's 'universals' became transformed from vague generalisations about the human condition into 'an expression of confidence in the knowability of the world'.[18] In this appropriation Heathcote was seen as using drama 'to produce knowledge in young people', that is to say real, unequivocal, objective knowledge of the world as it actually, indisputably, *is*. From such a perspective, to suggest that there might be shades of grey between the correct and the incorrect could be dismissed as, unforgivably, 'the standpoint of one who does not accept the knowability of things'.[19]

For me, the essence of the matter is that we are living in a decadent capitalist culture which is moving to ever higher state control in all walks of life, and which raises the very distinct threat of a nuclear holocaust in a final bid to perpetuate its existence ... Drama, on the other hand, working as art, would search out the truth in any particular situation and strengthen those participants in the struggle not to accept life as an object but to take up the challenge to become a subject.[20]

The stridency of this uncompromising appeal for unlimited self-determination stands in marked contradistinction to the wistful utopianism we have seen up until now. In 1984 the chair of the National Association for the Teaching of Drama (NATD) accused drama teachers of having too much 'tolerance of an ideology which played right into the hands of the present philistine, monetarist government which has brought us to the very edge of extinction',[21] while in 1986, and in the same journal, Jim Clark faced his fellow members with a series of forthright, rhetorical questions:

Is the system of which we are part too strong and clever for us? Do the powers that be just let us think we're different while actually absorbing us into their reality? ... we need to be positive about our achievements. BUT does our work fulfil its potential to challenge the patriarchal, sexist, racist, class-ridden context of the real world? Are we adding to the voices of our young people, are we giving them a way of challenging, a way of saying 'No!'?[22]

That same year, Clark shared the authorship of a political manifesto for drama teachers designed for adoption by the NATD. Among a wide range of statements and suggestions were modest proposals for the 'abolition of examinations' and the 'closure of all universities, polytechnics, colleges of higher and further education and adult education colleges'.[23] It has to be said, that while all the writers quoted here display a refreshing consciousness of the ideology behind the free-market ascendancy of the 1980s and make no attempt to reconcile their practice to it, and while they clearly prefer instead to ally themselves with those most at risk from that ascendancy, namely their least privileged students, the rhetoric ultimately fails to convince. There is just too great a gap between the radical fervour of the language and the lived realities of the classroom. It is doubtful that schools can so simply be dismissd as the unquestioning agents of capitalism, nor their pupils as the mute recipients of 'patriarchal, sexist, racist, class-ridden' values. Apart from anything else, to suggest that the battle lines can be so neatly drawn denies both the complex ambiguities of social life as well as the competence and intelligence of individuals. It is altogether too simple-minded a view of the relationship between society and those it sets out to educate.

Major influences on another (somewhat less dogmatic) section of the left alliance have been the deschooling theory of the Brazilian educationalist Paulo Freire and the dramatic techniques inspired by it of the Latin American director, Augusto Boal. Freire's *Pedagogy of the Oppressed*,[24] in which he describes ways in which language can contribute to the revolutionary struggles of underprivileged groups, has been influential in a whole range of Third World literacy projects. A South American Catholic increasingly drawn to Marxism, Freire rejects the idea of the revolutionary vanguard movement, and instead proposes that intellectuals and peasants should work together to identify, de-mystify and oppose specific forms of oppression. By doing so, he argues, the peasants would own their perceptions in ways which would then empower them to pursue their struggle for liberation with new insight into their historical circumstances. Always considering his Marxism to be an essential part of his Christianity, Freire has made a considerable contribution to the development of Latin American liberation theology, along with the famous deschooler, Ivan Illich.

I think the close links between Marxism and liberation theology are significant factors in the enthusiasm for Freire and Boal expressed by many advocates of drama-in-education on the left. On one level, the association with Illich and the deschooling movement evokes the anti-establishment progressivism of the 1960s with which drama-in-education sought to identify, while on another, the Latin American context anchors the theory in a most vivid and practical political struggle. The immediacy of that struggle has given Latin American Marxism a character of its own wherein ultimate theoretical questions have tended to be displaced by those of a more particular and pressing kind.

Importantly, the Christian ethic implicit both in Freire's and Boal's writings allows drama-in-education an anchor in the moral world once again. The unique combination of collective resistance and the self-liberating humanism of practical, non-dogmatic Christianity has for some practitioners unconsciously filled the ethical vacuum at the centre of the dramatic pedagogy project. Thus, Gustavo Gutiérrez, in his classic text on liberation theology, encapsulates their position entirely when he argues that 'an awareness of the need for self-liberation is essential to a correct understanding of the liberation process'.

> It is not a matter of 'struggling for others', which suggests paternalism and reformist objectives, but rather of becoming aware of oneself as not completely fulfilled and as living in an alienated society. And thus one can identify radically and militantly with those – the people and the social class – who bear the brunt of oppression.[25]

Augusto Boal acknowledges his debt to Freire in his own seminal work, *Theatre of the Oppressed*.[26] For Boal, theatre, like language, is a potential medium of liberation, but for it successfully to serve this purpose the traditional relationship between audience and performer has itself to be 'revolutionised'. In his productions, played out in the poverty-ridden *barrios* of Peru, the actors offer no solutions, but pause to allow the audience to discuss and redirect the story. Here, theatre becomes a laboratory of social change, where ideas can be tested in action, and where no outcome is preordained.

> ... the *poetics of the oppressed* focuses on the action itself: the spectator delegates no power to the character (or actor) either to act or to think in his place; on the contrary, he himself assumes the protagonic rôle, changes the dramatic action, tries out solutions, discusses plans for change – in short, trains himself for real action. In this case, perhaps the theater is not revolutionary in itself, but is surely a rehearsal for the revolution.[27]

The idea of drama as 'a rehearsal for the revolution' had obvious appeal to those seeking ways of confronting government policy in the classroom within an affirmative moral context. Here was a process by which pupils could be led, through drama, to a collaborative understanding of the overt and hidden oppressions of society. Inherent tyrannies of racism, sexism and class would be naturally exposed and condemned, not through the imposition of ideas by the teacher, but simply through the questioning, debating, and revising of dramatic pictures made by groups of actors or by the pupils themselves.

> In the forum theater no idea is imposed: the audience, the people, have opportunity to try out all their ideas, to rehearse all the possibilities, and to verify them in practice, that is, in theatrical practice.[28]

The introduction of Boal's *forum* and *image theatre* techniques represented an exciting development in drama education practice.[29] The idea that the audience could intervene and control from outside the dramatic action, opened the door to new perspectives on practices too long dominated by attention to the feelings of the participants. On the other hand, how successful Boal's methods have been in engaging with making sense of the ideological complexities of our advanced, consumer-dominated culture remains unproven. In the South American context of military coup, torture and exile, deprivation and oppression are easy enough to identify, as both Freire and Boal knew from personal experience,[30] but in the densely textured political ethnography of a post-imperial liberal democracy (one, incidentally, with long-standing theatrical conventions of its own), there is a real danger that Boal's technique can lead, not to enlightenment, but to simplification, to the reinforcement of the stereotypical position-taking of its exponents. In the context of the school there are considerable difficulties in regarding pupils as the equivalent of an oppressed social order, let alone in knowing what to take their side might mean. The traditional antipathy to education displayed by many white working-class groups, for example, which is held to be a major cause of inner-city truancy, would be likely to make them unreliable collaborators in the 'rehearsal for the revolution'.[31]

Nevertheless, the idea of a 'pedagogy of the oppressed' brought about through drama held many attractions for a loosely constituted group of practitioners acutely conscious of the social divisiveness engendered by the new times and anxious to press drama-in-education into the service of a resistance movement. The superimposition of the theories of Freire and Boal onto classroom practice enabled a significant number of those on the left of drama-in-education in the late 1980s to recast the drama pedagogy of Heathcote and Bolton in the rhetoric of social struggle.

The discursive imprecision of dramatic pedagogy made this project less difficult than might be supposed in the light of school drama's unimpeachable liberal credentials. For, as David Davis reminds us, had not Bolton himself once declared his aims to be; 'To help the student understand himself and the world he lives in', and 'know how and when (and when *not*) to adapt to the world he lives in'?[32] Like the pronouncements of ancient prophets, whose generalisaions and ambiguities can be gleaned to provide intellectual nourishment for all manner of causes, it became apparent that 'Dorothy and Gavin' could be as usefully enlisted into the service of the revolution as into the training programmes of the new utilitarianism.

Facing the future

In a contribution to a debate about the past and future of educational drama in 1986, Warwick Dobson offered a gloomy prognosis:

> It has been clear for some time that the school curriculum will undergo radical revision in the late 'eighties and early 'nineties, and few drama teachers expect their subject to emerge unscathed from the politics of curriculum planning.[33]

However, widely shared or not, Dobson's predictions were set out with some prescience.

... the government wants to see a return to the traditional curriculum consisting of so-called 'first-order' subjects like English, history and science ... drama is unlikely to figure very prominently – a more 'second order' subject would be difficult to find ... Given these circumstances, the question we should perhaps be asking is: does drama have any kind of future in the curriculum at all?[34]

Dobson answers this direct question with an argument drawn from his position on the radical left of the movement. For him, the value of educational drama as a learning agent in the service of political change is paramount; to advocate anything less is to embark upon 'a series of compromises'. The drama specialist should, in his view, see 'her institutional role as being inherently subversive', and use the processes of school drama 'as a means of challenging the values of the system within which she works'. 'Radical methodological processes', he argues, should be 'matched by a radicalization of content'. Concluding that 'marginalization is the *best* that can be hoped for under this particular set of circumstances', Dobson identifies 'two opposing courses of action'. One alternative is to see drama operating on the margins of formal education as a vehicle for political subversion; the other to 'legitimize the subject by moulding it into an acceptable academic discipline', to take 'refuge in a straightforward advocacy of theatre arts courses'.[35]

Here we are again with the old 'drama' versus 'theatre' argument, springing from Rousseau, endorsed by progressivism, and now ideologically reconstituted in the name of revolutionary politics. Dobson is not alone. David Davis clearly shares his judgement of this sharply differentiated duality:

I think these are the main opposites at the moment. The return to theatre arts on one side and those seeking developments in our work to meet the needs of young people on the other.[36]

Still caught in the loose mesh of moral relativism where 'achieving a change in understanding' has to stand awkwardly for 'seeing the world as we do', advocates of the pedagogy of dissent make claims for the efficacy of their practice no more substantiated than those of their less politically motivated predecessors. In the 1960s, Hodgson and Richards were happy to claim (without the support of any evidence) that, 'ample experience has indicated that improvised drama ... aids overall development of the personality'.[37] It is in this same confident tradition that twenty years later a new generation of drama practitioners was to desert the battlegrounds of radical individualism in order to pitch the tents of improvisation and role-play in the camps of the armies of the revolution. For some, still dressed in the uniforms of 1917, the campaign was simply part of the objective struggle of the 'oppressed' classes against world capitalism. For others, a version of the good, unconsciously owing much to a residual Christianity, revitalised the dramatic pedagogy project in the service of a shopping list of radical causes. Drama (it was now asserted) was uniquely placed to combat racism and sexism, for example, as well as to deal with issues of unemployment, the Third World, nuclear disarmament and the National Health Service.[38]

Of course, issues such as these are common enough subjects of attention in drama classes. Also, it is not difficult to see how properly contextualised role-playing can focus debate on issues of mutual concern, or how skilful and sensitive teachers might draw from their pupils new insights into questions of social and individual morality. Role-playing, in other words, can be an invaluable adjunct to rational discussion. Yet, once uncoupled from the distinctive concepts, procedures, knowledge and traditions of 'theatre arts', a pedagogic vagrant unprotected by the strong subject boundaries of the secondary timetable, drama as role-play is easily absorbed by the very subject which helped launch it into the curriculum in the 1960s. It comes to look very much like English. (See Appendix C.)

I fear that all those who have conspired to isolate school drama from the arts and to promote it as an educational utility, bear a heavy responsibility for this state of affairs. Ears have been closed to informed and sympathetic warning voices, and instead, an evangelical pursuit of a complex and elusive teaching methodology has ignored the reasonable dramatic expecta-tions of parents, headteachers and even the pupils themselves, and has resulted in the neglect of the very skills, procedures and insights which give drama its meaning in culture.

Nevertheless, despite the unfavourable climate, there are still grounds for some optimism. While drama might have been marketed as a learning medium, it is still manifestly present in our secondary schools as a creative art. The disproportionately modest effect the orthodoxies of dramatic pedagogy have had on actual classroom practice suggests that teachers themselves have been more healthily sceptical of its aims than is sometimes supposed. The majority of drama teachers remain sensitive to the enthu-siasm of their groups for improvised play-making and performance; in this respect, the basic elements of drama, those which link it conceptually to all the other arts, remain stubbornly in place. Through their abundant energy many heads of drama departments have built fine reputations for the subject within their schools, and in doing so have earned the respect of colleagues, governors and parents. Also, in their struggles with GCSE, records of achievement and curriculum reorganisation, drama teachers have become proficient in the kinds of skills which will help them push for their subject in the new structures of devolved responsibility.

What will help these teachers is a description of drama which will make sense to other arts teachers as they gather increasingly in creative or expressive arts groupings, to headteachers who will want to be reassured that precious curriculum time is being spent with sufficient rigour, and to governors who will soon be making difficult decisions about the allocation of resources. Such an account should attempt to provide an interpretative framework for what teachers *actually* do in their lessons rather than for what they *might* do given the peculiar circumstances of the demonstration class. In this respect, it should not reflect a favoured methodology but rather open doors to a multiplicity of practices. Above all, it must ensure that the language of drama is accessible to the pupils themselves, so that they can understand both how they are progressing in the subject and how what they do relates to the common understanding of drama outside the classroom.

The framework of any such description must be built upon strong theoretical foundations, and it is to those I now intend to give my attention. In the process some demolition work will undoubtedly be necessary. However, my hope is that what will emerge will ultimately be liberating, certainly for all those teachers who have for so long been persuaded to measure their practice against that of the great and the good and have, by specious comparison, been found wanting.

Part Two

Drama-in-education:
Interpreting the Text

It seems to me that the first principle of the study of any belief system is that its ideas and terms must be stated in terms other than its own; that they must be projected on to some screen other than one which they themselves provide ... Only in this way may we hope to lay bare the devices they employ to make their impact.

(Ernest Gellner, 1985.[1])

5

The Omnipotent Self

Authenticity and the self

In Chapter 1, I described how the progressive ideas which gave birth to drama-in-education had themselves evolved from a peculiarly English manifestation of Romanticism. The Arcadian individualism of Rousseau's 'uncorrupted conscience' found a home here, not as it had in his own country in the revolutionary agency of *sans-culotte* and *communard*, but in the imaginations of those who sought to oppose the less tangible tyrannies of industrialisation by cultivating the inner world of creative sensitivity and self-expression. I intend now to examine the relationship between this form of introspective rebellion and the model of the creative artist which it engendered, before moving on to look more closely at theories of arts education and at drama's place within them.

Until the late eighteenth-century makers of most of what we would be disposed to call art laboured within a framework of secular and religious patronage to which they were bound in greater or lesser degrees of servitude.[3] These 'artists', that is the painters, musicians, writers and actors who served society, expressed the unities and the riddles of the cultures in which they lived in forms which required no public reference to their own individual psychologies. The personality of the pre-nineteenth-century poet or performer was not generally considered to be of any particular interest; he [*sic*] was judged simply by his ability to echo and reflect the common experience of his class and his age. It was well into the seventeenth century before the word 'art' itself became restricted to what we now call the aesthetic field. Before then it would have been applied to all manner of human skills including medicine, astronomy and angling. The modern distinction between the *artist* and the *artisan*, which invests in the former intellectual and imaginative purposes absent from the craftsman or skilled worker, has a history of no more than two hundred years.

Under the influence of nineteenth-century Romanticism, of course, this special distinction was greatly reinforced. The work of art came to be considered not so much as the product of a particular form of skilled labour, but rather as a manifestation of the producer's *sensibility*. The artist, peculiarly equipped to give expression to this sensibility, thus relinquished his [*sic*] role as craftsman or servant and adopted instead the mantle of the extraordinary individual. Romanticism effectively internalised art, shifting the emphasis away from the skilled exercise of a craft, from *production*, in other words, towards the authentic expression of the psychological processes of the artist himself. The artist of the Romantic period created from the depths of his being, impelled by the energy of his creative inclinations: he became, for the first time, a *creative personality*.[4]

> ... the one thing that matters is the artist, so that he feels none of the blissfulness of life except in his art ... As for the gaping public, and whether when it has finished gaping it can justify why it has gaped, what difference does that make?[5]

Pierre Bourdieu describes how this internalisation of artistic endeavour, exemplified here by the young Goethe, also served to remove the work of art from the field of public judgement. If the audience has no say in the matter, then it follows that art's only critical reference point is the authenticity of the artist's intention.

> The declaration of the autonomy of the creative intention leads to a morality of conviction which tends to judge works of art by the purity of the artist's intention and which can end in a kind of terrorism of taste when the artist, in the name of his conviction, demands unconditional recognition of his work.[6]

The implications of this 'privatisation' of artistic endeavour were felt throughout nineteenth-century society. The spiritual elevation of the artist came about against the background of an increasingly insensible, mechanistic social world, where, in the face of a new materialism, powerful historic communalities of shared belief and moral purpose were rapidly dissolving. For many members of the new and prosperous middle class, increasingly confident of their independence from ancient secular and religious hierarchies while at the same time anxiously searching for forms of authentication to replace them, Romanticism provided a source of spirituality which reflected their own individualistic predilections. Indeed, the Romantic artist, with his unique ability to display the manifestations of his 'inner being', his 'creative spirit', might be said to have pre-empted the psychologist as the officiating priest of individualism.

While the influence of this new thinking on the poetry, visual art and music of nineteenth-century Europe was wide-ranging and complex, it was not without its contradictions. Apart from anything else, technological advances in printing and lithography were beginning to turn the reproduction and dissemination of art into an industry itself. The creative artist, mythologised as revolutionary and free spirit, was in fact no less dependent upon the material structures of society than anyone else. Writers and poets found themselves relying increasingly on a market of publishing houses, type-setters, printers and engravers, not to mention whole sections of that hidden army of unskilled wage labour whose aesthetic and economic deprivation stood in such stark contradistinction to the poetic ideal. In the very process of taking a stand against materialism, art had itself become a market commodity.

Twentieth-century arts educationalists share the heritage of this Romantic mythology. They have continued to champion the cause of individual identity and uniqueness against what they have seen as the pervasive and inhibiting influence of materialism. However, like the Romantics who inspired them, they have failed to take account of the cultural and economic circumstances within which this much-prized individuality is expressed.

For support, arts education turned instead to the new science of psychology. As a result, most creative theory is now entirely psychologistic, based upon the premise that we all have within us a 'creative faculty' which (and the horticultural metaphors are inescapable) requires careful cultivation if it is to blossom and flourish. Here is Carl Rogers:

> From the very nature of the inner conditions of creativity it is clear that they cannot be forced, but must be permitted to emerge. The farmer cannot make the germ develop and sprout from seed; he can only supply the nurturing conditions which will permit the seed to develop its own potentialities. So it is with creativity.[7]

Accounts of this kind decisively separate the created object from the process of creation, from the agent's *creativity*. The latter is removed conclusively by a sleight of etymology from the critical public domain and secured instead in the mysterious and untouchable recesses of the unconscious. At the same time, creativity, like imagination, becomes a function of ordinary human intelligence, no longer the preserve of the special individual but a faculty common to everyone. Twentieth-century psychology has succeeded in investing us all with the mystical powers of authentication previously the exclusive preserve of the nineteenth-century artist.

It is in terms like these that the argument for arts education is invariably framed. Children can best exercise and develop their creativity, it is claimed, in an environment free from the pressures of criticism and correction, where they can discover their own authenticity through the autonomous creative processes in which they are encouraged to engage. The quality of their work is seen as a measure of the authenticity of their relationship with it, of their spontaneity and sincerity. The teacher can support and encourage but should never interfere.

One of the most articulate modern exponents of this theory is Robert Witkin. Witkin writes about the arts in education from within the nexus of Romantic poetics and psychology described here, assuming a priori that the arts can be best understood as a function of the private, internalised world of the self, or more simply, as the creative expression of subjective feeling.

> If the price of finding oneself in the world is that of losing the world in oneself, then the price is more than anyone can afford ... In the case of the psychological system, it is the integrity of the world within the individual that is the source of his motivation, his enthusiasm, his feeling response to life ...[8]

By re-casting 'the arts' in the role of expressive agent for the creative faculty, Witkin and others have been able neatly to circumvent the discrepancies of categorisation and assessment which mark public distinctions of artistic value. However, Bourdieu has already drawn our attention to the fact that by adopting this simple expressionist position, with its assumptions about value circumscribed by theories of mental health, we are in danger of slipping into random self-regard. Furthermore, while it is central to Witkin's argument that the exercise of the individual's creative faculty is psychologically desirable, it is difficult to see upon what grounds this assertion is made as he denies himself any external evaluative reference points. Plainly he recognises the need to establish some criteria of worth; that it cannot be socially acceptable to endorse any kind of expressive act, by making no distinction, for example, between the considered arranging of colours by a child in the art lesson and the casual wall-daubing of a teenager's spray can. However, in his self-imposed exile from the aesthetic and ideological experience of public culture, Witkin denies himself access to the standards of worth by which society is accustomed to value its art. He thus is driven to manufacture a critical system which has no reference beyond the authenticity of the individual's response. In Witkin's confident epistemology, affirmative 'subject-reflexive' behaviour, for example, would adequately describe the child artist above, while the teenager's random spray-painting would be condemned as 'subject-reactive'. He even goes so far as to warn teachers of the danger of considering 'the implications and consequences of the behaviour in some social frame of reference', urging them instead to 'differentiate between behaviours in terms of their intrinsic character as action and knowing'.[9]

This instrumental view of the arts which sees them only as the manifestation of psychologistic processes, or 'sensate impulses', to use Witkin's formulation, has decisively shaped post-war arts education. Under the influence of writers like Bruner and Polanyi[10] the rationale for the arts in schools has been supremely constructed on developmental models which accord knowledge and expression of self primary status. Arts educationalists continue to emphasise the fragmented, behaviourist view of the self which they have inherited from the Romantic aesthetic, and which has been so successfully absorbed into the economic as well as the artistic consciousness of the late twentieth century.

School drama, as we have seen, owes its very existence to this particular picture of artistic creativity, and although many drama teachers are now trying to bring a political and social dimension to their work in the classroom, they are finding the old loyalties difficult to break. The result is often confusion and incoherence as ideological commitment grounds heavily on the intractable reefs of psychological self-reference. Thus, Bolton, for example, in a context where he seems to be trying deliberately to distance himself from 'the progressives', sees no ambiguity in claiming that 'drama is a *mental* state'.[11]

Any re-engagement in ideology, of course, raises its own problems for teachers. In a society increasingly devoted to the satisfying of de-politicised needs and interests, it may well be expedient to conduct the argument for the arts in a language which can claim to transcend politics and appeal to the self-regarding sensibility of its listeners. Certainly Malcolm Ross's particular brand of Romantic intuitionism, his commitment to 'feeling-form' and to the exclusivity of the aesthetic dimension in arts education, has enabled him to champion the arts in schools across a wide political spectrum.[12] If, on the other hand, teachers attempt to give the arts a history by relocating them in a social context, they pose a threat to the liberated, intuitionist self and lay themselves open to accusations of partisanship and bias. As we shall see, our therapeutic culture uses psychology as a powerful form of protection against such challenges.

The psychological imperative

The popular idea that the source of our views and preferences can be located in the depths of our psyches, and that psychology gives us an account of human agency which transcends politics and morality, was given added respectability in the post-war years by the no-nonsense positivism of Hans Eysenck. Eysenck, who always insisted on the strictest adherence to scientific rigour in psychological experiments, succeeded in popularising a particular brand of objective reductionism, which in an attempt to establish psychology as the bedrock of the human sciences set about systematically to redefine ideology in psychological terms. Put simply, Eysenck claimed that ideas, particularly political ideas, were nothing more than the rationalisations of emotions, outward manifestations of our unconscious 'inner world' of suppressed feelings.

> All other social sciences deal with variables which affect political behaviour indirectly ... The psychologist has no need of such intermediaries; he is in direct contact with the central link in the chain of causation between antecedent condition and resultant action.[13]

By means of psychological experiment and the analysis of statistical evidence (both subsequently much disputed), Eysenck set about demonstrating the temperamental instability of political 'extremists' of both left and right, in relation to a moderate 'centre' or psychological 'norm'. A simple-minded equation categorised Fascists and assorted totalitarians along with Communists and other left-wing radicals, and set their inherent 'tough-mindedness' against the 'tender-mindedness' of conservatives and liberals. The wide currency of this crude scientism, which has a superficial attractiveness in that it can render harmless the strongly held views of others by reducing them to psychoneurotic symptoms, has all too often allowed supporters of dominant political groupings to discredit radical opposition on grounds of mental instability. For the less than scrupulous popular press, 'loony', with its connotations of abnormality and even madness, is thus more than a useful alliterative prefix to 'left' in the face of serious challenges to the political establishment.

Influential well beyond the experimental school of English psychology, Eysenck's extreme but widely disseminated theories worked on a public consciousness that was warmly disposed to take the claims of psychology seriously. The psychoanalytic movement, for all Eysenck's reservations about its insufficiently rigorous 'scientific' approach, had already laid the ground for a model of the human agent possessed by an unpredictable inner life, a secular devil, which could be exorcised by submission to the psychiatrist's couch.

The unconscious world within the individual, the 'true self' so much loved and sought after by today's psychotherapists, is now widely accepted as a determining concept in our understanding of human agency. Although superficially we may consider ourselves in control of our thoughts and actions, in reality, so the familiar argument goes, deeper and less accessible forces are at work. This picture offers us a particular kind of internal reality to which we can gain access by self-knowledge. By 'knowing ourselves' we can recognise our real feelings, identify our real needs, and understand what things really mean (to us). In this way, morality, and truth itself, have been transformed by a relativistic scheme in which it has become acceptable to argue that a particular course of moral action is right for me, or even that a certain proposition, however widely disputed, is nevertheless true for me.

Epistemologically, of course, this deceptively attractive and widely held set of beliefs is infinitely regressive, as Gellner has amply demonstrated:

> The problem this approach faces, or ought to face (and which in practice it only evades) is this: how on earth is that 'true self' identified? Is it given by God, by nature, or self-chosen? The last of these alternatives is most in keeping with current background beliefs ... It involves the absurdity of assuming that the self must somehow choose or invent itself before it exists, and presupposes a curious and in practice arbitrary capacity to distinguish between ephemeral, capricious acts of choice or commitment, and those that are for real.[14]

Christopher Lasch's critique of the effect of this debilitating philosophy on the culture of the United States reveals an emotivist world where 'psychological man' struggles 'to maintain psychic equilibrium in a society that demands submission to the rules of social intercourse but refuses to ground those rules in a code of moral conduct.' Presiding over this profound cultural dislocation are the high priests of pychology the therapists, the psychiatric masseurs of the national neurosis. They administer to the 'anxiety, depression, vague discontents', the 'sense of inner emptiness' of modern society, but give 'no thought to anything beyond its immediate needs'.

> It hardly occurs to them – nor is there any reason why it should, given the nature of the therapeutic enterprise – to encourage the subject to subordinate his needs and interests to those of others, to someone or some cause or tradition outside himself. 'Love' as self-sacrifice or self-abasement, 'meaning' as submission to a higher loyalty – these sublimations strike the therapeutic sensibility as intolerably oppressive, offensive to common sense and injurious to personal health and well-being.[15]

Thus, in the laboratory of the feelings the encounter-group narcissist search-
es for a deep cleansing of the self from the destructive, polluting structures of all social institutions. This is pursued in the name of a perfect
purity of free aspiration, and realised in a series of personal intimacies
unfettered by dead conventions and traditions.

Politically, as recent American history vividly demonstrates, this over-
powering narcissism leads to disengagement and impotence. As long as the
criteria for moral action are determined by reference only to the integrity of
the self and are judged by the authenticity of the feelings associated with
them, then the subordination of those so-called 'needs' in corporate, public
action for a collective purpose becomes increasingly difficult. Narcissism
shapes a powerful form of political acquiescence; the individual is responsible for him- or herself and for his or her own self-knowledge, and for the
preservation of the community, whatever its holistic moral character, only
because he or she is aware that it is composed of other individuals with the
same kinds of problems in achieving self-authentication. In a narcissistic
society, 'awareness' becomes the vapid substitute for moral agency; the
pursuit of self as a legitimate end can only make meaningful ethical judgements impossible. With no yardstick beyond self-authentication, no actions
can be regarded as reprehensible if they are sincere, or indeed if they *appear
to be sincerely expressed*, because their sincere expression is their ultimate
justification. Thus, as an individual I look not for good or bad actions but
for sincere people, and because I have no means of knowing with what
degree of sincerity another person carries out an action, I can only assess
how sincere they seem. Or, conversely, if I can convince others of my
self-authenticity and of the sincerity in which I act, then I can reasonably
demand to be judged well. We are in the world of appearances, where what
counts is the effectiveness with which an agent adopts the appropriate role
in a society made up of improvised encounters.

> Society requires of us that we present ourselves as being sincere, and
> the most efficacious way of satisfying this demand is to see to it that
> we really are sincere, that we actually are what we want our commun-
> ity to know we are. In short, we play the role of being ourselves, we
> sincerely act the part of the sincere person...[16]

The self-justifying and self-referential naïvety of this scheme of things has
made it the ideological home of much charlatanry, as well as of the
simple-minded and insecure. The encounter groups and psycho-dramas,
happenings and love-ins of the 1960s were all manifestations of a form of
psychological escapism which had as its simple premise the deeply im-

plausible notion that the more individuals exposed their 'real' feelings to each other the better the world would be.

It has to be said that the extraction of the moral dimension from the truly therapeutic processes of mental health care can release some patients from unbearable personal pressure. For those who have suffered severe psychological distress through unreasonable feelings of guilt, such release may represent the first step towards recovery. However, for those of us fortunate enough not to have to inhabit the closed world of psychotherapy, the primacy of self-authentication over disinterested intellection can all too easily lead to the manipulation and exploitation of our perceptions. Richard Nixon's famous 'Checkers' speech on American television in 1952, for example, where, with tears in his eyes, he convinced the American voting public that he was a man who loved dogs, and therefore that they should forget about the election slush-fund in which he was implicated, taught that wily politician a lesson which served him well for nearly twenty-five years: voters can be deflected from scrutiny of a politician's inept or corrupt actions so long as he or she appears to display sincere feelings in public.[17]

Phenomenology, universals and the fallacy of individualism

It is my contention that it is within the discursive framework sketched here that theoreticians of drama-in-education have built their conceptual home. I am suggesting that in their denial of politics and culture they share this home with powerful forces within Western culture which also seek to de-politicise contemporary consciousness, but in the name of a naturalism owing more to Hobbes and Adam Smith than to Rousseau and Blake. It is, of course, profoundly paradoxical that drama-in-education should be grounded in a view of the world to which so many of its proponents are ideologically opposed, and yet which continues, unquestioningly, to inform its discourse.

In attempting to make sense of this paradox we should note that leading practitioners in the field are sometimes regarded as occupying philosophical ground which is, broadly speaking, phenomenological. Davis and Lawrence, for example, regard Bolton as quite explicitly 'embracing a phenomenological position',[18] and plentiful reference in the literature to 'personal meaning' and 'universals' suggests how the neo-Platonic apriorism of Edmund Husserl,[19] with his search for the Absolute, for an 'essence' beyond all criticism, upon which all knowledge can rest, could appeal to a discipline adrift in psychological theories of motivation.

Husserl saw it as the task of phenomenologists to identify and describe the essences which he thought made up our experience. Drawing extensively from psychology, he believed that close attention to our mental processes would reveal certain a priori truths intuited by the mind which could be isolated from any particular historical or cultural circumstances. In doing so, he set out to contain individualism within an epistemology of a-temporal imperatives concerning the nature of objective knowledge; under a transcendental phenomenological system of this kind it becomes possible to argue that simply 'knowing oneself' is the key to seeing the world as it actually is. To know oneself is to reveal the essential structures, the 'universals', through which all knowing becomes possible; for Husserl, taking things as they 'appear to the consciousness' is to know their reality.

The idea of phenomenological absolutes or universals fits neatly with the individualistic premises of drama-in-education, and has been widely, if only implicitly, accepted. Betty Jane Wagner, for example, in a much-quoted aphorism, claims that, 'True gut-level drama has to do with what you at your deepest level want to know about what it is to be human'.[20] Gavin Bolton goes so far as to list the 'universals' revealed by drama. According to him, they 'are to do with basic needs of protecting one's family, journeying home, facing death, recording for posterity, passing on wisdom, making tools, etc'.[21]

Latterly, Dorothy Heathcote turned increasingly to primitivism in what seemed to be a quest for forms of phenomenological absolute or 'universal truth'. Her students became accustomed to playing out the inter-cultural dilemmas of tribal communities, and to inventing their own 'rituals' for a wide range of simple activities such as choosing a leader or agreeing on laws. (For an example, see again, Appendix A.) Underlying this simple noble savage view of so-called 'primitive' societies are the phenomenological assumptions already indicated; notably, that there are certain realities, or *essences*, which form the common features of all human consciousness. Describing a drama session at an exclusive English public school, for example, in which Heathcote (somewhat improbably) had asked a group of boys in swimming trunks to 'assume roles of a primitive tribe', Wagner is confident that by 'identifying and creating' the boys could 'capture the essence of the primitive'.[22]

Both psychology and phenomenology can be seen as responses to twentieth-century secularism which seek to mystify the self and to create a morality of introspection. However, neither can provide a way out of the reductionist and self-regarding conceptual trap which drama-in-education has dug for itself, for neither system moves beyond the confines of the individual consciousness. Both represent views of the world which can only leave us ethically helpless in the face of the social, cultural and political dilemmas confronting us, for unlike pre-modern, traditional societies, we have lost the congruence of value through which a culture of membership confers identity and social meaning on the individual. We are faced instead with a curious kind of disembodied identity, self-contained and entirely self-referential, a 'specifically modern' emotivist self, which, according to the philosopher Alasdair MacIntyre,

> ... cannot be simply or unconditionally identified with any particular moral attitude or point of view just because of the fact that its judgements are in the end criterionless ... [It] has no necessary social content and no necessary identity can then be anything, can assume any role or take any point of view, because it is in and for itself nothing.[23]

Without doubt this is the vacuum at the centre of drama-in-education theory, the existential, narcissistic wilderness around which we circle in search of truth, value and meaning, but in which all the so-called social learning of the drama class, however conscientiously engineered, must in the end be condemned to wander aimlessly. In its desolate landscape the only deontological imperative is the absolute relativity of moral values; your actions need no other criterion to command my respect than that you should sincerely believe they are right for you. The moral attitude of an individual has value by *virtue of that individual's individuality*.

The transparent circularity of this argument has failed to dislodge it from its influential position in contemporary education, where individualistic, child-centred accounts of learning still predominate. But as John Dunn makes clear in his bleak account of modern liberalism, 'individuals might be all that, humanly speaking, was there; but this consideration alone would scarcely give one grounds for treating them as a commanding focus of value, or for acknowledging a duty to tolerate their idiosyncratic tastes and opinions'.[24] Nevertheless, individualism stands as the custodian of freedom in our society; challenge it in any terms but its own, so says convention, and that freedom is threatened. Thus, the traditional butts of the educational radical, progressivist or Marxist (state examinations, assessment, externally imposed curricula, vocationalism, and so on) are so categorised not for ideological reasons but precisely and solely because they are held to limit the free and arbitrary choices of individuals.

Denied ideology in a society inclined to reduce the strongly held ideas and beliefs of others to symptoms of psychoneurosis if they are unpalatable or inconvenient, all the radical teacher can hope for under such a scheme of things is that by demystifying the processes and contradictions of society in the classroom, significant numbers of individuals re-examining 'their own views and values' may eventually feel inclined to oppose them. It is what

David Hargreaves has called 'the fallacy of individualism', or 'the belief that if only schools can successfully educate every individual pupil in self-confidence, independence and autonomy, then society can with confidence be left to take care of itself'.[25] As a programme for the institution of egalitarian change it leaves much to be desired.

6

Happening on the Aesthetic

The art forms of school drama

In the previous chapter I sketched a history which showed nineteenth-century Romanticism and twentieth-century developmental psychology conspiring to shape post-war thinking about arts education. I argued that it was these two powerful forces that turned us away from thinking of art as a matter of making and appraising socially valued products, and towards the idea of art as a therapeutic engagement with the inner world of individuals. As a consequence of this reformulation, many arts educators have come to see the 'art process' originating in a kind of psychological drive perpetually striving to 'make sense of the life of feeling'.

> In music, painting, and drama and the other arts, we develop languages, symbolic forms through which we may understand this universe of personal response . . . They are the product of a compulsion to make sense of, express and communicate from, the inner world of subjective understanding.[1]

This particular view of the aesthetic has been popularised by many writers on arts education in recent years, most notably perhaps by Malcolm Ross. In the tradition of a line of expressive aestheticians like Marjorie Hourd, Arnaud Reid and Susanne Langer, Ross believes that the extravagant emotivism of the Romantic spirit is simultaneously awakened and tamed by the orderly exercise of creativity, so that education through art is 'education for emotional maturity'.

> The arts teacher helps children's emotional development by showing them how to express their feelings creatively and responsibly . . . Our

work differs from that of our non-arts colleagues in that we give pride of place to the formulation of feeling-ideas, to the creation and response to forms that must (and need only) in the final instance, satisfy strictly personal and subjective criteria.[2]

While Peter Slade and the early advocates of Child Drama had little doubt that drama was art of exactly this kind (Child Drama being an especially superior category 'of exquisite beauty', a 'high Art Form in its own right')[3], the promotion in later years of drama as a cross-curricular learning medium has meant some subordination of this aesthetic imperative.[4] In dramatic pedagogy, art (or 'art form') becomes a vehicle for more generalised learning outcomes. According to Gavin Bolton, classroom drama should no longer be considered as of necessity artistic at all. In his view, the 'art form' is only manifest when conditions of 'focus, tension and symbolisation' are present.[5] On the other hand, although what the children engage in, or produce, may not actually be 'art', he seems confident that participation in drama can nevertheless awaken their 'latent sense of the aesthetic'. This aesthetic turns out to be another form of phenomenological essence, or universal, which 'can be awakened in all of us'.[6] For Bolton, children's 'aesthetic sense' is something they 'feel in their bones'.[7]

Thus, in one of drama-in-education's more memorable concordances, 'focus, symbolism, tension, resonance, ambiguity, contradiction, ritual, simplicity, contrast, anticipation, resolution, completeness and incompleteness, humour, magic, ambiguity and metaxis, etc ... the inner forms of theatre that children of all ages can sense as significant', are supposed simply to swim into focus as the drama progresses.[8] Unfortunately, the random quality of Bolton's list serves only to obscure the hypothesis which it patently seeks to declare; that is, that art, and drama in particular, seems to have a special ability to engage with our apparent sense of *presence*, to illuminate for us that momentary consciousness of existential insight which, for Heidegger, was the key to understanding the complex relationship we have with our experience in its immediate aftermath.[9] I shall return later to this idea of presence.

While Ross has notably (and rightly) taken Bolton to task for the expansive pedagogic claims the latter has made on behalf of school drama,[10] neither seems to doubt the essential seaworthiness of the conceptual vessel upon which they both turn out to be embarked. When Ross expresses his dissatisfaction with the 'non-arts outcomes' of drama teaching, he does so in the context of his 'exclusive commitment' to an aesthetic with which Bolton would have no trouble in identifying. For both, the dramatic 'art form' is there to be discovered, its essential 'rightness' declaring itself through a process of developing aesthetic awareness. We are persuaded to see the creation and appreciation of art as a personal, subjective, and psychologistically self-validating process, measurable only against the 'integrity of the individual's feeling life'.[11] A drama teacher sums it up perfectly:

> The aesthetic dimension in Drama is to reveal deeper meanings so that children perceive universal applications personally.[12]

For all this, Ross has never been in doubt that school drama's difficulties with art originate in the 'wrangle between theatre and drama'. 'Drama-in-education', he claims, 'is a doomed mutant unless it can draw life from the theatre'.[13] By the 1980s we can observe attempts being made by Bolton and other writers to extend a somewhat limp hand of friendship to 'threatre art'. In 1988, for example, we find Morgan and Saxton speaking jauntily about rebuilding the bridge 'between Dramatown and Theatretown'.[14] However, efforts during the 1980s to reconnect the private, dispositional outcomes of educational drama to the demonstrably public ones of the theatre, mainly by the (strictly pleonastic) advocacy of the use of 'theatre form' in the drama lesson tended to lack conviction. Any progress on this front continued to be inhibited by traditional suspicions of public performance and an unwillingness to disengage from that overriding commitment to personal feeling-response that I have charted here. Thus, while Bolton was happy to acknowledge that 'drama' and 'theatre' might be less educationally incommensurable than previously thought, it turned out to be only to the extent that he seemed prepared to legitimate a limited number of suitably authentic 'theatre' experiences.[15]

The tradition of English

School drama has not been alone on the curriculum, of course, either in its dedication to personal feeling and experience or in its pursuit of the 'timeless truths' of the human condition. We can see in drama's long educational association with English a striking affinity of purpose between the two fields. In the 1960s, writers like David Holbrook, for example, evangelised a new kind of English lesson designed particularly to draw into the English experience those children traditionally alienated by the formal curriculum, those for whom 'creative drama', free as it was from the demands of the written text, seemed an ideal medium. Like the pioneers of educational drama, Holbrook too drew extensively on psychological theories of art and creativity, and succeeded in inspiring a generation of English teachers with the same kind of progressive idealism that we have already seen in the writings of Peter Slade and Brian Way.

In reality, it is hard to see how drama could have gained even a tenuous foothold on the curriculum without the wide acceptance of the centrality of English. Conceptually and ideologically, the tradition of which Holbrook was such an able representative and advocate provided much needed off-the-peg credibility for the emerging practices of drama in schools. That tradition, most commonly associated with the teaching and writing of F. R. Leavis and his fellow 'Scrutineers'[16] had such a pervasive influence that it is difficult to imagine that the study of English, as defined by these pioneers, has not always had its dominant position in our educational consciousness. But, as Terry Eagleton reminds us, in 1920 English was still considered the province of a tiny coterie of 'patrician dilettantes' on the fringes of academia. Within the space of ten years, these Cambridge radicals so revolutionised its status, that, by the outbreak of the Second World War, and in spite of fierce academic opposition, English could with justification claim to be the secular heir of classics and theology, the very yardstick by which what it meant to be 'educated' could be measured.

> English was not only a subject worth studying, but the supremely civilizing pursuit, the spiritual essence of the social formation ... English was an arena in which the most fundamental questions of human existence – what it means to be a person, to engage in significant relationship with others, to live from the vital centre of the most essential values – were thrown into vivid relief and made the object of the most intensive scrutiny.[17]

The tradition so influentially constructed by the Scrutineers was based on a belief in the existence of a transcendent humanism, an intense, Kantian morality that could be authentically felt through the experience of literature. This tradition defined and guaranteed an expressive and interpretative discourse which could be said to have usurped the value-inspiring role of religious education and to have secured for English a dominant position in the minds of curriculum planners thereafter.

We may see drama-in-education as having stowed away on this same humanising mission, happy to share with the tradition of English the apodeictic belief that beyond the messy uncertainties of history lie cosmic values, the eternal verities of liberal civilisation. The so-called 'universals' of the drama lesson, the phenomenological essences, turn out on closer inspection to be no more nor less than the moral assumptions of Leavisite humanism, whose truths it seems may be as satisfactorily soaked up in the suspended disbelief of the drama class as contemplated and absorbed through 'close reading'. In opting always for 'a level of greater generality or universality',[18] the dramatic pedagogues unconsciously guide their classes not towards the trans-cultural commonalities of their imaginations, but in fact to something very like the ideologically prescribed goals of the Scrutineers.

Thus it is that for all their professed commitment to the 'felt values' of the individual child, the choice of 'universals' and the approval or dis-approval of their outcomes is rarely in doubt. When Heathcote uses a drama about a refuse collectors' strike as 'an effective tool for gaining insight into the patterns and tensions of community life',[19] complex politi-cal and moral statements become muffled in the simple humanising mes-sage of tolerance and reconciliation.

However, as exemplified by the Victorian novelists, who felt sympathy with the poor until the moment they took action against their poverty, the liberal humanist tradition is notably silent on questions of social action or civic responsibility. In this context, Raymond Williams' comments on the author of *Hard Times* (a novel in which Leavis believed Dickens to be 'possessed by a comprehensive vision' of the 'inhumane spirit' of industrial-ism) could not be more apposite:

His positives do not lie in social improvement, but rather in what he sees as the elements of human nature – personal kindness, sympathy and forbearance.[20]

As Williams points out, attractive and desirable though they might be, these are not the values of the gods, but merely those elevated by a society anxious to preserve its social and moral fabric, if necessary at the expense of conflicting, yet historically more powerful, claims of justice and equality.

In drama-in-education, as in English, selective perspectives of this kind are additionally legitimated through appeals to the aesthetic. Tolerable feelings we might happen to have about something are elevated and recon-stituted as our 'aesthetic awareness' and their sense of 'rightness' further endorsed. Unfortunately, although Bolton insists that 'aesthetic meanings are *felt* rather than comprehended'[21] he has no Leavisite canon against which to measure them and thus no account of how we might distinguish between the feelings of aesthetic and non-aesthetic meaning.

The transcendence of this idea of the aesthetic, existing in a sphere beyond the mere intellectual and utilitarian concerns of society, accessible only through the imagination, insulates it perfectly from those inclined to locate artistic experience in our more earthly preoccupations. If the sub-text of the drama class reflects the ideals of Leavisite English, then its text is a masquerade of moral and aesthetic sensibility where experience and feeling too often stand in the place of interpretation and judgement, and where ultimately, in Eagleton's vivid and disturbing example, 'the truth or falsity of beliefs such as that blacks are inferior to whites is less important than what if feels like to experience them'.[22]

The difference between drama-in-education and the tradition of English, and it is a crucial one, lies in the latter's emphasis on criticism. However idiosyncratic and contested their conclusions, the Scrutineers were unambiguous about the need for aesthetic discernment, for the allocation of *value* in the arts. Their patrician acceptance that only a minority would be capable of the 'genuine personal response' necessary for the appreciation of their canon had at least the virtue of honesty, and they really did believe that, in return for the gift of insight, the few had a profound responsibility for the education of the many.[23]

The contrasting evasiveness of drama-in-education over matters of aesthetic and moral judgement has already been noted.

In recent years, English has made striking efforts to break away from the decontextualised, child-centred preoccupations of the past, and has begun to address itself seriously to the wider determining issues of culture and history. Probably more influenced now by the post-structuralism of Foucault and Barthes, and the cultural politics of Raymond Williams, than by the reassuring metaphysic of the Leavisite legacy, a substantial group of English teachers is now advocating a radical alternative prospectus.[24] For them, literature, like drama, does not transcend politics; they can see that the aesthetic which legitimated the surpremacy of their subject and which helped to give drama its entree into schools is as much a product of the processes of history as the alternatives which seek to replace it.

Naturalism and the theatre

If the aesthetic of drama-in-education owes much to the tradition of English, it is also, despite the recent emphasis on forms of pedagogy, deeply indebted to twentieth-century dramatic naturalism. To explain this we shall have to start by looking more closely at the form of the dramatic experience itself.

For drama in the classroom to *be* drama (and not social studies or English, for example) it must recognisably incorporate certain fundamental common features. Thus, if there were not groups of children in some sense taking on imagined roles or characters in a defined space for their own or an audience's satisfaction, strictly it would be difficult to describe a classroom activity as 'drama'. If we look carefully at this dramatic action as it is most commonly manifest (and that is to exclude any preceding or subsequent debate) I would argue that what we invariably find is deeply naturalistic in its form. Every day and across the country children are making up improvised plays with short, televisual scenes, or spontaneously taking on 'roles' which purport to place them in an imagined 'reality'.

This heritage of dramatic naturalism is readily identifiable in the statements of earlier practitioners. When Peter Slade, for example, assures us that 'there is no more certain way of understanding Drama than to act sincerely,'[25] and exhorts us to 'recognise how the vital characteristics of Child Drama, particularly Sincerity and Absorption, blossom on and on with the right handling',[26] it is difficult not to be reminded of Stanislavski's creative 'if', that 'imagined truth which the actor can believe in sincerely and with greater enthusiasms than he believes practical truth, just as the child believes in the existence of its doll and of all the life in it and around it'. Like Slade, Stanislavski believed that the successful actor had 'to develop to the highest degree his imagination, a childlike naivety and trustfulness, and artistic sensitivity to truth and to the truthful in his soul and body'.[27]

Few drama teachers today, I think, would fail to be similarly concerned with the truthfulness with which children portray reality in their improvisations, a truthfulness measured not by the accuracy of impersonation so much as by the apparent sincerity and commitment of the attempt, the so-called 'authenticity of feeling' associated with it. Indeed, it would seem that, given characters with whom they can empathise and situations close at hand, few children lack the potential spontaneously to enact human encounters with unselfconscious verisimilitude. In the right circumstances a child shares with the actor the ability to transform, in Stanislavski's words, 'a coarse scenic lie into the most delicate truth of his relation to the life imagined'.[28]

It is this unselfconscious commitment to an authentic 'inner truth', combined with progressivism's traditional mistrust of the critical or analytic, that binds drama-in-education to that same pervasive naturalism which so decisively frames television drama. The reluctance to make the step from describing the world through the eyes of individuals, from promoting children's or an audience's awareness, to any interpretation of those descriptions, draws both the drama of the classroom and that of the flickering images in our front rooms irresistibly back to that ideology of non-ideology which, for Terry Eagleton 'de-historicizes reality and accepts society as a natural fact'.

This draining of direction and meaning from history results in the art we know as naturalism ... Meticulously observed detail replaces the

portrayal of 'typical' features; the truly 'representative' character
yields to a 'cult of the average'; psychology or physiology oust history
as the true determinant of individual action.[29]

For all its pedagogic claims, I doubt that much classroom drama bears
resemblance to the dramatic didacticism of *lehrstück* and agitprop with
which its more radical advocates often seek to be identified.[30] The fundamental lack of specificity in its learning objectives, for one thing, makes it
difficult to see how dramatic pedagogy can be commensurate with the
didacticism of Brecht or Piscator. Also, drama-in-education's traditional
commitment to variations of such existentially passive aims as 'awareness',
'symbolisation' and 'significance' suggests that many practitioners would
be more at ease with the introspective symbolism of the later Strindberg,
'pre-eminently the dramatist of a dynamic psychology',[31] than with the
raucous theatrical polemics of the Weimar Republic.

The low-key emotional approach of Dorothy Heathcote clearly reveals
this commitment to naturalism. At first sight, many of her techniques, such
as the breaking up of narrative and the limiting of characterisation, seem
sympathetic to Brechtian practice. Where she parts company with Brecht is
precisely at the point where, in his own words, 'the means must be asked
what the end is'.[32] It is there that she invariably yields to that 'cult of the
average', denying both the specificity and the movement of history in her
attempts to universalise the dramatic experience. Heathcote claims that the
end product of the drama is changed students, 'changed in that their areas
of reference are widened, their growth as people is furthered, their understanding of humanity is extended'.[33] For her it is sufficient to assume that a
process of 'internalisation' has taken place, that the children have 'lived
through a problem' and have been encouraged to reflect upon it. Fine aims,
certainly, and a worthy description of the personal journeys made by the
characters in any Chekhov play. But, as we know, neither Ranyevskaya's
understanding of humanity nor her reflection upon her problems will save
the cherry orchard. These are precisely the limitations of a naturalism
which, as Eagleton makes clear, 'can create no significant totality from its
materials', where 'the unified epic or dramatic actions launched by realism
collapse into a set of purely private interests'.[34]

The high expectations raised by a dramatic pedagogy which seemed not
only to offer a new grounding for school drama, but also to restore to drama
teaching a sense of direction and purpose, a humane seriousness through
which the inner and outer worlds of our experience might be reconciled,
can only in the end be frustrated if practitioners methodically turn away
from the implications of its outcomes. For if naturalism's strength lies in its
'abstract objectivity', its ability to portray the suffering and injustice of the

world with startling clarity, its weakness is that it removes these perceptions from the field of human responsibility.[35]

According to the Marxist critic Ernst Fischer, there comes a moment of
decision when naturalism must either break through to forms of interpretation and action or 'founder in fatalism, symbolism, mysticism, religiosity,
and reaction'.[36] The so-called 'moment of understanding', the confident
achievement of the drama 'process', is also, and crucially, the moment of
choice. We are warmed by recognition, like Brecht's audiences for dramatic
naturalism, 'Yes, I have felt like that too,' but our new-found awareness
can too easily collapse into the self-regarding inertia and pessimism of a
Masha or a Vanya without a parallel understanding of the ideological
structures which are the key to change. In drama-in-education, the choice
which Brecht would wish to place for us at the heart of the dramatic
experience has too often been effectively obscured, usurped by a vicarious
submission to the changeless, where 'the specific nature of a historical
moment is falsified into a general idea of *being*'.[37]

The passive, internalised objectives of educational drama, the 'inner-
standings', 'awarenesses' and 'moments of significance', are products both
of traditional humanism and the naturalistic conventions within which they
are invariably acted out. They reflect a commitment to a transcendent view
of the aesthetic which is uncritical because it is beyond criticism. It is this
peculiar wrapping of the metaphysical in the commonplace that has contributed so profoundly to school drama's problems with evaluation and
assessment. Until drama-in-education can relocate its practices in the critical, public world it is unlikely that they will be resolved.

7

Significant Knowing

Knowing what you feel

From the end of the 1970s, largely under the influence of Heathcote and Bolton, ideas about creativity and personal development in drama were displaced with attempts to formulate theories of learning. This new project, with its emphasis on cognition, represented a determined attempt by leaders in the field to redirect the energies of drama teachers into areas less overtly reliant on the principles of progressivism. Conscious perhaps that school drama's roots in children's play gave them a hold on naturalistic theories of learning, they turned once again to psychology, and in particular this time to cognitive psychology, as a basis for the development of a comprehensive theory of drama as a way of knowing. The ideas that emerged looked to the internal processes governing the reception and ordering of our experience, the personal aspects of knowing, but ignored the social and cultural context in which knowledge is defined.

Thus, for Bolton, 'drama for understanding' was 'a process of personally engaging with knowledge'.[1]

> In play and in drama there is obvious learning potential in terms of skills and objective knowledge, but the deepest kind of change that can take place is at the level of subjective meaning. The learning ... has to be felt for it to be effective.[2]

The affirmation of the 'subjective response' indicated here, with its evocation of the Romantic ideals of liberated emotion and natural spontaneity, seems to be an attempt to raise the theorectical status of feelings. In a simple conflation of the 'objective' and 'subjective' worlds of our post-

Enlightenment consciousness, Bolton asserts that 'true knowing' is *what you know you feel.*

The teacher tries to put children in touch with what is deeply felt and then proceeds to initiate a slow process of disengagement from those feelings and values, not necessarily with a view to changing them but with a view to knowing what they are.[3]

By this account, because drama-in-education uniquely offers children access to this authentic emotional inner world, it is specially placed to help them 'feel their way into knowledge'.[4] In keeping with progressivism still, the objects of this knowledge are not, of course, to be the superficial facts of the traditional academic curriculum, the so-called 'value-free "detached" knowledge of subject disciplines'.[5] Instead, learning through drama involves a 'felt change in value',[6] and it is 'these felt values that contribute to the child's subjective meaning in playing and are a central feature of the activity of drama'.[7] It is not the teacher's place to examine these values in public, nor to mediate between variant moralities within the group. He or she should instead harness the capacity of drama to enable children *simply to realise what their values are.*

A teacher may from within the drama use her/his role to open up the door of opportunity for such Realisation. The teacher cannot know exactly what each child will learn or how significant the learning will be. That does not matter. Her/his responsibility lies in detecting which door and when to open it . . .[8]

It seems that the only criterion for the knowledge sought during this kind of experience is that it should be *significant to the learners*, that it should mean something (though not necessarily the same thing) to each individual. 'Meaning' would thus appear to be a goal in itself, circumscribed by its own intransitivity and revealed in those rare high points of dramatic concentration and focus that Heathcote once characterised as 'moments of awe'. Here is Bolton again, analysing a lesson he himself had recently taught:

. . . I could not be specific in terms of what was to be learnt – my intervention changed the mode of experiencing and thinking, an act of faith that the switch from the pupils' being outside the subject matter to inside it had some kind of learning potential . . . I am convinced that dramatic activity used for personal knowledge of this kind is educationally significant . . .[9]

For all the sanguinity of these assertions it is not easy to see how they can be classed as anything but acts of faith. Apart from anything else, as every school drama teacher knows, these apparent 'moments of significance' are in reality extremely difficult to achieve. Even Heathcote and Bolton in the controlled conditions of their demonstration workshops would often take several sessions to build up the required tension and commitment. In the pandemonium of the ordinary school day these 'awesome' dramatic occasions must be very rare indeed. It might reasonably be argued that the time and energy expended on such painstaking objectives, the ultimate justification of which seems to rest on intuitions no less questionable than those of the discredited 'drama for personal development', could be more profitably spent. It is tempting to conclude that for all the new dressing, this ambitious project reveals little genuine advance on the Newsom Report of twenty years earlier, which endorsed school drama as a way of helping young people 'to come to terms with themselves', working out 'their own personal problems' by acting out 'psychologically significant situations'.[10]

However, we must not forget that drama-in-education has also sought to link this idea of personal knowing to the wider project of liberal humanism through its claims to facilitate access to the transcendental essences of phenomenology. Implicitly agreeing with Husserl that only through self-knowledge can we unlock the fundamental structures of the world and see it as it really is, proponents of dramatic pedagogy have argued that the personal knowledge gained as a result of the drama experience is not as random and solipsistic as first made out, for it has as its object these selfsame trans-cultural essences. Under this system, therefore, meaning is both personal and universal.

The literature of drama-in-education is full of references to this concept of the hidden universal, from the surrealism of Heathcote's public-school boys in swimming trunks capturing 'the essence of the primitive' that we have already noted, to Bolton's hypothetical drama about the 1984–5 miners' strike revealing the 'fairly common universal' of 'how people cope under stress'.

> For example, the topic may be about an arrest on the picket line but it is really about a torn community ... Drama can normally only engage with a topic or issue obliquely, for drama's contextual meaning is but a vehicle for a level of greater generality or universality.[11]

The moral and political implications of this retreat from culture have already been noted; the 'obliqueness' in the above example really serves to fudge and obscure an issue rich in its particularily. Generalisations about 'torn communities' seem a poor substitute educationally for the dramatic learning potential in the politics of the actual, lived events.

Back in the classroom, the assumption that life can be reduced to a series of simple, timeless statements,[12] can lead all too easily to that kind of drama teaching in which the dense, thrilling language and brilliant thematic organisation of, say, the first scene of *King Lear*, are abandoned in favour of platitudinous improvisations about family squabbles, on the grounds that its themes are 'universal'.[13] Drama then becomes a form of reduction to the obvious, its learning objectives triumphantly achieved only because they are so undemanding.

Personal knowledge

However questionable the argument for personal and universal knowing, it is nevertheless plain that something quite unlike the normal scholastic knowledge transaction is going on in the manipulated make-believe of a successful educational drama session. Children under the pressure of sustained role-playing do indeed, on occasions, display surprising insights, and it certainly seems that by inducing deep emotional commitment to an idea in this way, the skilled drama teacher can stimulate high levels of expressive coherence in individual children.[14] Neither is it difficult to see how this might be interpreted as the manifestation of a special kind of learning, particularly as the circumstances surrounding such 'moments of significance' tend to be powerfully mesmeric. Many children *seem* to exhibit an unfamiliar capacity both for perception and commitment under these conditions.

However, the reliance of so much of the drama-in-education methodology on transient and unpredictable 'moments' of this kind make its outcomes difficult, if not impossible, to pin down. The process relies heavily on the intuition of the teacher, and although Bolton suggests that drama examiners should be primarily concerned with 'the quality of meanings the participants sought and found in the material',[15] he fails to indicate any quality criteria. While he seems satisfied that when he himself participates in drama he experiences 'a knowing in my bones', he obviously recognises the problems faced by drama teachers when arguing for the acceptance of their subject on these kinds of grounds. As he rightly points out, 'how do we argue a case for its inclusion in our school curriculum if we are not able to identify it? How do we know what we are teaching? What do we put in our syllabuses?'[16] How and what indeed?

Attempts to address these fundamental dilemmas have, not surprisingly, focussed increasingly on theories of knowledge which seem to give support to the primacy of the subjective experience school drama has staked out for its own. I have already indicated how aspects of phenomenology seem to have provided a conceptual framework within which Bolton and others have defended educational drama's agenda of essential meanings and inner knowing. For this complex and difficult epistemological brief, however, perhaps the most persuasive argument is available in the writing of Michael Polanyi, whose book *Personal Knowledge*[17] provides the title of this section. Polanyi's theories of 'tacit understanding' and 'intellectual passion' have proved irresistibly attractive to drama-in-education and deserve some attention here.[18]

I have already noted that in his claims for drama as a learning method Bolton remains loyal to the fact/value distinction. He has maintained that drama-in-education's unique contribution to understanding is made through its reference both to the 'objective' world outside the child, and to his or her 'subjective' internal world, the resultant meaning being (in his words) 'poised dialectically' between the two. Thus for Bolton, the creation of a drama is 'an opportunity for the child to express his feelings about the objective world'.[19]

Polanyi argues for a related distinction. For him, *explicit* knowledge is that most usually described as knowledge, such as information in libraries or the content of school syllabuses; it corresponds most closely to education-al drama's 'objective' category. *Tacit* knowledge, on the other hand, he describes as that pre-verbal, a-critical awareness which we share with all animals, and upon which our ability to understand what we explicitly know ultimately depends.

> . . . the function of understanding [is] that of knowing what we *intend*, what we *mean*, or what we *do*. To this we may add now that nothing that is said, written or printed, can ever mean anything in itself: for it is only a *person* who utters something – or who listens to it or reads it – who can mean something *by* it. All these semantic functions are the tacit operations of a person.[20]

However, as Polanyi makes clear, this tacit knowing, or understanding, while it is necessarily a function of the person, is not just another form of subjectivity, simply a question of the interpretation of 'reality' by an emo-tive inner world giving us each our 'personal meanings'. Polanyi here makes a crucial distinction between the passive feelings we all experience, such as pain, desire, jealously, and so on, and the active commitments of what he calls our 'moral and intellectual passions'. For him, it is these commitments which define the personal.

... we may distinguish between the personal in us, which actively enters into our commitments, and our subjective states, in which we merely endure our feelings. This distinction establishes the conception of the *personal*, which is neither subjective nor objective. In so far as the personal submits to requirements acknowledged by itself as independent of itself, it is not subjective; but in so far as it is an action guided by individual passions, it is not objective either. It transcends the disjunction between subjective and objective.[21]

Most importantly here, Polanyi attempts in this formulation to reconcile the individual with his or her cultural membership, by rejecting both the empiricist view that knowledge is simply objectively out there to be discovered and the relativist one that it is nothing more than the arbitrary construction of the knower. He proposes instead that the meanings we make for ourselves as individuals must be commensurate with those of the culture to which we belong, and that we are motivated towards this commensurability by our natural intellectual passion to discover correct solutions.

The sense of a pre-existent task makes the shaping of knowledge a responsible act, free from subjective predilections. And it endows, by the same token, the results of such acts with a claim to universal validity. For when you believe that your discovery reveals a hidden reality, you will expect it to be recognized equally by others.[22]

Thus, Bolton's 'knowing in my bones' and the sense of 'rightness' felt by participants in an improvised drama could be said to be manifestations of the tacit feeling of satisfaction gained from having successfully advanced from the problematic to a resolution. It is by this movement to an intellectual position of greater satisfaction, according to Polanyi, that 'we eventually come to hold a piece of knowledge to be true',[23] and, 'our adherence to the truth can be seen to imply an adherence to a society which respects the truth, and which we trust to respect it.[24]

At first sight, Polanyi's theory of personal knowledge seems to offer the knowing-through-drama project a new intellectual coherence. It clarifies and diffuses the objective/subjective dichotomy, it draws a distinction between the driving passions of intellect and morality and what are thought to be our simple, felt responses, and it seeks to identify these passions as unfailingly directed towards the satisfactions of universal truth.

Its weakness, which it passes on to drama-in-education, is that its essentially emotivist premises still fail to overcome Hargreaves's fallacy of individualism. Like psychology, it attempts to reduce human motivation to the

satisfaction of instinctual drives.[25] Thus, although the theory provides us
with a workable description of our feelings about the knowledge we possess,
or seek to possess, it cannot give an adequate account of the ways in which
those feelings are themselves determined by the ways we know the world.
Furthermore, its commitment to a paradigmatic liberal society which fos-
ters 'love of truth and of intellectual values in general',[26] and its concomi-
tant suspicion of ideology, leads its author to the same ontological source as
Popper and Eysenck. In much the same manner that Eysenck attempted to
portray ideological commitment as psychoneurotic disturbance, Polanyi
delivers a withering attack on Marxism, 'a fanatical cult of power',[27] on the
grounds that, by denying them their natural universality, it represents no
more than the propagandistic misappropriation of moral passions. Like
Eysenck, he sees little distinction between the 'extremism' of left and right;
he is anxious to remind us that 'Hitler greatly profited from the Bolshevik
example'.[28]

News from nowhere

The increasing acknowledgement of the political dimension of knowledge
and meaning by teachers on the political left of drama-in-education in the
1980s seemed at first sight likely to present an overt challenge to the
naturalism implicit in theories of dramatic pedagogy. However, what
emerged over that decade was in effect a complementary argument, claiming to reconcile a personal, individualistic theory of cognition, with an
understanding that knowledge is both public and contested.

For those on the left prepared to admit Gramscian theories of ideological
hegemony[29] into their class analysis, 'meaning' has been explicitly understood as the primary hegemonic battleground of the class war, with the
state, its institutions (including schools) and its governing class, intent on
maintaining their dominant position. For them, the answer to Bolton's
question is quite clear: children should be encouraged 'to challenge and
resist those unacceptable trends they see in the world around them'. The
knowledge pursued in the school drama class is unequivocally political.

> . . . if children are learning through drama, then *what* are they learn-
> ing? . . . above all, they are learning that drama and theatre provide a
> potent means of exposing and challenging the dominant ideology and
> its prevailing modes of intimidation.[30]

In the epistemology of the radical left the vocabulary of liberal progressivism is displaced by the axioms of struggle; the comfortable values of

'tolerance', 'understanding' and 'awareness' succumb to the robust vitality
of 'resistance', 'solidarity' and 'class-consciousness'.

> For example, in whose interests is it that women and men hold the
> roles that they do? It is in the interest of those who have social and
> political power. Knowledge therefore, is a social construct. Those who
> control knowledge have power.[31]

However, there are many problems with assertions of this kind. For one
thing, in the advanced capitalist democracies it is difficult to argue that
women or workers or children are generally and unqualifiedly exploited.
Our society certainly contains examples of 'intimidation', and thereby tasks
of emancipation, but the former do not hold as a general characterstic of
life, in schools, or out of them. There are logical inconsistencies, too.
Warwick Dobson, for instance, proposes that 'the drama work that goes on
in an institution' should serve to expose and challenge 'the values and
assumptions that constitute its very foundations'. However, he further
claims that his view of drama 'is based firmly on an acknowledgement of
the relativism of morality'.[32] While on one hand, it is easy to see how (in
support of his relativism) Dobson might wish to challenge the right of an
institution to make overwhelming claims about its moral codes, it is unclear
by what token such a committed relativist can imply just such a status for
his own scheme. On the same grounds, however much we may disapprove
of the meanings our children absorb from a culture whose values we reject,
we cannot as relativists, even were it practicably possible, simply replace
them absolutely with meanings of our own.
    Paradoxically, one major strength of the naturalism of Heathcote and
Bolton was that, intuitively, it avoided this central problem. A universality
of moral feeling, elevated above the everyday conflicts of moral choice, had
no need to engage in unseemly political debate. Once again, it is the fallacy
of individualism, limiting radical protest and progressivism alike to the
cause of the individual against the institution *per se*, which forces Dobson
and like-minded educators on the political left back into the world of
personal feelings and values. Clark and Seeley, for example, direct their
stern anti-racist polemic against those teachers who have failed sufficiently
to examine the authenticity of their inner understanding:

> We start from the recognition that every individual has her own set of
> meanings . . . This is why we as teachers – part of a power group in
> society – must be aware of these personal meanings at more than just
> a tokenistic level . . . Are we interested in giving children power and
> responsibility for change or are we just playing? . . . Maybe we have

stopped engaging with our personal meanings and are using the
'teacher-values' which are established by the institutions and systems
within which we work ... Unless we take oppression personally we
will remain self-oppressed.[33]

The transparent naturalism of these slogans, their clear, almost purify-
ing, commitment to the integrity of the self and to a vision of a potentially
corrupting world of hegemonising institutions, is more than a little remi-
niscent of Rousseau's diatribes against French public life. Its consistent pattern of self-reference certainly has little in common with the traditional
collectivism of the left. The 'developed person' of earlier theories of educational drama, notably those of Brian Way, owed much to the compassion-
ate and enlightened individualism of Rousseau's savage. What we seem to
be presented with here is an attempt to naturalise the Marxist ethic itself; a
new version of Natural Man, founded not on an emerging bourgeois consciousness, but on visionary socialism. Here, examination of 'the true and
uncorrupted conscience' will lead children and their teachers to the universal and unchanging freedoms, if not of *Das Kapital*, then at least of *News
from Nowhere*.[34]

These attempts to graft the ideologies of the political left onto prevailing
phenomenological models of knowledge and meaning, can lead only to
confusion and incoherence. If we are to establish a firm intellectual grounding for drama in schools, we shall need to re-examine the fundamental
premises upon which we base our theories of knowledge, and try to understand more completely not only how things come to mean what they do,
but also to what extent it makes sense to talk about making or changing
meanings for the children we teach.

8

Culture and Power

RITA   But when I looked round, me mother had stopped singin', an' she was
         cryin' . . . I said, 'Why are y' cryin', Mother?' She said, 'Because –
         because we could sing better songs than those.' And that's why I came
         back. And that's why I'm staying.

(Willy Russell, 1981.)[1]

Really useful knowledge and the tradition of dissent

My critique so far has sought to demonstrate that thinking about drama-in-education has been limited by an inheritance of psychologistic and phenomenological ontologies. These, I have argued, have conspired respectively to internalise and universalise the dramatic aesthetic, concealing in the process the ideological formations within which school drama has traditionally been held.

From a broader perspective it is also possible to see that the emphasis on the *private* implicit in this conspiracy is itself part of a wider historical movement in which the increasing subjection of public life to marketplace principles has been skilfully represented as a series of private emancipations. The approbative picture of the 'unique individual' in perpetual opposition to a shadowy and generally ill-defined 'system' or 'state' turns out to be just as important to the 'enterprise culture' as it is to the individualistic humanism of progressive education. Nevertheless, drama teachers are surely right to regard these forms of privatisation as a threat to many of their most deeply held principles.

We should not forget that for all its methodological quietism, drama-in-education had its origins in radical forms of educational thinking. It can still count among its allies those concerned to offer more egalitarian and humane alternatives to the present market-bound codes of the English school curriculum. Moreover, many of the values and principles implicit in the actual drama lesson can be seen to derive from a long, dissenting tradition in English education, a tradition deeply opposed to forms of narrow, self-seeking individualism. It is as the modern heirs of this tradition, and not as the standard bearers of the personal and the private, that drama teachers are likely to find themselves healthily at odds, and increasingly so, with the forces that are at present so energetically engaged in redrawing the map of English education.

At a conference in 1981, sociologist Michael Young called upon drama teachers to keep the dissenters' struggle going for a curriculum of 'really useful knowledge'.[2] For Young, it was the battle over who decides what counts as educational knowledge that should be central to our concerns. How does it come about, that certain categories of knowledge and skill are guaranteed a place at the core of the curriculum, other kinds are relegated to the perimeter, and still others, most, probably, fail to qualify entirely? However 'natural' they may seem, these choices represent a particular set of emphases and omissions reflecting consciously and unconsciously the history of what has been thought of as education in our culture.[3]

This does not mean, of course, that curriculum content is not powerfully contested. If for no other reason, the slow pace of cultural change guarantees a mixture of residual, dominant and emergent subjects, as Raymond Williams explains:

> An educational curriculum, as we have seen again and again in past periods, expresses a compromise between an inherited selection of interests and the emphasis of new interests. At varying points in history, even this compromise may be long delayed, and it will often be muddled. The fact about our present curriculum is that it was essentially created by the nineteenth-century, following some eighteenth-century models, and retaining elements of the medieval curriculum near its centre.[4]

When Williams wrote this in the early 1960s it was easier to believe that in the compromise between the new and the inherited, between the emergent and the dominant and residual, the liberal arts, vanguards of the new progressivism, were fast guaranteeing for themselves a central place in the curriculum of the future. Then the traditional methods and academic content of the grammar school curriculum could be easily represented as fusty and reactionary in the face of the new comprehensive ideal, for there was a Whiggish confidence in the slow but inevitable victory of progressive forces. Twenty years on, however, the ideological landscape must have looked less accommodating to the nurserymen and women of what now can only be described as 'traditional' progressivism, as a new set of interests, more concerned with consumer choice than intellectual autonomy, embarked upon a policy of systematic educational enclosure.

The current dominance of these interests, of course, has led to some scepticism as to whether history is, after all, ultimately on the side of the liberal ethic.[5] In appropriating the words 'radical' and 'reform',[6] these new interests have effectively redefined the spokespeople of the progressive optimism of the 1960s as themselves agents of outdated, inherited interest. Teachers, liberal college lecturers, once-thought-to-be-enlightened local authorities, are now said to *stand in the way of progress*. It is something of an irony that the world 'conservative' is widely applied to the assumptions and practices which at one time seemed as if they might change the educational agenda for ever. Those dissenters for whom the overthrow of the university-dominated school curriculum in favour of one made up of 'really useful knowledge' once seemed within their grasp, now find themselves out-manoeuvred and disinherited, fighting to 'conserve' what they can of the 1960s settlement.

Of course, drama teachers have long been accustomed to working at the boundaries of acceptable educational knowledge. Most probably perceive their work as constituting a modest challenge to traditional pedagogic practices and to the idea of 'fitting in'. Also, and commendably, they have become accustomed to taking their stand beside the less able and under-privileged in the latter's all too frequent confrontations with an unsympathetic world. Whatever their practical politics, therefore, it is apparent that most drama teachers are acutely aware in some sense that they, their subject, and probably most of their pupils, are threatened by historical forces which now seem deaf to the claims of the old humanist consensus.

Unfortunately, given the cultural and historical formation of drama in schools which I have outlined, with its suspicion of the intellectual and the analytic and its faith in psychology and personal enlightenment, it is perhaps hardly surprising that a coherent opposition from within the field to this threat has failed to materialise. There has, however, been a closing of ranks around two inviolable notions which we must now examine more closely. They are the imperative of 'need' and the idea of the moral relativity of cultures.

Reason not the need

In recent years the unpredicated use of the word 'need' has become ubiquitous. In education, children's 'needs' have tended to be identified either in the context of an individual child's psychological or physical capabilities ('Clare needs to work with a group more sympathetic to her needs') or of a group's social or ethnic formation ('Asian pupils need to have teaching materials suited to their needs'). The moral urgency implied by the use of 'need' in this way, as opposed, for example, to 'aspiration' or 'preference', its suggestion of the presence of the incontrovertibly necessary, gives powerful impetus to its use in the less prestigious areas of the curriculum. It elevates the preferences of individuals to the status of moral imperatives. An example demonstrates my point. In 1986 a speaker in a debate on the arts felt sure that it was now 'widely accepted that humans have a profound need to play'.[7] This familiar proposition would lose all its force if the 'profound need' were to be replaced by a 'marked tendency' or a 'common desire'. Similarly, there is a world of difference from my 'wanting' to do drama and my 'needing' to, let alone my 'learning to be very interested in it'.

The wide incidence of this idea in the 'caring services' may be seen as an honest attempt to escape from the economic rationalism of today's social and economic planners. The needs of individuals or minority groups acquire moral grandeur in the face of the grim utilitarians of profit and loss. Who could reasonably doubt that the needs of the disabled or maladjusted are indeed 'special'?

The problem is, that by invoking such claims upon the absolute, those unquestionably well-intentioned advocates of need are paradoxically in danger of putting at risk the very freedoms which they so earnestly seek to preserve. Thus, if need is to be established simply by assertion – 'Children need to express themselves freely' – then who is to arbitrate, and by what criteria, between rival claims, such as 'Children need to be disciplined'? Unless conscience can be mobilised over a broad spectrum, as in the formulation of Special Needs Education where disadvantage is unambiguously manifest, 'need' in its intransitive state can be an unreliable ally. Suitably predicated it may be readmitted to the discourse of value, but it will lose in the process much of its potency. Consider how the examples in this paragraph rapidly become contentious: '*In order to challenge and change society* children need to express themselves freely', and, 'Children need to be disciplined *to fit into the world of work*'. The child-centred premises of progressive education form only one of many ideological wagons to which the notion of 'need' can be harnessed.

A further characteristic of 'need' is that it is commonly ascribed by the privileged to communities of the powerless. In many ways it may be regarded as a discreet form of paternalism. 'Disadvantaged' groups tend to have their 'needs' identified not by their own members but those, however benevolently intentioned, with some control over them. Social workers speak of the 'needs' of children in care, the government of the 'needs' of small business, teachers of the 'needs' of racial minorities. It is perhaps a feature of our pride, or sense of solidarity, that while we ourselves are likely from time to time, in a self-regarding way, to refer to our individual 'needs', we are far less inclined to do so when we speak of groups to which we belong. Here we speak of 'demands', of 'rights', of 'equality' and 'justice'; we return, in other words, to an overtly expressed moral curriculum. Consider, for example, how the so-called 'right to manage', much celebrated by the selfsame managers of contemporary society, is neatly balanced in their parlance by the workforce's 'need to accept low wage settlements', or how teachers' 'rights' to fair pay and conditions are sometimes set against the 'needs' of those they teach.

The pervasive employment of the word 'need' tends not only to internalise and contain dissent – 'Clare's "need" to express her frustration with school' is a statement of a very different order from 'Clare's "right" to express her frustration with school' – but also, unless clearly predicated, implicitly perpetuates the powerlessness and underprivilege of those to whom it is applied. In our enthusiastic and doubtless well-meaning attempts to define and satisfy the 'needs' of our students we can all too easily fail to recognise legitimate aspirations which fall outside or even challenge our prospectus. In this way, and from the best of motives, we may be in real danger of reinforcing the social and educational divides we are so anxious to bridge.

For school drama, the emphasis on process has meant that the quality of the dramatic product has often been seen as of secondary importance of the 'needs' of the children engaged in producing it.[8] Many evaluation schemes place a child's contribution to the success of a group's social dynamic, for instance, as a primary criterion for success. However, it is by no means certain that groups made up of such mindful individuals will necessarily come up with drama of quality. Indeed, it is not uncommon for work of astonishing energy and concentration to originate from groups whose only common denominator is mutual dislike.

On the wider stage, our increasing dependence on the language of 'need' may be seen as an indication of the extent to which we have been forced to depoliticise dissent in a society which leans ever more heavily upon psychotherapeutic solutions to its problems.

Is eating people wrong?

Drama-in-education has traditionally put much store on the enacted projection into the lives of others. According to Brian Wilks, 'only in enactment can we explore what it feels like to be someone else'.[9] But how possible really is it to experience the world as others do through the medium of imaginative empathy?[10] Does closing our eyes and walking across the room, for example, *really* allow us to perceive the world as a blind person does?[11] Can we honestly say that the children in the tribal improvisation have *really* 'experienced the classic confrontation of the traditional tribal leader with members of the community'?[12]

These are, of course, not unimportant questions for a set of educational practices which advertises so confidently its ability to facilitate the brief occupancy by children of other people's moral worlds, and sets out to derive a pedagogy from it.

The social anthropologist Clifford Geertz is clear that we can apprehend such worlds 'at least as well as we apprehend anything else', but maintains that 'we can never apprehend another people's or another period's imagination neatly, as if it were our own'.[13] Instead, he insists that we are inevitably and inextricably bound by the imaginative and moral matrices of our own history and culture, which, while they will intersect in complex ways with other consciousnesses, will never allow the latter to be ours in the sense that we can inhabit them. In this respect, the generalities elided from tribal role-playing may turn out, on closer inspection, to be less like universals and more like very selective projections onto an unfamiliar social structure of the cultural matrices of our own.

Nevertheless, as Geertz points out, the idea of the cultural integrity of 'simpler' peoples is one of 'the most thoroughly entrenched tropes of the liberal imagination'.[14] Thus, when children take on the roles of American Indians in drama, they are likely to be doing so not so much in order to get to the roots of the Indians' imaginative world but to highlight two important principles. The first is that whatever their 'superficial' differences in customs, work patterns and social arrangements, there is a universal 'human-ness' which unites the children with the Indians: the second, that viewed from inside (a perspective, it is claimed, made possible through the adoption of role) a seemingly alien culture can both be understood and *justified* in terms of its own internal logic and sense of moral order.

In respect of the first of these principles, our attempts to mine fundamental truths from the superficially more accessible opencast workings of 'simpler' societies rather than from the deep pits of our own may lead us deeper than we imagined.

The image of the past (or the primitive, or the classic, or the exotic) as a source of remedial wisdom, a prosthetic corrective for a damaged spiritual life – an image that has governed a good deal of humanist thought and education – is mischievous because it leads us to expect that our uncertainties will be reduced by access to thought-worlds constructed along lines alternative to our own, when in fact they will be multiplied.[15]

Underlying the second principle is a familiar and understandable reluctance on the part of our post-imperial liberal consciousness to downgrade, or be seeming to patronise, unfamiliar cultural forms. But there is a profound dilemma here. What if the cultural practices portrayed turn out to be horrible? To what extent do we 'respect' a culture that is deeply racist, for example? Are tolerance and understanding really sufficient responses to a society which looks approvingly on female circumcision or acquiesces in the systematic extermination of Jews? What is our response to a Muslim community which expresses a wish for its women to be specifically excluded from equal opportunities legislation? Are our strong feminist and anti-racist convictions simply to be abandoned as we cross national or even local boundaries?

Written accounts suggest that in practice these difficult questions are rarely addressed in the drama class. As we have seen, the primitivism most commonly evoked is of a strictly acceptable kind, 'noble savagery' at its best; children line up solemnly to honour the tribe's dead or to choose a new chief.[16] The tenets of liberalism are rarely challenged.

In many ways, the Weismullerian tribalism of these rituals is harmless enough, so long as no great moral or anthropological conclusions are drawn from it. Also, to draw attention to the limits of liberal humanism in this context is by no means to deny its values, or its importance as a concept in the educational processes of a humane society. However, we should not forget the moral limitations of its comfortable consensus-seeking, and be clear that tolerance and understanding can be both a justification for oppression on the one hand and a recipe for feebleness on the other. If drama and the other arts are to have a liberating and empowering social function, then we will have to look beyond the simple assertion of the 'self-evident' truths of liberal individualism and examine more closely the complex relationship between culture and power in our society.

Singing better songs

The coupling of 'needs' to the idea of the moral integrity of cultural groups has led to the establishment of a simple but influential formula. This tells us firstly that we have an obligation to respect *ipso facto* the values, belief systems and cultural expression of any given community or cultural group. Then, by designating the furtherance of these values, beliefs and expressive forms as a 'need' (consequent upon a community simply *having* particular ideas and customs), any attempt to disseminate alternative cultural values among members of this community can be dismissed at best as an irrelevance and at worst as an unjustifiable imposition.[17]

This pious, although by no means uncommon, view is not only flawed in its casual and unpredicated use of 'need', but also because it seems not to recognise the community's place in a wider social and cultural context. In a commendable desire to empower those social groups at present alienated from the formal and informal hierarchies of the state, conclusions of this kind are drawn from a very narrow analysis of group identity and esteem. The limitations of such an approach – which assumes firstly that a 'community' is a consensual entity existing within fixed boundaries, secondly that its 'needs' are unambiguous and readily identified, and thirdly that they can be pursued in isolation from the interests of the dominant culture – are not difficult to see. In the context of a multi-racial society, for example, it is a perspective which 'reflects a white view of black cultures as homogeneous, static, conflict-free, exotic', and 'ignores the power relations between white and black people, both in history and the present'.[18]

While education clearly has an important function in fostering what David Hargreaves has called the 'dignity and solidarity' of communities (of which, incidentally, the school itself is one), to see schools as only, or even primarily, serving this end is to subscribe to a distinctly cross-eyed view of culture. To propose that different cultural groups in our society (Afro-Caribbean, Bangladeshi, working-class, middle-class, however one chooses to draw the divide) should be educated solely according to their ascribed cultural 'needs' is at best to enter into an organisational nightmare, and at worst to practice, as Hargreaves suggests, a form of 'educational apartheid'. As he points out, 'an exclusive focus on community regeneration in deprived areas distracts attention away from national regeneration. A community education which loses sight of the nation as a whole as a community is not worthy of its name and can justifiably be condemned as parochial'.[19]

In making claims on the 'common-sense curriculum', drama-in-education has deliberately set out to engage with the localised experience of specific groups of children. However, without any really satisfactory critical dimension, it has at the same time denied itself access to culturally endowed systems of appraisal, and thus to the means whereby this strictly local experience may be held up against greater wisdoms.

Above all, we should beware of mistaking this 'common-sense curriculum' for the 'really useful knowledge' of the dissenting tradition. As Gramsci has taught us, the whole idea of 'common sense' is elusive and deceptive, made up as likely of shared prejudice and ignorance as of collective sagacity (for Bertrand Russell, 'the metaphysics of savages'!). The Black Paper assaults on education, for instance, might be said to have been popular, not because they were presented as a series of carefully argued propositions, but precisely because, with their emphasis on standards, basic skills, freedom of choice, and so on, they appeal to 'common sense'. Who could reasonably oppose these principles? The point about 'really useful knowledge' is that it is jealously guarded, often far from obvious, and rarely displayed in the columns of the *Sun* or the *Daily Mirror* or in the 'popular' discourses of Coronation Street or Albert Square. Politics, sociology and philosophy, those disciplines at the intellectual core of moral understanding and social action are significantly absent from the 'common-sense curriculum'.

I believe there is a real danger that in our well-intentioned efforts to respond to the claims of children's sub-culture (their knowledge) we effectively deny them the knowledge through which they can effect change (our knowledge). Under such a scheme, we go to *Hamlet* at the National Theatre while they must be content with role-playing and improvisation, not only because we designate these latter activities as more relevant to their needs, but also because professionally we are not prepared to make qualitative judgements between the two experiences. Who are we (the argument goes) to impose our middle-class cultural values on working-class children, when their needs are so patently different?

There is more than a hint of hypocrisy here. In reality, of course, few of us are not disposed to pass critical comments on the dramas we see outside the classroom, and I suspect many drama teachers at the upper end of the secondary school slip more easily than they would perhaps be prepared to admit into the assessment rituals of GCSE and A level. The anxiety to protect the cultural authenticity of their pupils' work from the criteria of appraisal is rarely comprehensive.

Alongside this reluctance to admit the wider culture as a frame of critical reference there is sometimes a corresponding tendency to dismiss the art of the past as an irrelevance. In one sense this represents a recognition of the class-based domination of certain well-defined cultural forms and an understandable desire to challenge that hegemony at every point. However, I would argue that if such a challenge is to be effectively mounted, then it will require active engagement with the values of that hegemony and its vehicles rather than a simple rejection of its iconography. If teachers wish to take up arms against the dominant culture on behalf of their pupils then they will achieve little by turning their backs on it in the hope that it will wither away if suitably ignored. Its forces (to pursue the metaphor) are being continually reinforced from the ranks of the privileged and the powerful, and will not easily be dislodged.

Furthermore, it is less clear than is sometimes made out that the art of the past and its present day equivalents, however superficially 'middle-class', can so simply be dismissed on ideological grounds. To do so assumes the existence and recognition of an emergent alternative which is able in superior ways to engage with our sense of presence. Also, Georg Lukács surely had a point when he argued that a social class only thinking 'thoughts imputable to it' will be 'doomed to play a subordinate role' unless it can strike at the heart of 'the totality of existing society'.[20]

If as teachers we are really concerned to make equal opportunity for all our pupils a reality, whatever their racial or social identity, then we surely have a responsibility to equip them with the means to interpret and appropriate the world in which they live in the widest possible context. There is a real danger that the class-based exclusivity of certain cultural forms will be perpetuated and reinforced so long as we continue to assert that there are special kinds of cultural experience and knowledge appropriate for pupils, which they can somehow come 'authentically to know' through a set of intuitive, improvisatory processes with no reference to the lexicon of the culture. To deny young people critical access to the art of their society in the name of a specious commitment to sub-cultural 'need', is to remove them even further from meaningful access to the hierarchies of control. For drama teachers, this will mean opening up their classes to dramatic representations of all kinds, to dramas from the theatre and the street, to the popular narratives of the television screen. Most of all, however, it will mean restoring to drama-in-education a coherent discipline-based epistemology.

Part Three

Towards Dramatic Art

9

Practical Aesthetics and Dramatic Art

Criticizing the course of a river means improving it, correcting it ... A critical attitude of this type is an operative factor of productivity; it is deeply enjoyable as such, and if we commonly use the term 'arts' for enterprises that improve people's lives why should art proper remain aloof from arts of this sort?

(Bertolt Brecht, 1940.)[1]

Art and ideology

The most plausible case for the inclusion of drama in the school curriculum must surely rest on the publicly shared understanding that dramatic art is *ipso facto* a member of the arts community. For drama to survive and flourish as an independent discipline its case has to be made in these terms. At the same time, undoubtedly dramatic art has a very special contribution to make to education, one which places the emphasis not on generalised assertions about learning which presuppose the existence of elusive internal processes, but on the manifest centrality of drama in our social consciousness.

If drama is as unambiguously part of the arts curriculum as I am suggesting, then we shall require a serviceable aesthetic theory within which it may be placed. This must be capable of giving us an account both of dramatic art's critical place in culture and history and of the ways in which drama can reflect and articulate the ever-changing paradoxes of our common experience.

I have indicated already that the idea of the 'aesthetic' gains its affirmative power in the modern world when contrasted with the 'de-humanising' materialism of a prevailing technocracy. Ever since Matthew Arnold gallantly wrote about culture as 'Sweetness and Light',[2] the imaginative world of the spirit, the 'aesthetic domain', has been a cross of sensibility held out before the bloodthirsty jaws of mass production and consumption. This resistance, according to Raymond Williams, has meant that 'art and thinking about art' have been separated 'by ever more absolute abstraction, from the social processes within which they are still contained'. For Williams, aesthetic theory has been 'the main instrument of this evasion', giving us a picture of art-as-medicine in a sick and alienating social world.[3] Hence the emphasis placed by arts educators on 'creativity' as an idealised form of production dislocated from any idea of aim or social function, and 'aesthetic awareness' as unconscious and de-contextualised consumption. As we have seen, both these ideas have been central to the arts education project.

However, if we are seeking to put together a practical aesthetic which acknowledges the centrality of history and culture, then this way of regarding art as opposed and somehow superior to the vulgar uncertainties of contemporary experience will not suffice. Not only does it misrepresent the diverse relationships we actually have with art (we may, for example, make our living by it) but also its posture of detachment must be delusory. After all, we can only meaningfully 'create' within the critical parameters of a culture, we can only be 'aware' of what our historical moment and social conditions have on offer. The artist's roots in, and engagement with, his or her social and historical circumstances are inescapable.

In this respect, we may agree with Marx that it is not 'the consciousness of men that determines their being', but rather 'their social being that determines their consciousness'.[4] For Marx, aesthetics joins religion, law, politics, and ethics in the *superstructure* of society, all being constitutive of a 'social mentality', or *ideology*, which is derived from the material relations of production, society's economic base. 'Ideology', here, is probably best understood as constituting that rag-bag of values, metaphors, beliefs and ideas at the centre of our social consciousness, through which we perceive and interpret the world, and which is eventually absorbed into the vernacular of a society as its 'common sense'.[5] Contemporary Marxist aesthetics regards the nature of the relationship between art and ideology as a central question. So it must also be for us, for by releasing art from the dark recesses of the psyche into the public domain we must be careful that it is not then simply ensnared by popular categorisations of status and value.

Because ideology amounts to nothing less than the way we think about the world and form the grounds for our evaluative judgements, Marxist analysis argues that it will always be in the interests of the dominant social class to control it and redefine it in its own terms. This is achieved by widely advertising a more or less 'false consciousness' in order to disguise as 'natural' the particular forms of a class's historical advantages and to legitimate them as 'common sense'. History offers us many examples of how religious belief has been exploited to maintain hereditary power structures in just this way. In modern times ideological control has been attempted overtly by propaganda, as in Germany in the 1930s, and more subtly and unobtrusively through the everyday institutions of the state and its dependencies such as education and the media.

Under these circumstances, according to some Marxist critics, art becomes simply an agent of this 'false consciousness', helping to 'naturalise' class inequalities, another 'element in that complex structure of social perception which ensures that the situation in which one class has power over the others is either seen by most members of the society as "natural", or not seen at all'.[6] The paintings, books and dramas of previous ages are thus exposed as little more than expressions of past class-dominated ideologies, such as those represented by the Court, the Church, the State, the market, and so on. As historical artefacts they may have a place in museums or (suitably contextualised) in history books, but any resonances they may still have for us are dismissed as straightforwardly delusory, indications of our own submission to the same 'false consciousness'.

However, such a simple scheme of things is lacking in a crucial respect, as its detractors have pointed out. It offers no explanation of the ideological challenge offered to their societies by so many painters and writers. Art has often played an overtly subversive role. Büchner's *Woyzeck*, for a not exactly random example, uncompleted at his death in 1837, can hardly be said to embody, in its staccato scenes, its wild and disturbing caricatures and its working-class anti-hero, the confident false consciousness of its author's profoundly bourgeois circumstances. Contemporary examples are abundant, from Julian Beck's Living Theatre to *The Romans in Britain*, and we should not forget that even the great religious cycles of the Middle Ages were cast out into the town squares by the priests as soon as their rough but popular secularity began to undermine the dignity of the Church.

At this point, the aesthetic idealists would doubtless wish to assert that this is sufficient to refute the Marxist argument altogether. For them, Büchner's class formation and his place in history can simply be discounted in discussions about his art. As a playwright in pursuit of 'eternal values', they might say, nineteenth-century society can only be blamed for not recognising their expression in his work. Likewise, the medieval bishops were simply blind to the earthy naturalism, the 'universal humanity' of the mysteries; to speak in terms of class-based ideological conspiracies is to fail to see how art transcends the prejudices of the historical moment.

Marxist writers, of course, refuse to accept this, but they are faced with a problem. By maintaining that art is not accurately described in these metaphysical terms, and yet at the same time having to admit that it cannot be considered as straightforwardly the reflection of a dominant ideology, then art's relationship to the way we think and feel about the world has to be a more complex one than so far proposed.

The French critic Louis Althusser proposes that we can resolve this dilemma by understanding the relationship between art and ideology as intrinsically *dialectical*. Instead of the former being regarded simply as a reflection of the latter, they should be seen as dialectically linked. Ideology, that collection of signs representing 'what it feels like to live in particular conditions, rather than a conceptual analysis of those conditions', has art both in its service *and* as its unerring critic. Or, put another way, while critically reflective of our experience, art 'is held within ideology, but also managers to distance itself from it, to the point where it permits us to "feel" and "perceive" the ideology from which it springs'.[7]

The aestheticians of private experience might argue that this validates their position. Althusser's 'feeling and perceiving' is no more than that personal awareness of the universal which must, by their account, always be superior to the ideological or material. They have a point. If the fault of psychological accounts of art, with their emphasis on the subjective, the spontaneous and the transcendent, is that they offer no analysis of the social and historical forms within which art is created and invested with meaning, then the weakness of the purely materialist and analytic alternative is that it fails to give an account of 'what is actually being lived' in its attempts to describe 'what is thought is being lived'.[8] As a result of this neglect, materialism unwittingly further encourages the disconnection of the personal from the social that it sets out to refute. Its emphasis on the collective and the historical leaves the field of the individual, private response open to those who would wish to elevate such experiences to a level of superior truth and reality. Children's dramatic play, for example, with its beguiling sincerity and apparent structural anarchy, cries out its appeal to the present and the immediate. Small wonder that drama teachers have been so easily able to persuade themselves that they are dealing with a process with powers of intervention profoundly greater than those of 'mere intellection', nor that they hold in such esteem those of their number whose arguments take the form of appeals to experience, personal knowing and the immediacy of feeling.

These protests against the explicit, the formal and the analytic draw some of their inspiration from the perception that our experience, *while we are actually experiencing it*, cannot be reduced to the 'fixed forms' of class or ideological analysis, but is simply spontaneously 'felt'. Yet, as Wittgenstein has taught us, it is difficult to see how experience can even be recognised as experience outside the context of the language which articulates it. Kant, too, famously postulated that there can be no percepts without concepts, and Sartre has pointed out that even the spontaneous experience of fear is dependent on our at some time having perceived the fearsome propensity of some specific object.[9] For all three philosophers it is clear that in an important sense *we learn to know what to feel*. The immediate readings which constitute our 'experiencing', therefore, 'the experienced tensions, shifts, and uncertainties, the intricate forms of unevenness and confusion',[10] cannot simply be abstracted from our social consciousness, and recast in the mystifying language of the unconscious, the subjective and the symbolic. While they live in the present they may indeed defy the forms and structures through which we familiarly interpret and articulate experience, but as they slip inevitably into the past they gather coherence within subsequently emergent forms which they themselves help to shape.

What we have here is rather a form of *practical consciousness*, where, within the context of our ordinary lives, deeply felt appeals to the moral imagination form a continuing dialectic between received understandings and contemporary experience.[11]

Raymond Williams has called the sum of this practical consciousness, as it is manifest within a culture, and supremely in its art, at a particular historical moment, a 'structure of feeling'. That is to say, that tension which exists between formal ideology, as represented by the institutions of a society, to which its members will to a greater or lesser extent subscribe, and the meanings and values which constitute their life experience. Or, in Williams's words, 'the area of interaction between the official consciousness of an epoch, codified in its doctrines and legislation, and the whole process of living its consequences'.[12]

> We are talking about characteristic elements of impulse, restraint, and tone; specifically affective elements of consciousness and relationships: not feelings against thought, but thought as felt and feeling as thought: practical consciousness of a present kind, in a living and interrelating continuity ... Yet we are also defining a social experience which is still *in process*, often indeed not yet recognizable as social but taken to be private, idiosyncratic, and even isolating, but which in analysis (though rarely otherwise) has its emergent, connecting, and dominant characteristics, indeed its specific hierarchies. These are often more recognizable at a later stage, when they have been (as often happens) formalized, classified, and in many cases built into institutions and formations. By that time the case is different; a new structure of feeling will usually have begun to form, in the true social present.[13]

It is here, I would argue, in this space between our experience and our ability formally to articulate it, that art engages and challenges us. Here, surely, is that 'rightness', that 'knowing in my bones', that 'sensing as significant', which writers on school drama have been so concerned to identify and emphasise.

By successfully linking the ideological forms of society with the complex nuances of our immediate, lived perceptions in this way, Williams has made it possible for us to reclaim art for history and culture, with an account of its unique antagonistic presence within our social consciousness which needs no resort to 'aesthetic meaning', or 'feeling-form', or 'subjective knowing', or any other form of speculative introspection.

Concerning the dramatic text

The idea of art as commensurate with structures of feeling, engaging simultaneously with the content and form of dominant ideologies and with our practical consciousness, gives us the necessary aesthetic foundation for dramatic art. In now moving on to propose a structure for understanding drama education based upon it, I shall have in mind not only the traditionally accepted and familiar mainstream practices of drama-in-education, the creative improvisations and directed role-playing, but all those other less publicised manifestations of drama in our schools, such as visits to the theatre and the school play, puppetry and mime, design, play study and theatre technology. All these, and many other aspects of dramatic art evident in schools, have been for too long submerged beneath the prolific advertising of certain favoured methodologies. Dramatic art, however, is strictly non-sectarian. Nothing which can contribute to the making of dramas must be excluded from our consideration.

Firstly, we must bury for ever that historic but damaging distinction, unique to drama-in-education, between 'drama' and 'theatre'. It is my contention that conceptually there is nothing which differentiates the child acting in the classroom from the actor on the stage of the theatre.[14] Each is simultaneously taking part in and making a drama; each implicitly presupposes the existence of performer and audience. While for the actor in the theatre that audience will be a very real one, the solitary child's make-believe play will be likely to require only imaginary watchers. In the classroom context, to speak of audience-*less* drama is unintelligible, for critical observers and listeners are always present, even if they too are participants.

Also, although it is true that both actor and child are involved in a *process*, dramatic art, the outcome of that process, is itself inescapably a *product*. In more complex forms of drama making, such as the performance of a play in a theatre, many participants with a wide range of specialist skills are likely to have contributed to what we commonly know as the *production process*. But classroom improvisations also involve a production process, even though, of course, there may never be a formal, enacted presentation. Children experiment with a theme, they rehearse, reject some aspects, try again, abandon the idea. The teacher takes on a role and directs the action, the drama moves forward. Like the artist beginning a painting or the writer a novel, the possibility of arrival is implicit in the very act of starting the journey.

I wish now to borrow from the social sciences one of their most imaginative refigurations, one already widely adopted in film and television studies, and suggest that we may usefully describe the dramatic product, the outcome, that is, however provisional, of rehearsal, spontaneous improvisation or role-playing, as a *dramatic text*. It is important to stress that this use of the word 'text' allows it a far wider application than that limited to written scripts. A 'text' may indeed describe the script of a play but here it is extended to cover any form of active discourse or performance which can be *read* and *interpreted* by watchers.[15]

Production, then, is the making of the dramatic text, by writing, improvising, acting or role-playing. It has a meaningful application well beyond the school, of course, but for our purposes it is recognisably what children do in their drama lessons most of the time. In that context it extends as a category from the construction of make-believe play by infants in the play corner, through the making of more formal improvisations at primary and then secondary level, to the devised production and GCSE assessment pieces.

As an extension of this formulation, we may usefully describe the dramatic realisation of existing texts (preserved often in a written form) as *re-production*. At its most sophisticated, re-production may involve a range of non-acting skills such as lighting, stage-management or administration. The rehearsed presentation is the most public manifestation of this category, both in the theatre and in the school, but it also describes secondary work on written texts, aspects of GCSE and A level, and any dramatic activity where the children are concentrating on the performance rather than the making of a text.

The idea of the dramatic text, containing messages readable and open to interpretation by watchers, and encompassing any written, spoken or performed discourse, will also be invaluable to us in our attempts to locate drama in a critical context, for it provides us with the means to hold the products of classroom drama up to public examination. As in film studies, we may run sequences again, 'freeze-frame' moments to explore the messages they contain, we can deconstruct and reconstruct, interpret and clarify, edit and change. Under such a scheme, the drama-makers and their audience participate as craftsmen and craftswomen, honing the text to their collective satisfaction. The subjection to analysis of the form or content of a dramatic text in performance in this way, we may call *critical interpretation*. Most obviously, critical interpretation will apply to the written or vocal

discussion of a play after a visit to the theatre. However, it is extended here
to cover all the debate which surrounds the dramatic discourse, from the
critical comments of infants – 'No, *you* wear the hat' – to the teasing out of
meaning in the aftermath of role-playing, teacher comments in response to
improvisations, and group and individual self-appraisal at all levels as
members struggle to refine their work.[16]

Cultural narratives

This model of production, reproduction and critical interpretation, also
helps us to look afresh at questions of *form* and *content*. Under such a
scheme, artistic form is no longer understood as a latent, metaphysical
property of our dialogue with content, 'sensed as appropriate', but in terms
of its structural and ideological relationship to the readings it bears.[17]
Brecht's deliberately antagonistic use of form *inappropriately*, as in the
employment of the sentimental ballad to tell stories of economic
exploitation, provides a familiar but by no means exclusive demonstration
of the way these two fundamental elements of any drama can serve to
elucidate each other. In the drama lesson, this understanding should inform
work in all three areas of the model proposed, demanding an attention to
content in the face of an over-emphasis on form (when empty routines or
impersonations dominate the work, for example) and to form where the
pursuit of content has reduced the drama to mere debate (where a
preoccupation with discussions and meetings 'in role', for example, is
inhibiting the production process).

For art to be truly edifying in the ways expounded so far, then it must
both engage us with a sense of recognition and challenge us with the
revelation of the new. Thus, simply to put school children through their
theatrical paces, demonstrating, shall we say, the wonders of Shakespeare
or the correct way to move on a rake, amounts to little more than the
transmission of received opinion and residual form (the stubborn
persistence of the elocution lesson and the private drama class bears witness
to the continuing allure of this particular brand of social induction). Its
relationship to social change is thus a negative one, actively reinforcing
existing or past practices in the process of individual social advancement.
At best, it is reflective in an entirely non-critical sense; at worst, it amounts
to an attempt to keep alive forms which have long since passed from the
living consciousness of the culture.

By the same token, if it is not the aim of dramatic art to reproduce
uncritically dominant and residual dramatic forms, then neither should its
province be exclusively, as has sometimes been suggested, drama with an

overt commitment to social transformation. The idealised picture, painted by some on the left, of an alliance of pupils and teachers committed to emancipation-through-drama overthrowing the restricting 'oppressions' of bourgeois society is the product of wishful thinking based upon a deeply mistaken view of the role of art in social and economic change. While the art which evokes the most profound meanings for a society must be both reflective and critical of that culture, it cannot ever be historically in advance of the economic circumstances within which it is necessarily contained. Theatre may well, and in unique ways, critically articulate for us previously hidden or incoherent cultural shifts already in progress, stimulating our practical consciousness, but it is ill-equipped to be the sole inspiration for insurrection. In the end, the seditious undertones of Beaumarchais's *Le Marriage de Figaro*, suppressed by Parisian censors until 1784, pale retrospectively into puzzling insignificance against the conflagration which followed, and which the play may have presaged but hardly could be said to have caused. By the same token, contemporary attempts to resuscitate the tradition of agitprop theatre in the service of a variety of just causes have failed precisely because its exponents have not grasped that agitation/propaganda is a form of drama dependent upon a widely held revolutionary consciousness, present in post-First World War Europe and in late eighteenth-century Paris, but notably absent from the consciousness of Britain in the 1980s.

Also, such a view fails to take account of tne way theatrical forms and narratives from the past can in complex ways continue to provide us with paradigms against which our lives are sorted, judged and given meaning. To speak of them as 'false consciousness' is to misunderstand how, in many cases, they have become woven into that mesh of communally held meanings without which we would find it impossible to make sense of our world at all. Shakespeare, for example, in his time afloat on the full flood tide of English nationalism at the conjunction of the economic and ideological revolutions of the Reformation and the Renaissance, was highly successful in critically reflecting the diverse resonances of that tide and that conjunction. In doing so, not only did he capture the imaginations of his contemporaries, but he also succeeded in articulating the experience of subsequent generations in whose histories the sounds of those material and cultural collisions still reverberate. At the same time, the experience of those generations was itself perceived through structures of feeling evoked by a specific historical consciousness, a consciousness which Shakespeare, among others, helped to form.

If drama teachers are to be serious egalitarians then they must give their pupils access to the narratives of this historical consciousness, for these stories are the key to understanding, articulating and eventually determining the circumstances of their material and moral lives. Of course, in a culture itself composed of 'multi-cultures' these narratives will themselves reflect and celebrate a diversity of ethnic traditions within the context of society as a whole. It is for these reasons that there must be a place within dramatic art for the teaching of *dramatic literacy*.[18]

One consequence of the introduction of the idea of dramatic literacy will be that the 'moment of significance', previously born 'spontaneously' from hours of workshop preparation, can now simply be turned to in the lexicon of the culture, where invariably it will be found expressed with infinitely more acuity often in no more than a few lines of dialogue. The stylistic perfection of love expressed through the sonnet Romeo and Juliet share on the first meeting, or the fumbling silences as Lopakhin takes his leave of Varya in *The Cherry Orchard*, are just random examples of the kind of density of human experience collected within our dramatic history whose range and depth of meaning leave even the most accomplished role-playing far behind.[19]

In reality, the class-based exclusivity of certain cultural forms is perpetuated and reinforced if drama teachers offer their classes only a restricted diet of self-orientated, intuitive, improvisatory processes, while they reserve for themselves the satisfactions of traditional theatre-going. We should remember the teacher Vesovchikov in Brecht's play, *The Mother*. Well-meaning but hopelessly self-regarding, Vesovchikov's familiarity with the formal knowledge of his culture traps him into devaluing it, forgetting its crucial importance to the workers he is teaching and who must acquire it for the revolution that is about to come. 'Books are nonsense', he proclaims to his class;

> Men are only made worse by them. A simple peasant is a better human being for that reason alone, that he hasn't been spoiled by civilization ... Knowledge doesn't help, you know. It's kindness that helps.

The old woman, Vlasova, however, struggling with her chalk and slate, is in no doubt as to the value of the literacy which he has, but which she and her comrades lack. She snaps back at him:

> You give us your knowledge then, if you don't need it.[20]

Here the dramatist manages to gather together in one *gestic* moment the fragmented meanings of a particular historical struggle. It is truly a 'moment of significance', for it not only offers us that special insight into social and political content that only the metaphors of art can bring, powerfully illustrating, in this case, the argument about knowledge, but it also demonstrates how mistaken a view it is to dismiss our dramatic culture as of only marginal relevance to our children. After all, their struggle is Vlasova's struggle, if only they can realise it.

10

The Dramatised Society

Give your acting
That progression of one-thing-after-another, that attitude of
Working up what you have taken on. In this way
You will show the flow of events and also the course
Of your work, permitting the spectator
To experience this Now on many levels, coming from Previously and
Merging into Afterwards, also having much else now
Alongside it. He is sitting not only
In your theatre but also
In the world.

(Bertolt Brecht, 1936.)[1]

On the stage of life

Suggesting that we might describe what goes on in drama lessons as dramatic art is by no means to deny drama's potential contribution to the furtherance of understanding. I have argued that art engages with our practical consciousness and articulates structures of feeling in ways prior to, or beyond the reach of, other forms of discourse. Drama is a 'learning medium' to the extent that all art is edifying in this way. We may therefore regard dramatic art not so much as another way of knowing, but rather as a way of participating in dramatic conversations which can lead to new perceptions, to *us making better sense of things*.

Under the scheme proposed for dramatic art in the last chapter, these perceptions are likely to be gained at two levels. Firstly, through production, where children shape dramatic texts which express the consciousness of their lived present within the accessible context of familiar (though necessarily developing) ideological forms; secondly, through reproduction, where existing dramatic texts provide access to past structures of feeling now recognisably incorporated in dominant or emergent ideologies within the culture. Simultaneously, a continuing process of interpretation and appraisal means that dramatic art has the potential for critical articulations, both of the felt, social present, and of the ideological forms embedded in that present.

The reason that *dramatic* articulations of this kind are likely to be particularly useful to us in 'making better sense of things' is because dramatisation has always been a characterising feature of cultural life. I would suggest that dramatic forms are buried within the assumptions we make about ourselves and frame the way we perceive the world.

Four hundred years ago the Elizabethans attended the theatre to explore the possibilities of human action in a divinely ordered universe and saw society as a stage with men and women actors upon it.[2] Today, the pervasive presence of television in modern society has meant that we now have constant access to drama in ways never before possible. Drama has become built into the rhythms of our everyday lives, serving to confirm and reassure in a world in which active intervention in public life has come for many to seem futile and meaningless. We have in effect become the passive consumers of huge numbers of electronically reproduced dramatic fictions, fictions which pervade our consciousness and whose moral narratives shape how we think. Any casual observation of dramatic improvisation in school, for instance, will quickly reveal the extent to which pupils have absorbed the form and vocabulary of the dramatisations laid out for them by television.

I would argue that such incessant exposure to dramatic representation alone marks our society out as inescapably *dramatised*. In a sense, spectating has become another form of consumerism, serving the same ephemeral and short-term ends, determined by the same fabrications of need and promises of gratification. As atomised individuals in a culture where representations of political action are advertised on the pages of *TV Times* and electronically reproduced as a series of diverting images, and where political agency itself is legitimated in market terms, we live in a world where reality can quickly become indistinguishable from dramatic fiction. Distinctions between truth and myth, between fact and value, become blurred to the point of dissolution, as we watch film actors cast themselves as presidents, and prime ministers take on roles in patriotic melodramas.[3]

However, I think the pattern of cultural dramatisation is more profound even than this. As individuals, we are inescapably committed to a complex network of social relationships taking place against a background of culture and history. Such a network, I shall argue, can itself be described as a form of dramatic text, one which enables us to participate intelligibly in social life, and against which our participations may be measured. We are still, in this sense, actors on the stage of life. However, because of our extensive exposure to dramatised representations of reality, when we try to make sense of our actions we may do so with a consciousness which is itself dramatised. We are, so to speak, grounded in a complex matrix of meanings, over which we have only intermittent control, but which are nevertheless embodied in social action which we can recognise and understand, and which will make pressing claims to determine who we think we are and how we think we should act.

> Representations; typifications; active images; active parts to play that people are playing, or sometimes refusing to play. The specific conventions of this particular dramatisation – a country, a society, a period of history, a crisis of civilisation; these conventions are not abstract. They are profoundly worked and reworked in our actual living relationships. They are our ways of seeing and knowing, which every day we put into practice, and while the conventions hold, while the relationships hold, most practice confirms them.[4]

This matrix, I suggest, as it is manifest in action requiring the acknowledgement of conventions, the recognition of characters, and the adoption of roles, can be seen to be fundamentally dramatic in form. It presages intelligibility as a function of the distance between actor and meaning. As we watch and participate, we ask ourselves, 'What does this mean?', or more precisely, 'What drama am I in here?'

Roles and characters

These days we are all familiar with the idea that participation in social life can be regarded as a matter of playing different roles. For those concerned to turn this proposition into a science of human behaviour (notably the American ethnomethodologists), all human encounters have been categorised as 'real life' performances in which we attempt to be effective within a given social 'scene'.[5] In seeking success within these improvisations our aim is always to adjust our performance so that we remain in control of the situation. Erving Goffman has called this process of social manipulation, 'Impression Management'.[6]

In Goffman's role-playing social world, morality is atomised and self-referential. The only measure of moral behaviour is apparent appropriateness, and the only obligation is to observe the moral demands customarily associated with a chosen social role. The goal of the role-player is thus simply effectiveness, and success nothing but what passes for success.

> Society is organized on the principle that any individual who possesses certain social characteristics has a moral right to expect that others will value and treat him in an appropriate way. Connected with this principle is a second, namely that an individual ... ought in

fact to be what he claims to be. In consequence, when an individual projects a definition of the situation and thereby makes an implicit or explicit claim to be a person of a particular kind, he automatically exerts a moral demand upon the others ... The others find, then, that the individual has informed them as to what is and as to what they ought to see as the 'is'.[7]

What I think we have here is a rather more accurate account of the processes of dramatic pedagogy than those popularly advanced. It gives us a revealing picture of the power structures within which the dramatic purposes of a particular kind of drama lesson are worked out. The 'teacher-in-role' projects a 'definition of the situation' in just this way, and as a consequence is able to exert a similar 'moral demand' on the other participants. He or she informs them of 'what they ought to see as the "is"' and their degree of acquiescence in this picture then becomes the measure of their success in drama.

Certainly, if Goffman's thesis is right, and the human agent is accurately represented as little more than a role-player struggling to effect his or her will in a world defined by a continually changing matrix of performances, then of course it can make no sense to speak of the existence of any categorically sustainable theory of morality. Indeed, the most accomplished 'impression manager' in today's society must surely be the confidence trickster, whose very livelihood is dependent upon being able to project a deceptive image to potential victims.

> Goffman's social world is empty of objective standards of achievement; it is so defined that there is no cultural or social space from which appeal to such standards could be made ... imputations of merit are themselves part of the contrived social reality whose function is to aid or to contain some striving, role-playing will. Goffman's is a sociology which by intention deflates the pretensions of appearance to be anything more than appearance.[8]

For all this, Goffman's version of the human agent as role-player cannot be neglected in any reasonably comprehensive theory of dramatic art. I would wish to place it now alongside that of the omnipresent spectator in our developing picture of a dramatised society.

It must remain the case, however, that Goffman's morally disengaged performer gives us an insufficient account of our engagement in the dramatised society. Tolstoy was surely right when he said that science could not begin to address the most important questions which face us – what shall we do and how should we live? – and it is in their failure to take these questions into account that behavioural theories of this kind will always in the end be wanting. The truth is that in reality we do not simply seek to be effective. We may well choose to act on the basis of our moral convictions, quite possibly to our own immediate material disadvantage. We do things, quite simply, because we know them to be right.

Because of this, to complete our picture of the dramatised society, we will require a model of social agency which will enable us to regain a sense of active moral life as something more than the competition between the wills and preferences of role-playing individuals. For this, I am suggesting that we should turn to the idea of the *character*.

To understand how the idea of character differs from that of role within the dramatised society, we might usefully begin by looking at the purposes served by the stock characters of pre-naturalistic drama. In the European tradition, the character types of the comedy are conventionally traced back to late Greek and early Roman theatre, and probably reach their most refined form in the *soggelti* of the *commedia dell'arte* in the seventeenth and eighteenth centuries. However, they appear throughout world drama, developing often, like the plays they serve, from the confirming rituals of particular societies. Thus we find stock characters represented in the English medieval morality play, in the classic Noh theatre of Japan, and in the Balinese Barong dance, as well as in today's Christmas pantomimes and television soap operas. It is significant that the obsessive naturalism of twentieth-century theatre has made our consumer culture suspicious of 'stock types' in drama; we have tended to psychologise them into transcultural Jungian 'archetypes',[9] or in drama-in-education, to downgrade them as 'stereotypes', inauthentic representations of the true psychological self.

However, if we examine more closely how the stock characters relate to the movement and understanding of a dramatic piece, we see that they play a crucial part in delineating the possibilities of action and plot. Their inherent characteristics, which survive in an infinite number of settings, are immediately recognisable to an audience within the culture which has nurtured them, giving its members the key to interpreting their behaviour. The actors themselves, meanwhile, inform their performances with the same understanding. This shared process of performance and recognition is reflected in the social world, so that knowledge of the character provides an interpretation of the actions of those individuals who have assumed the character. It does so precisely because those individuals have used the very same knowledge to guide and structure what they do.

While stock characters are initially identifiable by their appearance (in the distinctive masks of the *commedia dell'arte*, for example), they are also the vehicles for familiar and quite specific sets of moral behaviour, which both performer and audience know will determine their action within the drama. A modern example of this form of dramatic signification may be seen in the employment by television advertising of actors who have come to be identified with a particular set of moral characteristics. Children, of course, use stock characters in their improvisations as an instantly recognisable shorthand for the expression of particular moral positions.

Thus, characters in this sense operate (both on and off the stage) in a very different way to the role-playing chameleons of dramatic pedagogy who will always match role to situation in the pursuit of effectiveness. It is most important that character and social role should not be confused. For Alasdair MacIntyre, characters 'are a very special type of social role which places a certain kind of moral constraint on the personality of those who inhabit them in a way in which many other social roles do not'.

> *Characters* are the masks worn by moral philosophies . . . [they] merge what usually is thought to belong to the individual man or woman and what is usually thought to belong to social roles.[10]

We can see cultures as literally *characterised* by the social roles which have become loaded with moral significance in this way. The characters of a dramatised society can be said to act as its moral representatives, allowing the moral premises and discourses of its communities a dramatic realisation in the social world. MacIntyre has identified some of the defining characters of Victorian England as 'the Public School Headmaster, the Explorer and the Engineer', and of Wilhelmine Germany as 'the Prussian Officer, the Professor and the Social Democrat'. In recent years I would say that the ubiquitous (though morally impoverished) Manager has emerged as a defining character in our own society.

This reformulation, emphasising character over role, allows us to entertain the thought that within the model of the dramatised society we may not be so conclusively condemned to a role-playing social world of competing individuals as Goffman and the ethnomethodologists would have us believe. Most importantly, by restoring a moral dimension to our thinking about dramatic action, it also makes possible conversation about social ends.

To set against Psychological Man, we now have in place the elementary framework for a model of human agency as socially defined dramatic action within a culture. Text, role and character are key co-ordinates in this framework. For the drama teacher, the idea of text as a sequence of dramatic actions which can be read by spectators offers the necessary conceptual basis for interpreting and evaluating the dramatic product. Far from being a narrow or restricting formulation, I shall argue that it may usefully be applied to dramatised interactions of all kinds, from theatre or classroom performances (implicit or otherwise) to the manifestations of the dramatised society itself. Role, of course, drama teachers will be familiar with, and although I have drawn attention to its limitations as a device for describing human action, it will continue to have an important part to play in the dramatic curriculum. Finally, by restoring the idea of character to the dramatic vocabulary, we now have the means whereby moral values may be enacted, debated and judged within the context of the discourse and popular representations of culture. It is this more generally educative function which I now intend to explore.

11

What Shall We Do and
How Shall We Live?

*So you are saying that human agreement decides what is true and what is false?' –
It is what human beings say that is true and false; and they agree in the
language they use. This is not agreement in opinions but in form of life.*

(Ludwig Wittgenstein, 1958.)[1]

Facts and opinions

It would be disingenuous to suggest that dramatic art could ever give us
answers to the dilemmas which have been troubling moral philosophers
since Socrates and before. However, by indicating how a theory of art based
upon culture and history, rather than private experience, gives us a
purchase on drama which is both interpretative and critical, it is possible to
see how we might use the model of the dramatised society in the drama
lesson to explore Tolstoy's fundamental questions.

To do this, we must first return to the epistemological arguments raised
in Chapter 7. We saw there how drama-in-education's claims on forms of
absolute, or 'universal', knowledge accessible through an authenticity of
feeling amounted to an attempt to justify drama in terms both of the
'objective' and 'subjective' realms. True knowledge was knowing what you
felt.

Education has not escaped the influence of that familiar distinction we
like to make between what we think we can know and what we might
happen to feel about it. The belief that we can unproblematically divide
our experience of the world into objective and subjective categories in this
way has been with us since the Enlightenment. Also, the continuing
domination of the curriculum by traditional 'knowledge-based' subjects,
such as maths and science, demonstrates the extent to which the 'objective'
category has achieved pre-eminence. While arts educators have become
used to making a case for the importance of the 'affective domain' in the
balanced development of young people,[2] as a culture, we have generally
accepted the epistemology of positivism, which allows only empirical
evidence and deductive logic into the sphere of legitimate knowledge.[3]

Thus, as both Eysenck and Polanyi saw, to be accepted as properly 'objective' subjects, the behavioural sciences (psychology, sociology and so on) had to be uncontaminated by people's views and opinions, by any taint of *ideology*. Legitimacy would only come from making the study of human behaviour 'value free'. Drama-in-education sought similarly to rid itself of ideology, but preferred transcendental phenomenology (where true knowledge of the world comes about through knowledge of the self) to the empiricism of behavioural science.

By the 1960s it was becoming apparent to some social scientists that the objective/subjective distinction claimed by the logical empiricists was less securely grounded than at first it seemed. The very idea of the possibility of objectivity was challenged. Apparently objective research was shown to be defined by a vocabulary of highly subjective assessment categories such as 'normal', 'deviant' or 'unacceptable', and even such commonly used words as 'role', 'status' and 'group' were shown to be open to a wide range of differing interpretations. For all our claims to disinterested cognition, they argued, we are constantly stuck by our own evaluative frameworks and the cultures which endorse them. The pursuit of scientific objectivity in the area of human behaviour is not only fruitless but actually an impediment to our understanding of the ways we act in society.

Pursuing this argument, I would suggest again that if we pause to examine how we think and act in the world, we discover that we often decide what to do not so much on the basis of disinterested empiricism, rationally weighing up the evidence available, but rather in terms of *grounds*. That is to say, our much vaunted 'objectivity' is inescapably circumscribed by the same distinctions of *worth* which made Goffman's model of competing role-players a less than adequate description of social interaction. It follows that values may indeed not be disruptive influences after all, but the very means whereby we are able to describe and interpret human behaviour in terms of action. What we are faced with is not so much a gauze of subjective value-judgements and appraisals, temporarily hiding from us univocal scientific explanations which require only to be illuminated by rigorous objective analysis, but rather a truly heterogeneous collection of *ad hoc* evaluative descriptions which can only be understood in the context of their particularity. By this account, human explanations can be judged only in their context; there is no 'objective' universal law, scientific or normative, to which we may appeal, no transcendent 'essences' to fall back upon.

Explanation, in Wittgenstein's phrase, is a family of cases, joined together only by a common aim, to make something plain or clear. This suggests that a coherent account of explanation could not be given without attending to the audience to whom the explanation is offered or the source of puzzlement that requires an explanation to be given. There are many audiences, many puzzles, and a variety of paradigmatically clear cases that give rise, by contrast, to puzzles about other cases.[4]

If scientific objectivity in the field of human behaviour turns out to be a chimera (and metaphysics an unreliable substitute), then all we appear to have to put in its place is an infinite number of personal subjectivities. Of course, this Nietzschean picture of society as nothing more than a collection of individual 'wills' governed by their own passions and desires has had a profound influence on twentieth-century society and the ways in which we speak about it. People think and talk *as if* it were true, no matter what their avowed theoretical standpoint may be; writers on drama-in-education are no exception.

So why, if this picture is so satisfying to the contemporary imagination, do we at the same time so tenaciously hold on to the idea of objectivity? I would suggest that our obsession with objectivity is twofold. It is partly born out of a desire to find secure foundations to which we might cling, indisputable frameworks beyond which we cannot stray, and partly out of our desire (once having reached tacit agreement about these objective frameworks) to be free to chart our own, self-determined (subjective) ends. The pursuit of objectivity thus represents simultaneously a search for confinement and restringency *and* a justification for unrestricted freedom of action. It turns the world into a neutral environment within which we can effect whatever purposes we choose.

The community of discourse

Such a model of the disengaged identity claims that what is out there is simply out there; how we then interpret it is entirely up to us as individuals. However, the language we use to make these distinctions cannot be a matter of individual choice. Alice was surely right to be sceptical about Humpty Dumpty's confident linguistic relativism.[5] The way we speak about the world and attempt to make it intelligible implies communally held agreements over language and meaning. Furthermore, as Wittgenstein was concerned to point out, these communally held agreements do not simply allow us to communicate but hold within them the very 'forms of life' by which meaning is itself made possible. Taking his cue from Wittgenstein, the philosopher Charles Taylor argues that we are inescapably part of 'communities of discourse' and it is these which structure the ways in which we think and speak:

The speaking agent is in fact enmeshed in two kinds of larger order, which he can never fully oversee, and can only punctually and marginally refashion. For he is only a speaking agent at all as part of a language community . . . and the meanings and illocutionary forces activated in any speech act are only what they are against a whole language and way of life.[6]

Taylor proposes that for practical purposes we might replace the objective/subjective dichotomy with a model of 'interpretation and action' based upon the idea of systems of 'inter-subjectivity'. Within such a model, we would seek to understand human agency not in terms of multiplicities of individual consciousness operating freely and independently in the epistemological landscape, but rather on the basis that there are inter-subjective standards of rationality by which we attempt to identify personal bias, or false beliefs, from objective claims. These standards will themselves depend on agreement within communities of discourse.

For Taylor, these inter-subjective meanings are not simply an intellectual device, another way of doing behavioural science, but actually constitute the social matrix in which individuals find themselves and act. They are embodied in the common and celebratory forms of cultural interaction, as *meaning-full* on the streets and in the homes of a society, as in its theatres, schools and pageants. They are continuously being played out and reformulated by human agents on the multiplicious stages of the dramatised society.

It is clear, by this account at least, that to speak of 'inner' or 'personal' meanings as if they could be self-sufficient objects of value is inherently to misunderstand the concept of meaning itself.[7] Mediated of necessity through the accumulated understandings of their percipients, the meaning of particular situations or utterances will, of course, vary in some respects between individuals, but at the same time those individuals can only make sense of themselves against a wider culture of meaning, the community of discourse. In the metaphors of the dramatised society, while I might be the star of my own life narrative, I am equally constituted as a bit-part player in the dramas of others and in the cultural text into which I am inescapably written. Whether I like it or not, I am part of a history, the bearer of a tradition. To be a policemen, therefore, is not, as Bolton's individualism would want us to believe, simply to be 'a man with a home and a family'[8] who happens to put on a helmet from time to time, but to receive elements of one's very identity from the meanings of a specific community of tradition and value and the characters who represent it.

By the same token, it makes little sense to speak of 'making' meanings for children. Their understandings are circumscribed not only by their own histories but by the cultural field against which they are identified. Certainly, teachers can demonstrate alternative ideas in an effort to encourage children to reorganise their understanding, but claims to be able to intervene strategically in meaning formation are highly tendentious. This is so, not least because teachers themselves 'mean' things to the children, they are themselves the objects of interpretation, as are all their pedagogic and non-pedagogic messages. Ideas perceived to be at odds with the received meanings of peer group and family will be filtered through that gauze of meanings before they can make a substantial impact on a child's world picture. It is naïve to imagine that drama teachers, by virtue of a set of superficially engaging practices, can operate beyond this framework; those much vaunted 'moments of significance' will in reality have widely variant meanings for teacher and taught. What appears to the former as essential revelation might well be more prosaically inspired, by a desire to please the teacher, for example, or a fear of 'getting it wrong', or by a host of considerations about 'what the others think'.[9]

Thus, while it might well be a legitimate aim of a pedagogy to challenge the fields of meaning by which assumptions are made, the efficacy of any such project, in terms of its ability to change the way children think about the world, must be strictly limited, however sophisticated its methodology:

> Already to be a living agent is to experience one's situation in terms of certain meanings; and this in a sense can be thought of as a sort of proto-'interpretation'. This is in turn interpreted and shaped by the language in which the agent lives these meanings. This whole is then at a third level interpreted by the explanation we proffer of his actions.[10]

It seems likely that it is only at this third level, the *interpretation of actions*, that drama-in-education or any other form of institutionalised pedagogy can intelligibly claim to make meaningful interventions. It can offer explanations, it can attempt to make sense of utterances and situations, but it can only do so within the structures of meaning already embodied in the self-interpretations of the participants (teacher and taught) and through the language of the culture by which those interpretations are both articulated and constituted. The drama teacher is engaged, not in revealing truths purporting to transcend language and culture, nor in the reduction of understanding to a matter of subjective preference, but in what Hans-Georg Gadamer has called a 'conversation' between researchers and subject matter:

> Understanding should not be thought of so much as an action of one's

subjectivity, but as the placing of oneself within a process of tradition, in which past and present are constantly fused.[11]

The teacher as critic

Informed by this theory of interpretation, I hope it becomes easier to see how the model of the dramatised society might offer us a serviceable conceptual structure for exploring through drama the fundamental questions of human agency. From the family to the state, through the dramatisation of individual encounters to analysis of the great dramatic rituals of nations, a whole range of formal and informal human institutions now offer themselves up for interpretation. Like classroom improvisations, we can read them too as *dramatic texts*, 'deconstructing' them for the messages they contain and the devices they employ to achieve their effect. For, as Clifford Geertz points out:

> The greatest virtue of the extension of the notion of text beyond things written on paper or carved in stone is that it trains attention on precisely ... how the inscription of action is brought about, what its vehicles are and how they work ... To see social institutions, social customs, social changes as in some sense 'readable' is to alter our whole sense of what such interpretation is ...[12]

However, we still have a problem. The fact that this theory of interpretation is not based on a naturalistic belief in predetermined realities, but is instead reliant upon the inter-subjectivity of meaning, will lay it open to accusations of complicity with the prevailing hegemony. It will be claimed, with justification, that simply to interpret society in terms of its own structures of meaning can only perpetuate those structures, and, by implication, the power relations embodied in them. For many teachers, in other words, interpretation alone will not be enough. As we have seen, there is a strong tendency within educational drama committed to challenge and to change.

So far, I have placed the teacher in the role of guide and collaborator in the interpretative project, responsible for structuring the investigation, setting up dramatic models for analysis, and stimulating questioning and reassessment. In many ways this functional relationship with the group and the material is recognisably similar to that of the 'teacher/facilitator' of drama pedagogy, although as we have seen, it serves a different end. To move the project forward into the realm of challenge, the teacher has now to stand outside the group, and become a critic. The critical teacher takes the 'adequate comprehensions' of the group, and subjects them to analysis, questioning the motivations and interests which are implicit in those comprehensions, exposing their origin, their distortions, and the purposes and functions they serve. Like the revolutionary in Brecht's song,

> He asks of property:
> Where d'you come from?
> He asks of factions
> Whom do you serve?[13]

By adopting a critical standpoint of this kind, the teacher attempts to get behind the resultant meanings by submitting them to what the critical sociologists have called, *ideologiekritik*.[14]

We may thus regard the drama teacher engaged in the critical interpretation of meaning in this way, as having two clearly defined, though interdependent, roles. Firstly, as a participant in the interpretative process, he or she must share and contribute to the understandings delivered by the group. This is not for non-interventionist 'child-centred' reasons of the kind which attribute equal value to the beliefs of individual children simply on the grounds that they are individuals, but because, as I have argued, meanings may not be arbitrarily imposed but are held only against a background of collective understanding. In this respect, the group represents not an aggregate of its individual members' personal knowledge, but a structure of understanding against which meanings are measured and modified. Thus, while it may not make sense to talk of the teacher 'making' meanings for the group, he or she can nevertheless participate, as an influential group member, in the processes whereby interpretations are produced. It is not in any way the object of this interpretative stage to produce unanimity of belief in relation to a subject, but rather, as we have seen, to reach *temporary satisfaction* with a shared understanding of how things are.

It is only at this stage, when the group is satisfied by and committed to the coherence of its interpretation, that the teacher can step outside in the role of the critic. *Ideologiekritik* can only be effective in this context if it can engage with perceptions which have already been organised and understood.

It is important to stress again that this analysis is not offered from the point of view of some kind of previously undisclosed objective truth; neither, on the other hand, can it be relativistically reduced to a collection of individual feelings and preferences. Any such analysis is itself the potential object of interpretation, modification and re-expression. The factors brought to bear by the teacher on the original interpretation are not revelations, 'universal meanings' standing beyond criticism, for they too are only articulated and made sense of against a field of meaning. At the same time, neither are they fully, or even partially, understood as the arbitrary prejudices of an individual teacher's subjective beliefs. They represent a critique formulated within the frames of what are generally understood to be the tests of evidence, of deductive thinking, and of approximation to an accepted reality. This critique may well not correspond to a consensus, indeed its purpose may often be explicitly to challenge consensus, but to dismiss it as biased, or 'purely subjective', is to succumb to the implied belief that there is something out there sufficiently objective for bias to be measured against it.

To summarise, we cannot make sense of things, including ourselves, outside meaningful structures with which we are familiar; we can only do so through the language by which those meanings are expressed. Our search for meaning is therefore dialectical, not in the simple subjective/objective construction favoured by drama-in-education, but in the sense that it is a continuous movement between preconception, revision and confirmation, Gadamer's conception of the 'hermeneutic circle'. The progression is thus not from 'the particular to the universal' towards ever more diffuse levels of generality, but rather a circle of modification, where participants in, or observers of, the drama return to reassess, or even reject, their understandings in the light of dramatic explorations which are themselves continually being modified. The outcome is not a moment of a-temporal revelation, but an adequate comprehension of the meaning of the object under consideration. Teacher and taught unite as researchers, using the dramatic model to interpret human interaction, organisation and meaning, counting success as the achievement of a level of intelligibility in relation to the subject matter sufficient to satisfy the investigation. As human agents we have all sorts of governing beliefs and attitudes; what unites us is that we justify them in the terms that our society *counts* as justification. Thus, the teacher's final critique of these 'adequate comprehensions', while it makes no claims on objectivity, must nevertheless be justifiable in this way.

Learning how to act

I have shown how the apparently unlimited choices offered us by modern individualism seem to drop us helplessly into moral relativism, where values themselves become 'personal' and where there seems to be no possible recourse to moral imperatives beyond the individual conscience. However, if, as I have suggested, the ways in which we think and act are in fact governed by decisions about grounds and these evaluations are not individualistically preferential but socially defined, then our judgements about values must take place not in psychological isolation but within the context of standards agreed by communities of discourse.

By such an account, our actual lived politics and morality originate not in the depths of our psyches nor in the semi-mystical essences proposed by the phenomenologists, but reside instead in the multifarious communities of which we are, of necessity, members. Our self-understanding depends not so much on the 'inner' and the 'personal' as on our characterising ourselves as moral agents in our communities of discourse. The family, the gang, the school, the nation: these are our moral constituencies, the spaces defined by distinctions of worth, within which, and only within which, we can comprehend the self. In this sense, the community actually tells who we are. Our 'self-interpretations' are 'drawn from the interchange which the community carries on'; the community 'provides the language by which we draw our background distinctions', and without which human agency 'would be not just impossible, but inconceivable'.[15]

In this way, not only are the moral dilemmas which accompany us through our lives usefully made sense of in terms of our overlapping membership of many such commnities, but our selfhood can also be understood as being worked our against the conflated 'interchanges' of the networks of moral loyalties they imply.

The gradual secularisation of western culture, accompanied historically by the development of increasingly sophisticated forms of communication and by an expanded social mobility, allows individual members of today's national community to owe allegiance to a vastly more complex and contradictory range of moralities than could have even been imagined in our ghostly versions of the relatively stable, pre-industrial past. This complexity, of course, makes the actions of the moral agent easily mistaken for those of the 'disengaged identity' favoured by drama-in-education. However, as Durkheim reminds us,

> Morality begins, accordingly, only insofar as we belong to a human group, whatever it may be. Since, in fact, man is complete only as he belongs to several societies, morality is complete only to the extent that we feel identified with those different groups in which we are involved – family, union, business, club, political party, country, humanity.[16]

For teachers, many of the day-to-day problems of discipline and commitment are ascribable to conflicting moral loyalties; yet without these complex networks of membership, in which, of course, teachers them-selves share, our sense of ourselves would be severely diminished. David

Hargreaves makes the point that the predominance of the 'fallacy of individualism' in English education has in many cases blinded teachers to a hidden curriculum of collectivism. Drama teachers too, he suggests, 'have unwittingly become victims of the cult of individualism, and in so doing they are in real danger of ignoring the powerful corporate potentials of drama'.[17] Educational drama's commitment to 'group work', for instance, is ironically always framed in the individualistic language of co-operation, tolerance and empathy, reflecting the idea of the group as simply an aggregation of individuals relating to each other. Significantly absent from the discourse are the complementary concepts of duty, loyalty and obligation, unintelligible, of course, to the spirit of the disengaged consciousness, but utterly comprehensible and reassuring to children. Moral behaviour of necessity requires submission to a set of rules, to a moral authority, which, as Hargreaves points out, 'must be obeyed not in a spirit of passive resignation but out of *enlightened allegiance*'.[18]

A conceptual scheme of this kind which postulates moral knowledge as a form of social solidarity allows us to break conclusively with psychologism and its narrow, emotivist premises. As agents, we do not in fact 'discover' our values by dredging our unconscious, but rather actively mediate between the differing claims of many allegiances. In doing so, we exercise our moral imagination, weighing up consequential considerations against higher, deontological claims, measuring a whole range of 'oughts' against our perceptions of the moral environments in which we are compelled to be agents; we assess the strengths of our loyalties. Our moral feelings are reflections of our relative commitments to membership. Our social class, our ethnic group, our trade union or our church are communities of moral discourse to which we belong and which, in crucial ways, tell us not only how we should feel but also what we should do and how we should live.

We can now perhaps see more clearly how the dramatised society is moved by the characters representing its moral communities, those fusions of role and morality which so profoundly characterise its distinctions of worth both on and off the stage. It becomes possible to demonstrate how the 'stock type' has a vital part to play in the dramatisation and interpretation of our social lives. If our morality turns out to be the result of the contracts we make with communities and the (often conflicting) loyalties they demand from us, then the collisions of these loyalties, sometimes the result of very stark contradistinctions, while disturbing to our moral equanimity, create the tensions which inform the dramatic art of secular society.

Romantic individualism sought legitimacy for our choices through reference to the 'truth' of our emotional experience. We have seen how drama-in-education conceptualised itself simply as a vehicle for the exposure and expression of personal moral feelings or 'subjective knowing'. Employed as a kind of living laboratory, however, where decisions about what moves us morally can be made in the dialectical context of rival commitments after rigorous experiment and analysis of the kind described above, drama education can be released from the confines of psychology to engage with the political and moral structures of contemporary society. Like all art, drama can expose and articulate the deepest and most significant dilemmas of our culture, but like all art it negotiates and articulates in the public domain by which it is both valued and defined.

Summing up: dramatic art and the dramatised society

Dramatic art dissolves the old distinction between 'drama' and 'theatre' and proposes a programme of drama education located in the public world. Within it, drama is described as a textual message system crafted specifically to convey meaning to watchers. A tri-partite structure of production, reproduction and critical interpretation makes it possible to formulate the dramatic text as the product of the drama lesson and to make it available for evaluation and revision by the participants.

As a fully paid-up member of the arts community, dramatic art shares with the other arts the potential for engagement with the structures of feeling of our historical moment. At the same time, it is instrumental in the promotion of dramatic literacy, for by seeking as wide an appropriation of dramatic tradition as possible while making no easy or patronising assumptions about cultural relevance, dramatic art is the genuine servant of cultural egalitarianism.

The model of the dramatised society is the backdrop to dramatic art. In it, we are described not simply as role-playing individuals acting out our preferences against a known 'objective' world, but rather as moral agents making sense of ourselves and our actions through our membership of communities of discourse. In this way the institutions of the dramatised society may themselves be regarded as dramatic texts containing representative characters who act as yardsticks for our actions and beliefs.

The reading of these dramatic texts constitutes a way of approaching questions of understanding and meaning which rejects the objective/subjective distinction and replaces it instead with a commitment to interpretation. In the classroom, dramatic strategies enable the teacher both to establish a framework for the collective interpretation of the meanings expressed in the dramas produced and to subject those dramas to criticism.

Above all, dramatic art gives us an aesthetic located in the dramatised inter-subjectivities of our social being and in contact with the moral and political implications of that being. As actors in the dramatised culture, we write and perform our dramatic texts according to the dramatic forms which that culture, its traditions, its conventions, its history, make available to us. However, as we have seen, our cultural membership is diverse and the forms with which we are familiar and which tell us who we are, often contradictory. It is here that the dramatic aesthetic most powerfully engages, for it is able to connect us with history in ways which liberate our understanding, while simultaneously (and necessarily) connecting us to the communities of value and meaning by which we make sense of our lives.

12

The Dramatic Curriculum

The 'particularity' of the drama education in any school will emerge from the skills and predilections of the drama staff, the material resources of the school, and the dramatic needs, abilities and tastes of the children. Any particularity will do, provided the conceptual base of the curriculum is sound. There are, however, certain basic conditions and resources essential to education through drama – enacting human beings, space, light, a surface to move on, silence, and, invariably, audiences.

(Malcolm Ross, 1978.)[1]

Wider landscapes

When Peter Slade introduced the concept of 'Child Drama' in the 1950s, he sought to categorise it as an exclusive form of educational activity, quite distinct from what was generally understood as theatre practice. I have traced the effects of the 'drama' and 'theatre' dichotomy which has been the debilitating legacy of this distinction, and I would wish to stress again that in restoring the synonymy of drama and theatre, dramatic art makes no such division. It is genuinely inclusive, as happy with the vulgar spectacle of carnival and circus, for example, as it is with the metaphorical complexities of Elizabethan verse or the dramatic play of the infant classroom.

It follows that, unlike dramatic pedagogy, dramatic art has a curriculum of its own which can be practised, developed and taught. It is un-ambiguously a discipline. This is not to suggest that the wide variety of issues and concerns which have offered themselves as the subject matter of dramatic pedagogy now vanish from the drama teacher's prospectus. Effective teaching of contemporary plays, for example, can hardly be expected to avoid contact with the moral and political dilemmas which characterise our times. Nigel Williams's *Class Enemy*, for example, set in an inner-city classroom of such savage repute that no teacher dare enter, raises profound questions about school and society. Similarly, Ena Lamont Stewart's *Men Should Weep* says things about the exploitation of women far beyond the reach of the most earnest anti-sexist role-playing. Even *Henry the*

Fifth can hardly fail to raise issues of war, history and patriotism. In my view, a carefully designed dramatic curriculum makes these kinds of exploration more rather than less likely; for all the rhetoric, the solipsistic freedoms of drama-in-education have often been an excuse for the inconsequential and banal.

The clear subject identity engendered as a consequence of placing dramatic art generically within the arts grants educational drama a disciplinary coherence which has been notably lacking in the past. The speculative colonisation of the curriculum suggested by dramatic pedagogy more often than not stood in stark contrast to a limited and limiting practical agenda, where rigid adherence to the complexities of methodology effectively stifled a whole range of alternatives. Dramatic art, on the other hand, simply encompasses all that is the art of drama. Its limits come where that categorisation is least distinct, where drama merges with other forms of human expression, such as in performance art, or music theatre and opera perhaps, or at the edge of certain forms of religious ritual. For most purposes, dramatic art's unequivocal identification with such culturally familiar concepts as plays, theatres and actors, gives it an identity readily accessible to a wide constituency.

In terms of curriculum theory, Basil Bernstein's classic model of the classification and framing of educational knowledge[2] shows the infinitely weak classification of dramatic pedagogy being replaced with the far stronger subject identity of dramatic art, so that the frames within which knowledge is transmitted during the drama class can themselves become much weaker. 'Strong frames', says Bernstein, 'reduce the power of the pupil over what, when and how he receives knowledge, and increases the teacher's power in the pedagogical relationship.'[3] The implicitly authoritarian presence of charismatic drama teachers like Dorothy Heathcote set up the strong framing necessary for the pedagogy. *Ad hoc* rules about what was and was not acceptable were quickly assimilated by Heathcote's classes, as indeed they had to be when the subject-defining boundaries were effectively non-existent. Dramatic art, on the other hand, presupposes the shared understanding of its parameters by teacher and pupils alike. This in turn allows for a relaxation of framing and a consequent expansion of the range of transmittable knowledge. Thus, a drama lesson might simultaneously involve one group of children researching, another planning some lighting, yet another improvising a scene. The relatively strong classification of dramatic art, and the weak framing thus allowed, increases opportunities for both individual and collective motivation, giving children the freedom to explore and learn within clear contextual limits.

I am convinced that only by a shift of emphasis of this kind will drama teachers be able to advance their practices with confidence. The dramatic art curriculum offers opportunities for pupils and students at all levels to explore the expressive potential of theatre, as performers possibly, but equally as writers, designers, directors, technicians, *animateurs* and experimenters. It encourages them not only to share the deep, corporate satisfactions of the dramatic experience, but also to carry forward a developing expertise and appetite for drama into life outside the school. While in practice, pupils in the school drama lesson may well still be confronted by forms of role-playing and improvisation, they will now be able to make sense of those activities in a wider theatrical context. For the children, their work in the classroom or drama-studio, their out-of-school play rehearsals, their parents' involvement with amateur dramatics or the community play, their visits to the theatre, even their absorbing of the conventions of *East Enders*; all these will be perceived as legitimate elements of dramatic art.

The formulation of dramatic art, therefore, represents not a new set of rules and methodologies but rather a conflation of the best of existing practice in the field of drama education. Its eclecticism insists that the meanings of the word 'drama' must be allowed a wide interpretation, and cannot be unilaterally confined by a section of the dramatic community and employed exclusively to describe its own idiosyncratic practices. Dramatic art in education is thus a wedding of these wider perceptions with the lived priorities, skills and inclinations of drama teachers.

Practising dramatic art

Because dramatic art has no aspirations to be an educative *system*, it makes no essential claim on the moral or psychological development of the children. That is not to say that individual teachers or institutions may not have strong views about the educational requirements of young people (nor indeed that mine are not reflected in this book). The fact that my classes study Caryl Churchill rather than Terence Rattigan, however, or improvise around contemporary themes and neglect Restoration comedy, is a choice I make as a teacher; like all other syllabus choices it will be a product of more diverse perceptions. It is not a function of dramatic art itself. Instead, in the same way that the visual art teacher would encourage students to develop manipulative skills in a range of media (painting, sculpture, graphics, pottery, ceramics and so on), the practical exploration of all aspects of theatrecraft is central to the study of dramatic art. In drama, as in art, dance and music, without skills in their chosen medium, the most creative children in the world can only fumble. Creative play is not necessarily theatre. Drama specialists have a fundamental responsibility to equip those they teach with the tools of dramatic expression.

I would argue, therefore, that there are certain basic elements which constitute dramatic art, and proficiency in these is how we measure progression in drama. Our pupils get better at handling the medium, become more adept at producing and understanding dramas of all kinds. Thus, in the same way that visual art may wish to make judgements of worth, between, shall we say, the design of a cornflakes packet and a Rembrandt self-portrait, so dramatic art has its criteria of value, eclectic and contested certainly, but held and understood within the context of cultural. Of course, it is important that these criteria should not be exclusively Euro-centred. They should encourage rather than inhibit cultural diversity, both through the use of mother tongue and by the incorporation of a wide range of historical and ethnographic reference.

Quite how we describe these basic elements will, of course, be a matter of some debate. For this reason, the categories I propose here are not inflexible or closed to reformulation. Neither are they set out in any particular order of importance. The point is that something like this sketch of curriculum content will be always be necessary if we are to articulate what it means for young people to progress in drama.

For example, if pupils are to practise drama successfully then they must learn how a playing space can be used to good effect and how the sounds made within it combine to convey mood and ideas. The physical language of gesture (movement, mime, facial and bodily expression)[4] as well as the spoken language of drama will also deserve attention. Students must learn how to manipulate the conventions of dramatic discourse. *Space*, *sound*, *gesture* and *discourse*, therefore, might reasonably be said to be four essential elements of dramatic art.

I have already suggested that we might regard much of what goes on in the drama lesson as a production process leading to the formation of dramatic texts. Whether we call these texts 'dramatic fictions', or improvisations, or plays, most of the drama teacher's working day is probably spent developing dramatic narratives of one kind or another with pupils. Unfortunately, the non-interventionist policy of Peter Slade has often allowed groups of children to get away with the most appallingly self-indulgent acts of improvised 'creativity'; a more rigorous and critical approach to the making of dramatic texts in this way has to be developed. Also, despite assurances, children do not simply 'stumble upon' the appropriate theatrical forms for the expression of their ideas, but need to have demonstrated both the structures and the disciplines which can help them. They have to be taught about documentary, street theatre, pantomime, the well-made-play, farce and so on. All these are examples of specific forms of popular dramatic expression which children should be able to appropriate and use to their advantage. It follows that we can add *text* and *form* to our list of basic elements.

The dramatic texts produced by groups of students are invariably made for presentation. That is to say, while the process of making the text may well be a private affair, the intention of a group in working to achieve satisfaction is in terms of an implicit or explicit showing of some kind. As casual spectators we may not be welcome visitors in a band rehearsal or looking over the shoulder of the sketching artist, but this is not to deny that ultimately communication to some audience is intrinsic to the aims of aesthetic production (it may be, of course, that the audience is composed only of the artists themselves). Dramatic art acknowledges this. In the same way as the art teacher imbues children's paintings with value by displaying them on the walls of the classroom, the drama teacher will encourage the presentation of dramatic work in suitably supportive contexts. The art of dramatic reproduction will entail learning about the complex relationship between audience and performers, and the ways in which *mise-en-scène* can draw all these elements together.[5] To help them as they progress here, students will have to be introduced to the technical aspects of theatre such as design, lighting and sound, set-construction and backstage organisation. I shall thus conclude my list of basic elements with the art of *mise-en-scène*, or *scene-making*. (For a practical application of this scheme, see Appendix B.)

The methodologies employed to achieve ends of this sort are not new. Improvisation, role-play, script-work and technical training will all have a part to play in the delivery of attainment in dramatic art. While it is certainly possible to devise formal Attainment Targets for drama (the extracts in Appendix C. would form the basis for such a project), achievement in the different elements should not be regarded as a set of educational hurdles, but as markers in programmes of study which aim to develop pupils' ability to produce and critically interpret dramas.

Making and interpreting dramatic texts remain at the core of dramatic art. As processes neither will be unfamiliar to drama teachers. For one thing, what goes on in the classroom is still predominantly characterised by pupils dividing into small groups to rehearse and appear in improvisations of various kinds (including that ubiquitous *non sequitur*, 'the polished improvisation'). What this most tenacious form of group scene-making has always lacked, however, has been suitable forms of teacher intervention. A tacit commitment to the so-called 'spontaneous response' has inhibited teachers from the kind of work-in-progress criticism accepted by visual art. As a result, presentations are often ill-prepared and repetitive, and it is difficult to identify advance either in form or content.

If we stop regarding improvisation as the uninhibited manifestation of the creative spirit, and instead treat it rather like the rough-cut of a film, then teachers have direct access to the crafting process. Presented at some time during the lesson, the teacher can ask for the improvisation to be run again, can suggest alterations, can examine 'freeze-frames', can send the group away to 're-cut' their work. Other watchers, the remainder of the class, can participate in this *editing* process, becoming essential collaborators in a form of collective evaluation. By intervening during the production process in this way instead of waiting to offer comments at the end (when it is too late), the drama teacher is thus able to monitor development in the basic elements and set tasks which address particular weaknesses. A group showing considerable skill in 'discourse' but failing to reflect their message in their body language, for example, might be restricted only to 'gesture' for the following lessons. Like the music teacher restricting a pupil to arpeggios with the left hand or the art teacher insisting only on monochrome, there are times when close attention to form is necessary for progression.[6]

Borrowing from film-studies in this way draws attention to the importance of the audience in dramatic art. In describing the dramatised society, I suggested that the electronic media have enabled us to witness dramatised fiction on an unprecedented scale. Few of us appear in plays, but millions of us watch them, even if only on television. While theorists of drama-in-education have remained largely silent on this most elementary form of dramatic participation, public assessment schemes, notably at GCSE level, are increasingly expecting secondary pupils to show a critical aptitude in relation to theatre performance.[7] Lacking a suitable vocabulary, drama teachers sometimes fall back on forms of criticism which depend upon privileged knowledge of the play as literature. Unfortunately schemes of this kind not only favour the more scholastic child, but also perpetuate the idea of theatre as 'high art', and turn out to be impotent when faced with the unfamiliar or unconventional. But critical interpretation plays a leading part in dramatic art, both in the classroom and in the theatre, so we have to develop a language which can accommodate very diverse theatre forms, such as slapstick or music-hall, for instance. Fortunately, there is now a growing discipline of semiologically based *performance analysis* which could be usefully adapted for use in schools.[8] (See Appendix D.)

Finally, but most importantly, dramatic art does not neglect the wider curriculum. It offers the drama room as a kind of laboratory in which the content of our lives in the dramatised society can be explored and interpreted. The form in which this process of critical interpretation and adequate comprehension takes place is that of the dramatic narrative. We learn through the stories we and others tell; in a dramatised culture these stories will themselves take the form of dramatisations. We are presented with a series of interlocking dramatic narratives which are the substance of our social lives, and in which we are both participant and spectator. In dramatic art, we test out our performances against the distinctions of worth which give our actions meaning in the social world; we make sense of the dramas we watch and in which we are participants in the context of the culture and history upon which they are grounded. To render this act of interpretation conscious, and dramatic art makes claims to be able to this, is to make both understanding and critical judgement possible.

In appearance, this process will not be unfamiliar to drama teachers. To take an example. The *interpretative* stage might involve a teacher and a class exploring the relationships within a family – father, mother, two children. The class divides up to improvise scenes designed to provide models for study, an initial mediation of the material. These models become the dramatic texts which are then interpreted, reassessed and modified by performers and observers. Changes are made, the texts are altered, in the light of what is jointly perceived to be an insufficient correspondence between them and the lived experience of the class. One group now chooses a fatherless family, another a motherless one; there is an extended Asian family, an only child. The process is repeated, the texts further modified. In one text, a son's seemingly irrational outburst of anger becomes a focus of attention; in another, a single mother's frustration.

Under the guidance of the teacher, an exploration of these texts leads to an interpretation of how the family sees itself in relation to other families, or to the state through its dependence on social benefit, or to the conventions of an unfamiliar culture. How the Asian daughter interprets European teenage customs, and how her parents interpret her involvement in them. How the whole is itself interpreted by a social worker, a statistician, the next-door neighbours, the political parties.

In the *critical* stage the teacher subjects these interpretations to analysis, exposing, possibly, the play of surreptitious economic interests which underlie the dramatic texts, demonstrating, perhaps, how society stig-matises unemployment, how advertisements sell us seductive images of the nuclear family, how received meanings of male and female lead to discri-mination and frustration as satisfactory role-fulfilment under those terms becomes less and less possible.

What I have offered here is very far from prescriptive. These few pages consist merely of suggestions, map-references in the landscape of dramatic art. My intention has been to indicate possibilities rather than to dictate formulae. My hope is that drama teachers will see this conceptual sketch as an opportunity to clarify, enhance and expand their own classroom strategies and not as an attempt to impose yet another set of specialised practices.

The arts, the school and the community

Dramatic art, with its capacity for animating, co-ordinating and providing a focus for the other arts, has a central role to play in a successfully functioning arts faculty. Unfortunately, little or no attention has been paid within drama-in-education to the conceptual or structural links that drama might have with the other arts.[9] *The Arts in Schools*, however, is quite clear about the value of collaboration:

> The need should be recognised for a policy for all of the arts in schools and arts teachers in the same school should therefore discuss and co-ordinate policies wherever possible, and especially in relation to the allocation of time and facilities.[10]

Traditionally, in the secondary school, the drama specialist has been a somewhat isolated and marginalised figure. The experience of those lucky enough to teach within thriving drama departments with well-equipped facilities and a team of colleagues is becoming an increasingly rare one. More often, drama in the secondary school is associated with a single teacher, fighting lone battles with caretakers, timetable-planners and the headteacher, while holding the drama banner as high as he or she dares in what is often a less than sympathetic educational environment. For one thing, drama has never been a very neat activity, tending instead to spill over into corridors and to employ school furniture in unconventional ways not likely to endear it to school managements.

Part of the problem is that the private world of the drama class is rarely if ever exposed to the wider school community, so that the only opportunities the drama teacher has to demonstrate his or her worth tend to be the extra-curricular ones offered by the public performance. As we have seen, the concept of performance to an audience has been given only the most cursory acknowledgement by the guardians of drama-in-education. The drama teacher may thus have to live with the fact that success in the terms of the subject orthodoxy will neither be seen nor understood by the school community, while the popular, public achievements of performance are regarded as marginal by the advocates of dramatic pedagogy.

By bringing the idea of production and reproduction in from the cold within the context of dramatic art, the question of legitimacy, of course, ceases to arise. The upgrading of performance allows the drama teacher to emerge from the wings and to regard public acknowledgement as entirely consistent with classroom practice, so that the school or class play becomes an element of the dramatic experience to be made available to all children as they pass through the school. A whole range of alternative performance options might be offered, so that pupils would have the opportunity of participating in lunch-time shows, festivals, TV and radio dramas and so on.

David Hargreaves has described the school play as 'a paradigm for other aspects of the creative arts', 'an exemplar of differentiated team work' remembered by pupils 'longer than almost anything else about school.'

> Yet in most schools the play is part of the *extra-curriculum* – an optional and occasional (perhaps annual) activity involving a minority of the pupils in their spare time ... Most pupils' experience of drama must be confined to 'drama lessons' and the easiest way to conduct such a short lesson is to devote it to *improvised* drama and movement, with its focus on individual objectives. One of the central functions of drama is thereby distorted.[11]

Traditionally, of course, school productions have often been exploited by headteachers as ways of demonstrating the cultural pretensions of their institutions with routine performances of the classics. Alternatively, the fare has been light musical comedy. Either way, the nights of the play have long been occasions for the informal gathering of a school's constituency. The potential of such events for more substantial community involvement is immense. The rare times where I have had a sense of the school being at the centre of the lives of those it serves has been where the children, their families and their teachers have come together to celebrate through drama. On one particular occasion, over two hundred children from all parts of a large city comprehensive had researched, written and performed a play, with songs, about their locality and its old mining tradition. Almost all their parents, and many of their grandparents, had been involved in one way or another, as had the school's music and art departments, the latter to the extent of structuring lessons around projects associated with the show. In the hall, on a first night packed with mums and dads and grannies and aunties and babies and dogs, as well as with children and their teachers, the atmosphere was electric. Anyone who has experienced the massive outpouring of energy and enthusiasm harnessed by a successful community play of this kind will know what rich and unforgettable festivals they can be.

The flexibility of a well-structured arts faculty should be able to make this kind of learning experience possible, with the teacher of dramatic art able to feel committed to such projects as an integral part of his or her teaching and no longer an after school 'extra'. It goes without saying that it is quite wrong that for so many drama teachers their best and most rewarding work should be conducted on a voluntary basis, particularly since the advent of directed time. Given the will, it cannot be beyond the capacity of schools to find ways of integrating performance work into the mainstream of the curriculum, and by doing so avoiding a reliance upon the drama specialist's extra-curricular time. The introduction of modular arts curricula would help to facilitate this, allowing a drama production to be an assessable module of a two-year GCSE course, for instance. (See Appendix B.)

Not only would moves of this kind greatly enrich the work of drama departments, but they would also increase the confidence and self-esteem of individual teachers. By bringing drama out into the open, so that it is no longer regarded by the rest of the school as freemasonry conducted behind the closed doors of the drama studio, but as an intelligible set of skills and expressive practices frequently made manifest in performance, dramatic art allows drama teachers to shed their role as curricular missionaries and the evangelical defensiveness which grew with it. It should be possible for them to share intelligible accounts of what they hope to achieve with colleagues, parents, headteachers and, above all, with the children themselves.

This then, is the case for dramatic art. At its heart is my contention that drama occupies a place at the very centre of the way in which we make sense of ourselves and order our lives. I have argued that in the theatre and on the street, in televised reproductions and in the school, we have multiple versions of our dramatised society displayed for our interpretation and critical analysis. Dramatic art allows us to engage with these social forms as we emerge from the reverent and self-referential silences of dramatic pedagogy into the altogether brighter light of the public world. Above all, drama is about stories. Like Brecht's actors, we should pay a visit

... To that theatre whose setting is the street.
The everyday, thousandfold, fameless
But vivid, earthy theatre fed by the daily human contact
Which takes place in the street ...

There, on the street corner, says Brecht, a man is telling a story, demonstrating how an accident took place. He uses narrative and imitation, holding his street audience with his skills as a performer. In exactly the way that I have been proposing, he is able simultaneously to make sense of the accident, to describe, in other words, the actions of the driver and the victim, and to leave us knowing its senselessness.

The accident
Becomes in this way intelligible, yet not intelligible, for both of them
Could have moved quite otherwise; now he is showing what
They might have done so that no accident
Would have occurred. There is no superstition
About this eyewitness, he
Shows mortals as victims not of stars, but
Only of their errors.[12]

It need not be further stressed that the aesthetic and cognitive forms of dramatic art are ineradicably 'social and sociable'. They give us the necessary social ground of practical moral reasoning, which, as Aristotle tells us, is where politics happen. They enable us to enter into the discourse of morality in dramatic action, so that moral and social questions are released from the private preferences of emotivism onto the stage of critical judgement. Politics is restored to the curriculum, for morality as collective agency and belief is the political text of the drama.

Appendix A

The three accounts of drama lessons in this appendix cover a period from 1965 to 1981. Real and imaginary, illustrating the idealism and the reality of nearly twenty years of drama-in-education, they are set out here as insistent reminders of classroom aspiration

Lesson one: 1965

A drama lesson is just ending. The class lines up quietly and begins to file out onto the foyer, joining other children already beginning to move to different classes. The empty hall seems vast and gloomy, full of interesting corners and patches of light. The curtains are closed and spotlights cast irregular pools of shiny light on the floor, emphasising the pattern of polished wood blocks. An intense orange light shines in your eyes. It fades to a full glow, and with a clatter the drama teacher jumps from the stage and beings to sort through some records by the gramophone. With a slight movement he signals to the class next door to come in, and the hall is once more full of children.

They enter excitedly chattering to one another, removing jackets and pullovers as they go, each finding a safe spot to dump satchels, books and the many things that children always seem to carry with them. The teacher takes little apparent notice, but the children are obviously aware of his presence, and he seems to be summing up the mood of the class while experimenting with brief snatches of music on the gramophone. Some of the class are discussing something important in pairs and small groups. Some are leaping and weaving around the others as if they are casting spells. A small boy in one corner is walking stiffly, like a clockwork toy. A few children make straight for the gramophone and, as they ply the teacher with questions, try to read the name on the record label as it revolves. They admire the sleeve – an arresting picture – it is *The Firebird*.

A loud crash from the gramophone speaker, set high on the wall, temporarily halts most of the class. They turn and look, not at the loudspeaker but at the teacher, who takes this opportunity to give a sharp clap, followed by a gesture which obviously says, 'Come and sit down over here'. There is a brief jockeying for places, but very quickly the class is in a semi-circle round the steps on one side of the stage. Some lean on the stage, some sit cross-legged, while others lie with their heads propped in their hands. All seem quite relaxed, especially the teacher. From this distance what he says is barely audible, but soon hands shoot up and the children seem to be offering suggestions. A rucksack ... camera ... sandwiches ... primus stove ... thermos flask ... At a decisive movement from the teacher the semi-circle disintegrates, and the children are scattered around the hall, some sitting, some lying, some seeking the splashes of light, some preferring the dark corners. A few children perch on the edge of the half-dozen rostrum blocks placed haphazardly about the floor. Stacks of metal chairs line one wall; the occasional child finds a haven near them. The teacher's voice is now quite clear. The whole class is silent as he begins a story: 'It is early on a summer's morning. Outside the sun is shining. We are asleep in bed; very soon the alarm clock will sound ...' The children seem asleep – some restlessly, some deeply. The teacher meanwhile has moved imperceptibly over to the stage, and suddenly he rattles a side-drum, and the class reacts – some quite violently. They seem absorbed in the real process of getting out of bed. Some manage it straight away, some roll over and pull bedclothes over their faces, while others are quite obviously finding cold lino under their bare feet. 'Go into the bathroom and have a good wash. Don't forget behind your ears! Clean your teeth and get dressed.'

The children's activities begin to vary. Some obviously wash in their pyjamas, while others get partly dressed first. Some make tap noises as they fill their own wash basins. A general hatred of washing is shown by perfunctory and noisy splashing, but just a few hold their heads under the taps. The narration continues, and the children rush down to breakfast, cut sandwiches and pack things to take for a day in the country.

They set off to catch the bus in a happy mood, whistling, running and skipping. To help them music blares throught the loudspeaker: a 'pop' record from the past – *Jumping Bean* – just the thing to convey the spirit of setting off, and the children respond to it well. They meet friends and begin the bus journey, amid much slapstick comedy with imaginary bus conductors.

The transition from one activity to the next is quite natural. The teacher never says things twice, in fact he hardly interrupts the action: the children seem to hear every word without apparently listening. Most of the time they are completely absorbed in what they are doing, and only occasionally, when they need to sort out some snag, do they become conscious of the hall and their neighbours. The hall is transformed every few moments into a fresh location, sometimes by sounds from the gramophone, sometimes simply by the sincerity and absorption with which the children create their own ideas for the story. Moods vary tremendously, and the class is at one moment noisy and lively, at the next quiet and intent.

The only control over mood is by the teacher suggesting where they are and what they are doing, or by the type of sound they can hear. Now, for instance, they are searching for wild flowers and listening for bird songs. 'Morning', from *Peer Gynt*, sets the quiet atmosphere. They cross a farm-yard and feed ducks and dogs, providing their own noises (some of the walkers forsake their walk to become, briefly, a farm dog). They choose a spot, eat their meal, rest and begin to play ball games. An unusual record is used for this – an almost forgotten 'hit' – a clever, twangy, fast guitar piece called *Little Rock Getaway*. After the games, and a short spell of fishing, everyone goes in for a swim. The children swim with lazy strokes to *The Swan of Tuonela*, covering vast areas of the hall. All sorts of interesting experiments are going on: someone in the corner is trying a backstroke, blowing bubbles as she goes.

Soon the excursion comes to an end, the children pack up their things and head for home – a shower of rain causing a mild panic on the way. At last when they are back in bed all is still, once more. Quietly, and only gently breaking the spell, the teacher calls the class to him. In a very different mood from when they came in, the class is again clustered in a semi-circle round the gramophone at the foot of the steps. The children seem relaxed and satisfied. Quiet discussion is taking place now, and it seems to draw naturally to a close with a few of the class getting up and collecting their things, while the teacher returns to re-sort his records. Ties are replaced, blazers and cardigans put on, as the children drift towards the door into what is obviously the routine of forming quiet lines ready to go. The timing was just right, the bell rings and the teacher sees the class out into the foyer.

This is just one example of a drama lesson, and is the sort of work that a first-year class in a secondary school might be doing.

(R. Pemberton-Billing & J. Clegg, *Teaching Drama*, 1965, pp. 11–15.)

Lesson two: 1976

Frequently Heathcote will deliberately set a drama back in time to a more primitive age when tribal conflicts are acted out face-to-face and issues can be seen more clearly. An example of this occurred in the tomb drama . . .

. . . Jerry (a tall black 12-year-old), takes over the leadership of the tribe. He has secured the support of the dead bodies (who are by this time sitting on chairs rather than lying in the tomb). When he addresses the community, he can get their attention by using a formal posture, coupled with phrases like 'The spirit of our fathers has spoken.'

... when the children come in for this last day of drama, there, along the end of the long hall, are stretched scrolls with the descriptions and interpretations the adults have written on them. The session begins with the reading of this record.

After reading the record, the children drape or tie swatches of black and brown fabric about them and go back into their roles as tribe members. Before long, Jerry is instructing the corpse of the dead man for his role in the ceremony to come. He tells him what to say and directs him to speak in a deep voice.

When he and the man-in-role as the dead man are ready, Jerry calls the group together to listen to the words of the spirits. 'Spirits!' he calls ceremoniously.

'Spirits!' Heathcote repeats.

'Come, Spirits!' Several other tribe members join her in repeating this invocation ritualistically.

Then the voice of the dead resounds in an authoritative, sepulchral tone: 'Let the dead be worshipped. May the words of those who watched be destroyed.'

Jerry turns to his tribe. 'You have heard the Spirit tell us to tear up the reports that they wrote.' With a long spear he points to the back of the large hall. 'Let every tribe member go over to the papers and tear up those papers.' Heathcote is clearing her throat and visibly tense at this point. She values the written word and efforts of the adult students very highly, so she finds Jerry's leadership painful to follow.

A girl, looking up at Heathcote's agonized face, shouts, 'I cannot bring myself to tear them.'

'What the Spirits said, we must do,' warns Jerry. He ceremoniously tears the first sheet, saying, 'In the name of the Spirits.' The tribe hesitates. 'Go ahead, tear!' They join him. After a few moments of frantic tearing, Jerry looks as the shredded bits of paper and says with conviction, 'These are not our words, not our laws. We have wrote our own laws.'

'Then we can never learn from others,' Heathcote says in a soft, regretful tone.

'No, we will not learn from others. I want all the tribe to grab these and put them in a pile over there.'

After they dutifully do that, Heathcote says humbly to her leader, 'The unlaw is now piled beside the true law.'

Jerry points to the pile. 'I have read it, and these Spirits have read it, and they know it's the wrong law. Now we shall learn our own law.' He then leads a procession down to the other end of the large hall and again invokes the Spirit of the dead.

'Spirits! Spirits! We have done what you have asked. What is your wish?'

The Spirit doesn't answer. 'Spirits! Spirits!' Jerry calls again. 'The words of our tribe are now the only words.'

'Behold the words of the past,' the Spirit says solemnly. 'Thus have died those words that are not our words. May they never return.'

'Yes, oh Holy One.'

Then the tribe follows Jerry's lead and sits in a circle. The begin to think about what they have just done. One girl in role as a woman of the tribe thoughtfully confronts Jerry, 'You have just torn up what our tribe is about. What are we if we are not that?'

'That we have not wrote. This we have wrote,' he says, pointing to their records. 'That is not our law,' he says, forcefully gesturing with his spear.

'How do we know?' asks the girl.

'The Spirits have spoken. No reporters will come on our land.'

'But I trusted the words of those reporters.'

'Why did you trust them?'

'Because they spoke true about our tribe.'

Another woman says, almost to herself, 'It is against our law to destroy.'

Jerry is hard pressed now; he calls on the Spirit again. 'Why did we tear up the laws of the strangers? this woman asks. Our law says not to destroy.'

The Spirit replies, 'Let those of our tribe behold the words of the past. You are as we were, and thus it shall be done and understood in our tribe. That which is gone is of the eyes of those who are not of us.'

'You hear?' says Jerry, vindicated. 'After this, no one shall come in and visit us.'

When the drama is over, the children discuss what they have done. They have experienced the classic confrontation of the traditional tribal leader with members of the community who are ready to open themselves to new understandings ... The problems on both sides are the heart of anthropological investigation.

(B-J. Wagner, *Dorothy Heathcote: Drama as a Learning Medium*, 1979, pp. 206–8.)

Lesson three: 1981

'An Air Disaster'

The teacher has the use of the hall for thirty-five minutes, has a class of thirty ten-to-eleven-year-olds of mixed ability and with slightly more boys than girls. The class is used to this pattern of lesson and is always anxious to show its work.

As they enter the hall the class is noisy and untidy, so in order to create a more self-disciplined atmosphere, the teacher decides to try some 'warm-up' exericses. The first one involves running everywhere and 'freezing' when the cymbal is struck. The movement produces quite a few collisions and people giggle during freeze-times. Clearly the children need a more static piece so they are put in pairs to work a mirror exercise. They have to match each other's movement without speaking. There is a great deal of talking and laughter and the imitation is not accurate. There is a feeling that this is a very familiar exercise for the class and one which does not provide much interest any more. The teacher feels valuable time is slipping away and that perhaps it would have been better to have started as he had originally intended. So he stops the class and calls them to sit round him. The proximity of the boys sitting closely in a tangle of children leads to horseplay which the teacher resolves by separating offenders.

His questions quickly produce from the children the focal point he requires. They have much more information than he requires and having appeared to be soliciting their knowledge of the recent disaster he is constrained to allow more random talk than he really wants or time allows. So he cuts through the wealth of information that the raised hands and voices represent, to announce that they are going to make their own disaster. When he dismisses them, he tells them that they must form a group and work out whether they are the crew, the passengers, ground control, etc. The class is already full of planning talk while he is still dealing with a boy who is asking if it is alright if he is the hijacker who makes the plane crash. Although that was not his intention, the teacher allows this as the class is already moving away into noisy bunches. The parted combatants now reunite and immediately begin to wrestle as hijacker and guard. Indeed an alarming number of the boys seem to have cottoned on to the idea. Where a quieter group are simulating the cabin and the controls they are set upon by another group of lusty hijackers. This is not part of their plan and they protest ultimately to the teacher as they are not as strong or as numerous as their attackers. The teacher stops the class and warns the children that they will not be allowed to make their play if they don't behave. He sorts out the groups and sets them to work once more, making sure that the difficult boys are settled to plan their piece. He has even suggested to them that they are survivors, dazed and injured who have to find help. The boys are excited by the prospect and soon the teacher feels able to leave them to get on by themselves.

The rest of the class is busy, not apparently working to a plan but making it up as they go along. They shout instructions to each other as the noise is intense. They have set out chairs more or less elaborately and these clatter over as the crash occurs in different parts of the hall. The teacher is aware that the noise level is such that it might invite intervention of the headmaster and also the time indicates that only seven minutes are left. He stops the class and asks them to sit down to watch their pieces. Talk immediately resumes and this he quells, stressing that they have to pay attention to the scenes of others to be able to criticise them, especially as they will put the scenes together to make a play. As some semblance of quiet is apparent he invites the naughty boys' group, with which he had planned, to show theirs first. The piece starts as he might expect with the survivors reeling about like drunken men. But soon a dispute about food and water arises and the exhausted men fight with remarkable energy. Already people are walking through the hall and embarrassed by what appears as riot, the teacher stops the piece. As he asks for the next, the bell rings and amid cries of frustrated actors, the chat of the naughty group, the increasing horde invading the hall and the clatter of the dinner ladies, he promises they will see the rest next time.

Nothing has worked as he had planned, he feels exhausted and depressed because the idea was a good one. He dare not evaluate the lesson because the lofty aims remain as an indictment of his ability to produce drama with the class. For the children there is no such heart-searching. In the playground they are doing much the same as they were previously doing in the hall. The lesson was very much as usual with the opportunity for some fun and a break from the more formal task of writing. As usual, one had to make up a story about a given idea, and act it with friends – if there was time. 'Sometimes it get boring when you have to do the same idea again or when you have to do the same thing, like being mirrors, and that.' To be honest neither class nor teacher could really justify the work to an anxious mother, irate father or sceptical deputy head.

This imaginary incident might seem a cruel exaggeration of an unfamiliar scene; it is not. Its details are fictional, but the experiences they exemplify have been seen again and again.

(B. Watkins, *Drama and Education*, 1981, pp. 64–6.)

Appendix B

A modular GCSE in dramatic art

The following extract is from an Inner London Education Authority Mode II submission to the London East Anglian Examinations Board. With some modifications, this modular syllabus was offered in the Authority's schools from September 1988.

Originating from the ILEA Arts in Schools Project, the syllabus matches similar modular programmes in Art, Music and Dance. Each shares a common conceptual base, so as well as following single subjects it becomes possible to assemble combined arts courses made up of a selection of modules.

As it restores arts-subject status to school drama, the syllabus reflects many of the themes and emphases of dramatic art indicated in this book. Copies of the complete syllabus may be obtained from the London East Anglian Examinations Board.

GCSE Drama & Theatre Arts (Dramatic Art) – Mode II (Modular)

Syllabus aims

1 To develop the ability to respond creatively through dramatic art to a variety of stimuli.

· 2 To develop a critical self and cultural consciousness through the exercise of and engagement with the dramatic aesthetic.

3 To develop the ability to communicate using space, movement and

language in both conventional and experimental dramatic forms; to develop the skills, techniques and conventions necessary for effective dramatic presentation.

4 To use dramatic art to interpret, challenge and revalue cultural assumptions, notably those concerning race, gender, class and attitudes to disability.

5 To develop the ability to analyse and reflect critically; to evaluate one's own work and that of others against an understanding of their social and historical contexts.

6 To develop the capacity for independent study and investigation by encouraging response to direct dramatic experience, and in particular that involving professional companies and performers.

7 To develop, through dramatic art, the imagination, sensitivity and self-confidence of the individual.

Assessment objectives

The assessment objectives of each module are grouped under four main headings. The examination will assess the extent to which candidates are able to give evidence of achievement in the following:
INVESTIGATING
EXPERIMENTING
RECORDING
PRESENTING

1 Investigating
Candidates should:
a) observe, select, interpret and record responses to first hand experience;
b) select and use reference and resource material to form and develop ideas.

2 Experimenting
Candidates should:
a) develop skills and techniques in the selection and control of material;
b) experiment with a wide range of different starting points, working methods and ideas.

3   Recording
Candidates should:
  a) see their work in its widest curricular, cultural, historical and environmental context;
  b) use written, oral, visual or electronic media (or any combination thereof) to record and evaluate work.

4   Presenting
Candidates should:
  a) select, organise and use the techniques of dramatic art in shaping appropriate material for the expressive transmission of ideas;
  b) sustain chosen studies from conception to presentation.

Syllabus framework

The syllabus framework is constructed to provide the maximum flexibility. Centres will be able to develop a broadly based modular syllabus appropriate to their specific circumstances, expertise and resources. There is no intention that each, or even a specified number, of the 'Processes and Procedures' or 'Practices' should be included in any specific course of study. For the purposes of clarity, the 'Processes and Procedures' have been separately listed but in reality they overlap and are interdependent. It is hard to imagine any work which would not involve, for example, 'critical appraisal'.

Basic elements	Processes & procedures	Practices
SPACE	Project-based thematic enquiry and response	Improvisation
SOUND	Sequential development of ideas, study and practice	Representation and Interpretation
GESTURE	Expressive response, unrestricted exploration	
DISCOURSE	and development	Critical reflection
TEXT	Structured discussion, critical appraisal and analysis	
FORM	Experimenting and restricted exploration	Stagecraft
SCENE-MAKING	Research, analysis, observation and recording	Cultural and historical studies

The following sections present a range of possible content from which an appropriate programme of modules may be constructed by centres.

Basic elements

1 Space
This refers to all aspects of dramatic art concerned with the manipulation of space to create dramatic meaning. Modules are likely to include:
a)   The use of space appropriate to a given role.
b)   'Shaping' – the use of space and the relative placing of people or objects within it.
c)   'Focus' – the direction of attention to specific aspects of the drama.
d)   The manipulation of objects to convey meaning – eg. puppets, props, scenery.
e)   The naturalistic and non-naturalistic use of dramatic space.
f)   The creative designing of space as an environment for dramatic action; light, colour, balance, etc.

2 Sound
This refers to all acoustic aspects of dramatic art other than spoken language. Modules are likely to include:
a)   Ritual sounds and singing.
b)   The use of the pause; silence.
c)   The use of sound to create dramatic mood.
d)   Sound-effects and music.
e)   The use of recorded sound.

3 Gesture
This refers to all aspects of dramatic art concerned wit h the use of physical movement to create dramatic meaning. Modules are likely to include:
a)   Facial expression and gesture.
b)   The use of physical signs or symbols to convey meaning.
c)   Body language appropriate to a given role.
d)   The use of tableaux (still-pictures).
e)   Stylised movement and the use of ritual.
f)   Non-verbal discourse. Mime.
g)   The development of physical clarity and expressiveness.
h)   The linking of physical expression and movement to costume, lighting, etc.

4 *Discourse*

This refers to all aspects of dramatic art involving spoken language. Modules are likely to include:
  a) Spoken language appropriate to a given role or character.
  b) Vocal clarity and expressiveness.
  c) The use of language registers appropriate to the dramatic situation.
  d) The conventions of dramatic dialogue.
  e) Technical appropriations such as radio drama.

5 *Text*

This refers to improvised or script-based drama in action. Modules are likely to include:
  a) The use of narrative and plot.
  b) The interpretation and realisation of dramatic scripts.
  c) The shaping of dramatic movement within role-play and improvisation.
  d) The critical analysis of dramatic enactments.
  e) The use of lighting, costume, effects, etc. to enhance the text in action.

6 *Form*

This refers to all aspects of dramatic convention. Modules are likely to include:
  a) The nature and formation of dramatic conventions. Genre.
  b) The importance of form in relation to history.
  c) The appropriateness of dramatic form to creative intention.
  d) The exploration of new forms of dramatic action.
  e) Form as a structure of cultural expression. (Carnival, ritual, community drama, etc.)
  f) The relationship of costume, lighting, scenery, etc. to dramatic form.

7 *Scene-making*

This refers to the combining of aspects of dramatic art in the form of a production or presentation. Modules are likely to include:
  a) The combining of elements of drama to create dramatic resonance.
  b) The editing and presentation of 'polished' improvisations.
  c) Understanding the role of the director.
  d) The devising of research-based dramatic presentations.
  e) Understanding the collaborative quality of scene-making.

f) The technical, managerial, and administrative aspects of production.

Processes and procedures

1   Project-based thematic enquiry and response
This refers to a scheme of work which sets out to explore a particular topic.
Although the maximum opportunity should be given to develop the topic in
a variety of ways, it will be constrained by its theme. For example:
   a)   an exploration through discussion and role work of the influence of
        social conventions on power relations within the family;
   b)   improvisation based upon stories in the popular press;
   c)   teacher-led background work in social studies, history or
        anthropology;
   d)   the preparation of related selections from written texts.

2   Sequential development
This refers to a scheme of work planned on a structured system which aims
at an accumulation of specific skills, knowledge and understanding over a
fixed period of time. For example:
   a)   an introduction to the naturalistic use of tableaux or still pictures
        through the construction of dramatic 'photographs'.
   b)   the use of the same technique to express individual abstract ideas or
        emotions, such as depictions expressing 'jealousy'.
   c)   the application of the technique to more complex concepts, such as
        tableaux representing Shakespeare's 'Seven Ages of Man'.

3   Expressive response
This refers to the unrestricted exploration and development of ideas and
feelings through dramatic art. This way of working would usually be
preceded by exposure to a particular stimulus, perhaps a current event of
particular interest to the candidates, and might include:
   a)   responses to photographs, poems, stories, music, script extracts,
        videotapes, offered by the teacher.
   b)   the expression of fantasy.
   c)   personal interpretations of things seen, imagined and felt.

4   Experimenting and restricted exploration
This refers to specific task-setting closely related to established dramatic
theory and practice wherein candidates might be required to consider a
range of ideas and solutions and select appropriate media. For example:
   a)   candidates see examples, live or videorecorded, of a theatre-in-
        education company working with primary children;

b) techniques are analysed with the help of the teacher and/or the company concerned;

c) candidates prepare their own programme on a subject of interest to them;

d) the programme is played in a local primary school. Work in progress as well as the end product is evaluated and recorded by the candidates.

5 Structured discussion, critical appraisal and analysis
This refers to the formulation and articulation of value judgements about dramatic art and might include:

a) group or individual tutorials on candidate's own work;

b) reaction and response to a theatre visit;

c) comparison between candidate's own work and that of established practitioners;

d) discussion, 'editing' and restructuring;

e) analysis and criticism of technical aspects of a project.

6 Research, analysis, observation and recording
This covers methods of approach, appropriate technical skills and the use of information retrieval and reference systems, and might include:

a) selection from an arranged collection of stimulus material such as pictures, poetry, newspaper cuttings, written observations and sketches;

b) material related to a thematic project which requires substantial individual research, such as the recording of oral history, ideas for presentation, transcripts from improvisations, and copies of relevant documentation;

c) preparation notebooks in specific skills, such as design, production, or individual performance;

d) analyses of performances.

Practices

1 Improvisation
This refers to those practices through which we can experiment in dramatic art. It includes the forms of improvisation, 'spontaneous' and 'prepared', which are common in drama lessons, but also more stylised forms such as *commedia dell'arte* or clowning. The nature of improvisation makes it impossible for any list to be exhaustive, but consideration is likely to be given to practices that fall into two categories:

a) activities which take place in 'real time' – that is, situations which are naturalistically 'acted out'. For example, pair work in role, small group improvisation whole group improvisation and simulation.

b)   those activities which involve non-naturalistic dramatic conventions. For example, characters speaking the thoughts of other characters, re-enactments, tableaux, and the use of stock-characters.

2   Representation and interpretation
This covers the forming and shaping of work specifically for presentation to a defined audience, where the content has been broadly determined in advance. It will embrace performances of work devised by the candidates themselves as well as plays by established playwrights.

Attention will be paid to the effectiveness of chosen dramatic forms and conventions in conveying the intentions of the group in relation to the dramatic text. This will involve:

a)   the use of dramatic elements such as space, movement and discourse;

b)   the manipulation of tension and conflict to create dramatic interest;

c)   the use of narrative or other forms of dramatic delivery;

d)   a recognition of the implications of the text in performance for a defined audience.

3   Critical reflection
This refers to the means by which evaluation of a candidate's own work and the work of others is encouraged and refined. Normally an essential part of classroom practice such evaluation will extend to the critical appraisal of contributions from external arts agencies, theatre visits and independently pursued projects.

Some modes of this practice are well established, such as group discussion and written accounts. This submission gives equal weighting to evaluative practices occurring outside, or as part of, the drama process; occurring orally, in written or diagramatic form, using audio or video recording, or using computer-assisted profiling. Consideration is likely to be given to responses relating to:

a)   improvised work;

b)   presentation work;

c)   script studies;

d)   live performance;

4   Stagecraft
This refers to the conditions and organisation of representations on the stage. It will include specific acting techniques, such as use of mask, or

vocal projection, as well as technical skills, such as make-up, lighting and sound. Consideration is likely to be given to:

a)   performance skills (voice, movement, dance, singing, stage conventions, interpretation);

b)   design (set, lighting costume, props, make-up, puppets, masks);

c)   instrumental skills (set building and painting, lighting rigging and operation, costume making, props acquisition and making, make-up application, puppet and mask making, health and safety considerations);

d)   organisation and management (stage management, administration, publicity);

5   Cultural and historical studies
This aspect of the course would be incorporated into its general structure Studies would aim to establish the idea of dramatic art as cultural expression in a historical context. This would be achieved by the employment of a wide frame of reference inclusive both of European and non-European forms. The emphasis would be on the enrichment of candidates' own practice by allowing them access to the work of practitioners from a range of cultures, past and present. These studies might include:

a)   ritualised drama (Classical Greek drama, Balinese ritual theatre, 'Theatre of Cruelty', pageant and ceremony);

b)   drama of cultural affirmation (medieval cycles, Shakespeare's histories', drawing-room comedy, Noh Theatre);

c)   drama of protest (Boal, Piscator, Unity Theatre, Chilean Theatre, Commedia dell'Arte, Women's Theatre);

d)   'non-legitimate' drama (melodrama, soap opera, pantomime, musicals) . . . .

Appendix C

Attainment in drama

The National Curriculum Council's Arts in Schools Project argued consistently for the arts to be regarded as a generic area of the curriculum, like the sciences. In the Project's publication, *The Arts 5–16: A Framework for Development* (Longman, 1990), a structure for understanding attainment in the arts is proposed. Based upon what the Project sees as the two fundamental ways in which we engage with the arts, *making* and *appraising* (corresponding to the production/reproduction and critical interpretation categories identified here), three profile components and seven attainment targets are identified. These acknowledge the creative and imaginative dimension peculiar to arts education as well as the necessity for the development of knowledge and skills. Within this framework, it is possible to deliver attainment in the arts through individual art forms.

Any programmes of study in dramatic art based upon the Arts in Schools' model must also take account of the developing programmes of the national curriculum alongside and within which they will of necessity have to be delivered. Sections of two key documents are reproduced here.

1   English 5 to 16: Proposals of the English Working Group

The English Working Group's proposals recommend drama specifically as a 'learning medium' for their Speaking and Listening component. While programmes of study for speaking and listening are a long way from forming a coherent dramatic curriculum, drama teachers will find much here which is familiar.

15.24 Attainment target one speaking and listening

The development of pupils' understanding of the spoken word and the capacity to express themselves effectively in a variety of speaking and listening activities, matching style and response to audience and purpose.

Level Description

1 Pupils should be able to:
  - i Participate as speakers and listeners in group activities, including imaginative play.
  - ii Listen attentively, and respond, to stories and poems.
  - iii Respond appropriately to simple instructions given by a teacher.

2 i Participate as speakers and listeners in a group engaged in a given task.
  - ii Describe an event, real or imagined, to the teacher or another pupil.
  - iii Listen attentively to stories and poems, and talk about them.
  - iv Talk with the teacher, listen and ask and answer questions.
  - v Respond appropriately to a range of more complex instructions given by a teacher, and give simple instructions.

3 i Relate real or imaginery events in a connected narrative which conveys meaning to a group of pupils, the teacher or another known adult.
  - ii Convey accurately a simple message.
  - iii Listen with an increased span of concentration to other children and adults, asking and responding to questions and commenting on what has been said.
  - iv Give and receive and follow accurately precise instructions when pursuing a task individually or as a member of a group.

4 i Give a detailed oral account of an event, or something that has been learned in the classroom, or explain with reasons why a particular course of action has been taken.
  - ii Ask and respond to questions with increased confidence in a range of situations.
  - iii Take part as a speaker and listener in a group discussion of straightforward issues, or in a group activity, commenting on what is being discussed.
  - iv Participate in a presentation, *eg of the outcome of a group activity, a poem, a story or a scene.*

5   i   Give a well organised and sustained account of an event, a personal experience or an activity.

    ii Contribute to and respond constructively in discussion or debate, advocating and justifying a particular point of view.

    iii Use transactional language effectively in a straightforward situation, *eg an eye-witness account of an event or incident; reclaiming an article which has been lost.*

    iv Plan and participate in a presentation, *eg of the outcome of a group activity, a poem, a story, dramatic scene or play.*

    v   Talk about variations in vocabulary between different regional or social groups, *eg dialect vocabulary, specialist terms.*

6   i   Contribute considered opinions or clear statements of personal feelings to group discussions and show an understanding of the contributions of others.

    ii Understand and use transactional language effectively in a variety of relatively straightforward situations where the subject is familiar both to the pupil and to the audience or other participants.

    iii Participate in simple presentations or performances with some fluency.

    iv Talk about some grammatical differences between spoken Standard English and a non-standard variety.

7   i   Express a point of view cogently and with clarity to a range of audiences and interpret with accuracy a range of statements by others.

    ii Understand and use transactional language effectively on occasions where the situation or topic requires more than one outcome and is less readily familiar to the pupils and/or their audience.

    iii Take an active part in group discussions, contributing constructively to the development of the argument in hand.

    iv Talk about appropriateness in the use of spoken language, according to purpose, topic and audience, *eg differences between language appropriate to a job interview and to a discussion with their peers.*

8   i   Express a point of view on a complex subject cogently and with clarity, and interpret alternative viewpoints with accuracy and discrimination.

    ii Understand and use transactional language effectively in a variety of complex situations which involve a range of audiences.

iii   Take part in group discussions, actively and critically, showing an ability to summarise and evaluate arguments effectively.

iv   Talk about the contribution that facial expressions, gestures and tone of voice can make to a speaker's meaning, *eg in ironic and sarcastic uses of language.*

9   i   Give a presentation involving a personal point of view on a complex subject cogently and with clarity, integrating talk with writing as appropriate, *eg using hand-outs or visual aids,* and respond appropriately to the presentations of others.

ii   Take an active part in group discussions, displaying sensitivity, listening critically, *eg to attempts to persuade,* and being self-critical.

iii   Talk about ways in which language varies between different types of spoken communication, *eg joke, anecdote, conversation, commentary, lecture.*

10   i   Express a point of view on complex subjects cogently and with clarity, applying and interpreting a range of presentational strategies and assessing their own effectiveness accurately.

ii   Take a leading role in group discussions, *eg by taking the chair,* listening with concentration and understanding, noting down salient points, summarising arguments and, where appropriate, formulating a consensus.

iii   Talk about some of the factors that influence people's attitudes to the way other people speak.

(National Curriculum Council, *English for ages 5 to 16: Proposals of the Secretary of State for Education and Science and the Secretary of State for Wales,* Department of Education and Science and the Welsh Office, June 1989.)

2   HMI's Drama from 5 to 16

While acknowledging the contribution drama might make to the delivery of attainment in English, HMI take us a step further in the process of identifying a specific dramatic curriculum. Drama from 5 to 16 does not specify attainment targets as such, but instead proposes learning objectives appropriate for pupils of 7, 11 and 16.

Objectives
11   The following learning objectives are cumulative. Those at the first stage should lay a foundation for pupils' experiences of drama. Subsequent stages should extend and deepen previous achievements.

These objectives will need to be considered in conjunction with the attainment targets and statements of attainment for English in the National Curriculum, particularly those within the profile components for speaking and listening and for reading. Although they are presented separately, in practice they will be interrelated through a variety of opportunities for dramatic activity. This activity will, by the age of seven, enable pupils to:

- play inventively and with concentration, both on their own and with others;
- understand and take pleasure in the difference between pretence and reality;
- identify with characters and actions through role-playing, for instance in a dramatised story, and as spectators of a live performance;
- have the confidence and ability to put across a particular point of view;
- realise that the views of individuals do not always coincide;
- learn how to work together to solve human and practical problems;
- explore the differences between right and wrong in simple moral dilemmas posed through drama.

12 By the age of 11 pupils should be able to:
- invent and develop convincing roles in specific situations;
- create and take part in improvised scenes in order to explore particular issues which could, for instance, have a practical, social or moral dimension;
- know how to structure dramatic sequences in order to convey meaning;
- carry out dramatic intentions with a clear but unforced control over movement and voice;
- organise and deploy physical materials, colour, light and sound to create a space for drama;
- be able to use artefacts or properties as symbols in dramatic action;
- experience the power of ritual and display and other structural means in order to appreciate the contribution these make to dramatic meaning;
- select and use first-hand material which is relevant and dramatically significant;
- recognise good work in drama through a detailed and critical observation of the characters created, the issues involved and the processes employed.

13 By the age of 16 pupils should be able to:
  • demonstrate a knowledge of the basic concepts of drama (fictions, symbols, characters and roles, situations and settings, plotting, rules and conventions, dialogue).
  • use appropriate structures to control dramatic action;
  • try out different ideas or unorthodox approaches in experimenting with improvisation and text;
  • recognise that there may be alternative interpretations of dramatic meaning which have equal validity;
  • appreciate dramatic ambiguity, for example when language and action work in opposition;
  • call upon a range of subtle skills in voice, posture, movement and gesture in order to sustain and develop dramatic action;
  • integrate sound and silence, movement and stillness, light and darkness to make effective use of spaces where dramatic action takes place;
  • create improvised or written dramas for others;
  • understand the main characteristics of different kinds of drama and have practical experience of suitable classic and contemporary examples;
  • experience the organisation, discipline and teamwork necessary to perform drama to others, formally or informally, in or out of school;
  • recognise social conventions and stereotypes and be prepared to re-examine them;
  • show insight into, and sympathy for, human and cultural differences.

(Department of Education and Science, *Drama from 5 to 16: Curriculum Matters 17*, HMSO, 1989.)

Appendix D

Performance analysis

The questionnaire reproduced here originates from the Institute of Theatre Studies at the New Sorbonne. It was devised by the theatre semiotician Patrice Pavis to help drama students with no particular knowledge of semiology to identify aspects of theatre performance for interpretation and analysis.

With some adaptation and simplification, and used selectively, drama teachers might find elements of this questionnaire useful for looking at performance with their pupils.

1 *General discussion of performance*
   a) what holds elements of performance together
   b) relationship between systems of staging
   c) coherence or incoherence
   d) aesthetic principles of the production
   e) what do you find disturbing about the production; strong moments or weak, boring moments.

2 *Scenography*
   a) spatial forms: urban, architectu-

ral, scenic, gestural, etc.
   b) relationship between audience space and acting space
   c) systems of colours and their connotations
   d) principles of organization of space
      – relationship between on-stage and off-stage
      – links between space utilized and fiction of the staged dramatic text
      – what is shown and what is implied.

3 *Lighting system*

4 *Stage properties*
   type, function, relationship to space and actors' bodies.

5 *Costumes*
   how they work; relationship to actors' bodies.

6 *Actors' performances*
   a) individual or conventional style of acting

b) relation between actor and group
c) relation between text and body, between actor and role
d) quality of gestures and mime
e) quality of voices
f) how dialogues develop.

7 Function of music and sound effects

8 Pace of performance
a) overall pace
b) pace of certain signifying systems (lighting, costumes, gestures, etc.)
c) steady or broken pace.

9 Interpretation of story-line in performance
a) what story is being told
b) what kind of dramaturgical choices have been made
c) what are ambiguities in performance and what are points of explanation
d) how is plot structured
e) how is story constructed by actors and staging
f) what is genre of dramatic text.

10 Text in performance
a) main features of translation (script to stage)
b) what role is given to dramatic text in production

c) relationship between (written) text and image.

11 Audience
a) where does performance take place
b) what expectations did you have of performance
c) how did audience react
d) role of spectator in production of meaning.

12 How to notate (photograph and film) this production
a) how to notate performance technically (SM's book?)
b) which images have you retained.

13 What cannot be put into signs
a) what did not make sense in your interpretation of the production
b) what was not reducible to signs and meaning (and why).

14
a) Are there any special problems that need examining
b) Any comments, suggestions for further categories for the questionnaire and the production.

(P. Pavis, 'Theatre analysis: some questions and a questionnaire', *New Theatre Quarterly*, 1:2 (May 1985), p. 209.)

Notes

Chapter 1

1 Rousseau's noble savage was certainly no Caliban. In a significant sense he epitomised the ideal family man [*sic*] of the bourgeois imagination; a responsible and considerate husband and father inspired with a natural kindliness and possessed of all necessary natural wisdom.

2 This view of human nature is, of course, in marked contrast to that of the seventeenth-century English philosopher Thomas Hobbes, whose argument for a strong state was based on his belief that, in nature, man's life would be 'solitary, poor, nasty, brutish and short'. It is from Hobbes's individualism (through Adam Smith) rather than from Rousseau's that modern economic theory derives.

3 G. Bolton, 'Teacher in Rôle and Teacher power', in *Positive Images: 1985 Conference Publication* (Joint Committee (NATD, NATFHE Drama, NAYT, NADECT, NADA), 1986), p. 38.

4 J.-J. Rousseau, *Politics and the Arts: The Letter to M. d'Alembert*, tr. A. Bloom (Free Press, Glencoe, Illinois, 1960).

5 Ibid., p. 126.

6 I wander thro' each chartered street,
   Near where the chartered Thames does flow,
   And mark in every face I meet
   Marks of weakness, marks of woe.

> (William Blake, *Songs of Experience*, 1794.)

7 Gavin Bolton is right to point out that a village school headmistress of the same period, Harriet Finlay-Johnson, was also using drama in her

classroom. See H. Finlay-Johnson, *The Dramatic Method of Teaching* (Nisbet (undated)).

8   H. Caldwell Cook, *The Play Way* (Heinemann, London, 1917).

9   Ibid., p. 4.

10   In philosophical terms, Nietzsche's vision of the absolute liberty of the will cannot co-exist with Aristotle's belief in 'honour through merit'. The fact is that we, like Caldwell Cook, sometimes *do* succeed in persuading ourselves that it is possible simultaneously to hold these two irreconcilable views of moral action, and in doing so we fall victim to the forms of moral rationalisation against which Nietzsche warns us.

11   K. Groos, *The Play of Man*, tr. E.L. Baldwin (Heinemann, London, 1901).

12   M. Klein, P. Heimann, S. Isaacs and J. Rivière, *Developments in Psychoanalysis* (Hogarth Press, London, 1952), p. 111.

13   Board of Education, *Report of the Consultative Committee on the Primary School* (The Hadow Report) (HMSO, London, 1931), p. 76.

14   Ministry of Education, 'Report of Informal Committee', under chair of A. F. Alington (later HM Staff Inspector for Drama), and then G. Allen (HM Staff Inspector for English), unpub., 1951.

15   P. Slade, *Child Drama* (University of London Press, 1954).

16   P. Slade, *An Introduction to Child Drama* (Hodder & Stoughton, London, 1958).

17   In the 1960s, the number of full-time teacher-training courses offering a qualification in Drama rose from six to over one hundred.

18   Slade (1958), p. 2.

19   Ibid. For a fictional paradigm of this aesthetic in action, see Appendix A, Lesson 1.

20   Ibid., pp. 64–5.

21   Ministry of Education, *Half our Future* (The Newsom Report), (HMSO, London, 1963), p. 157.

22   B. Way, *Development through Drama* (Longman, London, 1967).

23   Ibid., p. 2.

24   Some examples are: R. Pemberton-Billing and J. Clegg, *Teaching Drama* (University of London Press, 1965); J. Hodgson and E. Richards, *Improvisation* (Eyre Methuen, London, 1966); P. Chilver, *Improvised Drama* (Batsford, London, 1967); B. Walker, *Teaching Creative Drama* (Batsford, London, 1970); J. Goodridge, *Drama in the Primary School* (Heinemann, London, 1970); D. Bowskill, *Drama and the Teacher* (The Pitman Press, Bath, 1974).

25   See J. Pick, 'A little food for thought', *English in Education*, 1:3 (Autumn, 1967), p. 58; J. Pick, 'Skeletons in the prop cupboard', *Higher Education Journal* (Summer, 1970); J. Pick, 'Five fallacies in drama',

Young Drama, 1:1 (February, 1973); J. Clegg, 'The dilemma of drama-in-education', *Theatre Quarterly* (1973), No. 9.

26　D. Heathcote, *Theatre Quarterly* (1973), No. 10, pp. 63–4.

27　D. Heathcote, 'Drama as Challenge', in *The Uses of Drama*, ed. J. Hodgson (Eyre Methuen, London, 1972), p. 159.

28　In L. McGregor, M. Tate and K. Robinson, *Learning through Drama* (Report of the Schools Council Drama Teaching Project (10–16), (Heinemann, London, 1977).

29　J. Fines and R. Verrier, 'The work of Dorothy Heathcote', *Young Drama*, 4:1 (February, 1976), p. 3.

30　B-J. Wagner, *Dorothy Heathcote: Drama as a Learning Medium* (Hutchinson, London, 1979).

31　A good example is: A. Lambert and C. O'Neill, *Drama Structures* (Hutchinson, London, 1982).

Chapter 2

1　P. Slade, *Child Drama* (University of London Press, 1954), p. 52.

2　D. Bowskill, 'Drama in secondary education', *English in Education*, 1:3 (1967), p. 13.

3　D. Heathcote, 'Improvisation', *English in Education*, 1:3 (1967), p. 27.

4　'Dorothy Heathcote in interview with David Davis', *2D*, 4:3 (Summer, 1985), p. 75. Earlier in the interview, Heathcote speaks of how she has been 'building the possibility of thickness'. The point is, nowhere is this idea of 'thick description' explained. We may only surmise that she has been reading Gilbert Ryle, who introduces 'thick description' as a way of doing ethnography in G. Ryle, *Collected Papers, Vol 2: Collected Essays 1929–68* (Hutchinson, London 1971).

5　Ibid., p. 77.

6　E. Gellner, *The Psychoanalytic Movement* (Paladin Books, London, 1985), p. 154.

7　R. Lee, 'Two mules waiting', *Drama Broadsheet*, 3:1 (Winter, 1984), p. 9.

8　J. Kelly, '652 Theatre Project; a session with Dorothy Heathcote at Earls House Hospital', *Drama Broadsheet*, 3:2 (Spring, 1985), p. 4.

9　L. Johnson and C. O'Neill (eds) *Dorothy Heathcote: Collected Writings* (Hutchinson, London, 1984), p. 13.

10　A. Seeley, 'A woman that attempts the pen: a look at the work of Dorothy Heathcote', *2D*, 6:2 (Summer, 1987), p. 7.

11　Kelly (1985), p. 4.

12　B-J. Wagner, *Dorothy Heathcote: Drama as a Learning Medium* (Hutchinson, London, 1978), pp. 14–15.

13   Seeley (1987), p. 8.
14   D. Heathcote (1983), p. 20. The epigram for this piece is the chorus
     from Yeats's poem, 'The Only Jealousy of Emer':

     ... How many centuries spent
     The sedentary soul
     In toils of measurement
     Beyond eagle or mole ...

15   J. Neelands, 'Whose art is it?', *Drama Broadsheet*, 2:1 (Autumn, 1983),
     p. 21.
16   J. Fines, 'The edges of the matter', *London Drama*, 6:8 (Summer,
     1983), p. 4.
17   R. Sennett, *The Fall of Public Man* (Cambridge University Press,
     1977), p. 270.
18   G. Fairclough, *The Play is NOT the Thing* (Basil Blackwell, 1972), p. 8.
19   S. Welton, 'Towards the swamps?', *Drama Broadsheet*, 3:2 (Spring,
     1985), p. 13.
20   Neelands (1983), p. 21.
21   Lee (1984), p. 9.
22   C. Skoogh, *Drama Broadsheet*, 2:2 (Spring, 1984), p. 5.
23   For example, writing about the 'psychological and educational im-
     plications' of school drama, Bolton has this to say about Robert
     Witkin:

     In this connection Robert Witkin has built a huge conceptual
     framework in this *Intelligence of Feeling* but I regret I cannot use
     it because I cannot understand it!

     G. Bolton, 'Drama in the Curriculum', in *Gavin Bolton: Selected Writ-
     ings*, ed. D. Davis and C. Lawrence, (Longman, London, 1986),
     p. 227.
24   Johnson and O'Neill (eds) (1984), pp. 9–10.
25   J. Neelands, 'I'm coming out of the closet', *Drama Broadsheet*, 3:2
     (Spring, 1985), p. 13.
26   D. Rowntree, *Assessing Students: How Shall We Know Them?* (Harper &
     Row, New York, 1977), p. 1.
27   Midland Examining Group, GCSE *Leicestershire Mode III Drama*
     (1986), pp. 2–3.
28   G. Bolton, 'Theatre Form in Drama Teaching', in Davis and Lawr-
     ence (eds) (1986), pp. 178-9. For a full account of this workshop, see
     G. Bolton, *Towards a Theory of Drama in Education* (Longman, London,
     1979), ch. 8.

29   N. Morgan and J. Saxton, *Teaching Drama: 'A Mind of Many Wonders
      ...'* (Hutchinson, London, 1987), p. 206.
30   B-J. Wagner (1979), p. 231. See also Appendix A, 'Lesson two'.
31   C. Hill, in *The World of the Muggletonians* eds C. Hill, B. Reay and W.
      Lamont (Temple Smith, London, 1983), p. 12. Although much less
      well known than other radical groups of the English Revolution,
      such as the Levellers and the Diggers, the Muggletonians continued
      to attract followers into the twentieth century. The historian E. P.
      Thompson befriended the last member of this obscure religious sect,
      Philip Noakes, and before Noakes died in 1979, succeeded in rescuing
      the Muggletonian archive for posterity. Its eighty-eight volumes,
      which include the seventeenth-century correspondence of the
      prophets and their followers, are now stored in the British Library.
32   Hill et al. (1983), p. 12.

Chapter 3

1   See B-J. Wagner, *Dorothy Heathcote: Drama as a Learning Medium*
      (Hutchinson, London, 1979).
2   *Education Reform Act 1988* (HMSO, London, 1988).
3   Centre for Contemporary Cultural Studies (CCCS), *Unpopular Educa-
      tion* (Hutchinson, London, 1981), p. 65.
4   Anthony Crosland: Secretary of State for Education and Science,
      1965–7. Edward Boyle: Minister of Education, 1962–4; Minister of
      State for Higher Education, with a Cabinet seat, 1964.
5   Ministry of Education, *Report of the Committee on Higher Education* (The
      Robbins Report) (HMSO, London, 1963(1)), ch. 19.
6   Ministry of Education, *Half our Future* (The Newsom Report)
      (HMSO, London 1963(2)).
7   B. Morris, *The New Curriculum* (HMSO, London, 1967), p. 6.
8   Ministry of Education (1963(2)), p. xvi.
9   B. Way, *Development through Drama* (Longman, London, 1967), pp.
      2–4.
10   For example, and famously, see L. Stenhouse, *Schools Council Humani-
      ties Curriculum Project* (Longman, London, 1969).
11   Particularly after the school leaving age was raised to sixteen in 1972
      (ROSLA).
12   In the first instance, two issues in 1969 of the *Critical Survey*, a
      periodical associated with the literary *Critical Quarterly*. Edited by C.
      B. Cox and A. E. Dyson, they appeared under the titles, 'Fight for
      Education' and 'The Crisis in Education'. Over the following five

years, further 'Black Papers' appeared echoing the right-wing sentiments of the original contributors.

13   For examples from the press see CCCS (1981), ch. 10.
14   C. Burt, in *Black Paper 2. The Crisis in Education*, ed. B. Cox and A.
      Dyson (Critical Quarterly Society, 1969), p. 23.
15   R. Boyson, in Cox and Dyson (eds) (1969(2)), p. 57.
16   R. Pedley, in Cox and Dyson (eds) (1969(2)), p. 85.

17   ... the simple fact, well known to any teacher and available to
          all at the cost of a little reflection, that if you pack your class
          with thicks you will either have to ignore them and teach only
          the bright people or, if like most teachers you feel responsible for
          all levels of pupil, you will compromise, i.e. lower your stan-
          dard.

      Kingsley Amis, 'Why Lucky Jim Turned Right', in *What Became of
      Jane Austen, and Other Questions* (Penguin Books, Harmondsworth,
      1981), p. 198.
18   From Prime Minister James Callaghan's Ruskin College speech (18
      October 1976), in *Education*, 148:17 (22 October 1976), p. 333.
19   Cox and Dyson (eds) (1969(2)), p. 15.
20   Department of Education and Science, *Education in Schools* (HMSO,
      London 1977(1)), pp. 8–13.
21   Department of Education and Science (1977(1)), pp. 8–13.
22   See E. Boyle, A. Crosland and M. Kogan, *The Politics of Education*
      (Penguin Books, Harmondsworth, 1971), p. 123.
23   Notably, M. Blaug, *An Introduction to the Economics of Education* (Pen-
      guin Books, Harmondsworth, 1976).
24   J. Ellis, *Life Skills Training Manual* (Community Service Volunteers,
      London, 1983), p. 3.
25   'Letter from a drama teacher', *2D*, 3:1 (Autumn, 1983), p. 2.
26   K. Joyce, 'Drama in Personal and Social Education', *2D*, 3:1 (Au-
      tumn, 1983), p. 13.
27   D. Morton, 'Drama for capability', *2D*, 2:3 (Summer, 1983), p. 6.
28   L. Johnson, Editorial, *London Drama*, 6:9 (Spring, 1984), p. 3.
29   E. Fennell, 'Teacher or trainer? – the dilemma of YTS', *London
      Drama*, 6:9 (Spring, 1984), p. 19.
30   D. Davis, 'Drama for deference or drama for defiance?', *2D*, 3:1
      (Autumn, 1983), p. 35.
31   *The Arts in Schools* (Calouste Gulbenkian, London, 1982).
32   *The Times Educational Supplement* (6 February 1981), quoted in *The Arts
      in Schools* (1982), p. 28.

33   Ibid.
34   Department of Education and Science, *Curriculum 11–16* (The Red Book) (HMSO, London 1977(2)), p. 6.
35   Inner London Education Authority, *Improving Secondary Schools* (The Hargreaves Report) (1984), p. 59.
36   Department of Education and Science, *Better Schools* (HMSO, London, 1985), pp. 20, 22.
37   A. Rumbold, *Speech by the Minister of State at the Annual Conference of the National Association for Education in the Arts, 28.10.87.*, Department of Education and Science (1987), para. 42.
38   See *Education Reform Act 1988*, 1988, p. 2:

> (1)   Subject to subsection (4) below, the core subjects are
>   (a)   mathematics, English and science; ... ·
> (2)   Subject to subsection (4) below, the other foundation subjects are –
>   (a)   history, geography, technology, music, art and physical education:
>   (b)   in relation to the third and fourth key stages, a modern language specified in an order of the Secretary of State ...

Chapter 4

1   W. H. Auden, 'New Year Letter, January 1940.'
2   Department of Education and Science, *Training for Jobs* (White Paper) (HMSO, London, 1984), p. 14.
3   First piloted in 1983, the Technical and Vocational Education Initiative aimed to make pupils better equipped to enter the world of work. Courses emphasised initiative, motivation and enterprise, as well as problem-solving skills and other aspects of personal development.
4   B. Reid and M. Holt, 'Structure and Ideology in Upper Secondary Education', in *Education and Society Today*, eds A. Hartnelt and M. Naish (The Falmer Press, London, 1986), p. 92.
5   Department of Education and Science, *National Curriculum: Task Group on Assessment and Testing Report* (The Black Report) (HMSO, London, 1988), para. 163.
6   T. McElligott et al., *Report on TVEI* (Assistant Masters and Mistresses Association, May 1988). Reported in the *Guardian* (31 May 1988).
7   Health Education Authority, *High Stress Occupations Working Party Report* (June, 1988). Reported in *The Times Educational Supplement* (3 June 1988).

8   This ironic assessment appears in F. Inglis, *The Management of Ignorance* (Basil Blackwell, Oxford, 1985), p. 17.

9   In the 1983 General Election, a MORI poll for *The Times Educational Supplement* showed the Tories commanding 44 per cent of support among teachers in England and Wales, followed by the Alliance with 28 per cent and Labour on 26 per cent. By 1987, Tory support had dropped to 24 per cent, the Alliance being the main beneficiaries at 46 per cent and Labour more or less the same at 28 per cent. (*The Times Educational Supplement*, 29 May 1987.)

10   D. Self, *A Practical Guide to Drama in the Secondary School* (Ward Lock Educational, London, 1975), p. 7.

11   D. Dorne, 'What Future for British Political Community theatre?' Unpublished essay (1987). See also Appendix A, 'Lesson three'.

12   P. Slade, *An Introduction to Child Drama* (Hodder & Stoughton, London, 1958), p. 2.

13   For a classic compendium of time-fillers, see A. Scher and C. Verrall, *100+ Ideas for Drama* (Heinemann, London, 1975). It and its sequel have slipped neatly into the pockets of a great many drama teachers since their publication.

14   M. Wootton (ed.), *New Directions in Drama Teaching* (Heinemann, London, 1982), p. 4.

15   G. Readman, 'Drama in the Market Place', *2D* 7:2 (Summer, 1988), p. 11. Saxton and Verriour go further in their enthusiasm for the market, assuring us that 'the idea of putting one's money into something one can own, is looking more and more attractive'. As a consequence, they express no surprise that 'educational drama is in the vanguard of the new thinking'. See J. Saxton and P. Verriour, 'A sense of ownership', *The NADIE Journal* (Australia), 12:2 (March 1988), p. 9.

16   I am conscious that television folk heroes like Yosser fade quickly from the memory. Played by Bernard Hill, he was one of the unemployed 'Boys from the Blackstuff' in the 1982 series by Alan Bleasdale. Desperate for work, Yosser's manic 'Gizza job' and 'I can do that' became catchphrases as unemployment soared in the early 1980s.

17   The Standing Conference of Young People's Theatre (SCYPT) has long been characterised by the schismatic nature of its Marxist political affiliations. For many years, and until the split in that movement, it was dominated by the Workers' Revolutionary Party, and its conferences and debates were marked by the internecine feuds between factions of the radical left.

18 G. Gillham et al., Editorial, *SCYPT Journal*, 14 (September 1985), p. 6. For a reverential but convoluted example of this bizarre appropriation, see also G. Gillham, 'What life is for: an analysis of Dorothy Heathcote's "Levels' of explanation", 2D, 8.2 (Summer, 1989), pp. 31–8.

19 Gillham et al. (1985), p. 6.

20 D. Davis, 'Drama for deference or drama for defiance', *2D*, 3:1 (Autumn, 1983), p. 35.

21 W. Dobson, 'Professors who live in glasshouses', *Drama Broadsheet*, 4:1 (Winter, 1985), p. 7.

22 J. Clark, 'An introduction to conference 1986', *Drama Broadsheet*, 4:2 (Spring, 1986), p. 3.

23 J. Clark and J. Spindler, *Education for Change in our Society* (National Association for the Teaching of Drama (NATD), 1986), p. 21.

24 P. Freire, *Pedagogy of the Oppressed*, tr. M. Bergman Ramos (Penguin Books, Harmondsworth, 1972).

25 G. Gutiérrez, *A Theology of Liberation: History, Politics and Salvation*, tr./ed. I. Caridad and J. Eagleson (SCM Press, London, 1974), p. 146. See also D. McLellan, *Marxism and Religion* (Macmillan, London, 1987).

26 A. Boal, *Theatre of the Oppressed*, tr. C. and M. O. Leal McBride (Pluto Press, London, 1979).

27 Ibid., p. 122.

28 Ibid., p. 141.

29 Chris Vine and the Greenwich Young People's Theatre have been leading exponents of Boal's practices in this country. See 'Augusto Boal interviewed by Chris Vine', in *Augusto Boal: Documents on the Theatre of the Oppressed*, ed. A. Hozier (Red Letters, London, 1985), pp. 4–17.

30 Freire's work devising literacy programmes in Brazil was cut short by the military coup of 1964. Exiled, he carried on his work in Chile. Boal was imprisoned, tortured and exiled after the military coup in Brazil in 1971.

31 Deirdre Griffin's account of working with Boal out of context, at a conference in Austria in 1982, is revealing in this respect. She describes a workshop based upon:

> ... experiences from the lives of people who had not suffered the oppression of Peruvian landlords, or, for that matter, been on the receiving end of police brutality. The problems focussed on included the oppressions of: – hierarchy; sexual discrimination; corruption; systems; noise ...

Important though these issues are, even put together they fall a long way short of a comprehensive critique of the oppressions of late-capitalism. D. Griffin, 'Augusto Boal's "Theater of the Oppressed"', *2D*, 2:2 (Spring, 1983), p. 7.

32 Davis (1983), p. 34.

33 W. Dobson, 'The benefits of "marginalization"', *New Theatre Quarterly*, 2:8 (November, 1986), p. 371.

34 Ibid., p. 371.

35 Ibid., pp. 372–3.

36 D. Davis, 'Drama as a Weapon', unpublished address to the 1987 conference of the National Association of Drama Advisers.

37 J. Hodgson and E. Richards, *Improvisation* (Eyre Methuen, London, 1966), p. 9.

38 See J. Neelands, 'Issues or contexts?', *Drama Broadsheet*, 4:1 (Winter, 1985), pp. 10–13:

> How are drama teachers going to deal with questions like:–
>
> Why can't I get the job I choose?
> Why is my dad never going to work again?
> Why do we let blacks in when there aren't enough jobs for whites?
> Why has my gran got to wait three years for a hip operation?
> Why are babies starving in Ethiopia when we destroy food in Europe?
> Why can't women walk alone in safety?
> Why do we spend money on bombs rather than jobs?

Chapter 5

1 E. Gellner, *The Psychoanalytic Movement* (Paladin, London, 1985), p. 5.

2 J-P. Sartre, *Kean* (1954), Act 1, Scene 1, tr. F. Hauser (Davis-Poynter, London, 1972).

3 Alongside this there existed, notably in the theatre, systems of commercial production of which Shakespeare's early joint-stock company at The Globe and Blackfriars theatres is a famous example, although this too required noble patronage to protect its members from vagabondage.

4 The word 'creative' is a product of this same etymology. For centuries creation was generally understood as the prerogative of gods and monarchs and quite beyond the presumptions of ordinary mortals. Attempts to prefix with 'creative', in its modern sense, a universe-

creating Jehovah or even a royal decree, reveal the word's redundancy in a pre-Enlightenment context. It was only when eighteenth-century humanism had established the centrality of human agency in the ordering of the world that the idea of acts of creation being dispositional could gain currency.

5   J. Goethe, *Samtliche Werke, XXXIII*, 17–18. Quoted in M. H. Abrams, *The Mirror and the Lamp* (Oxford University Press, 1953), p. 90.

6   P. Bourdieu, 'Intellectual Field and Creative Project', in *Knowledge and Control*, ed. M. Young (Collier-Macmillan, London, 1971), p. 165.

7   C. Rogers, 'Towards a Theory of Creativity', in *Creativity*, ed. P. E. Vernon (Penguin Books, Harmondsworth, 1970), p. 146.

8   R. W. Witkin, *The Intelligence of Feeling* (Heinemann, London, 1974), pp. 1, 2.

9   Ibid., p. 33.

10   See particularly J. Bruner, *On Knowing: Essays for the Left Hand* (Harvard University Press, 1962); *Toward a Theory of Instruction* (Harvard University Press, 1966); *The Relevance of Education* (George Allen & Unwin, London, 1971).

     Also, M. Polanyi, *Personal Knowledge: Towards a Post-Critical Philosophy* (Routledge & Kegan Paul, London, 1958); *The Study of Man* (Routledge & Kegan Paul, London, 1959); *Knowing and Being* (Routledge & Kegan Paul, London, 1969).

     Polanyi's theories of knowledge are considered in Chapter 7.

11   G. Bolton, 'Changes in thinking about drama in education,' *Theory into Practice*, 24:3 (Summer, 1985), p. 155.

12   Malcolm Ross, through organisations like the National Association for Education in the Arts (NAEA), was particularly active on behalf of the arts during the passage of the 1988 Education Bill through the House of Lords. His essentially non-political account of arts education gave him access to many influential peers across a wide ideological spectrum.

13   H. J. Eysenck, *The Psychology of Politics* (Eyre Methuen, London, 1954), pp. 9–10.

14   Gellner (1985), pp. 89–90.

15   C. Lasch, *The Culture of Narcissism: American Life in an Age of Diminishing Expectations* (Sphere Books, London, 1980), pp. 12–13.

16   L. Trilling, *Sincerity and Authenticity* (Harvard University Press, 1971), pp. 10–11.

17   See R. Sennett, *The Fall of Public Man* (Cambridge University Press, 1977), p. 263. The televised testimonies of Colonel Oliver North at the 'Irangate' hearings in 1987 offer a more recent example of how someone appearing to be sincere in public can persuade public opin-

ion to put aside its doubts about their actions. At the same time, in their assessment scheme quoted in Chapter 2, Morgan and Saxton would surely have been pushed not to give 'Ollie' North an 'A' for 'maintaining role'. A serious (and worrying) point.

18   D. Davis and C. Lawrence (eds), *Gavin Bolton: Selected Writings* (Longman, London, 1986), p. 194.

19   See E. Husserl, *Cartesian Meditations: An Introduction to Phenomenology*, tr. D. Cairns (Martinus Nijhoff, The Hague, 1960).

20   B-J. Wagner, *Dorothy Heathcote: Drama as a Learning Medium* (Hutchinson, London, 1979), p. 76.

21   G. Bolton, 'Drama in the Curriculum', in Davis and Lawrence (eds) (1986), p. 226. This simple primitivism is always mystifying because it denies contemporary experience. How often, I wonder, do we *make tools?* Would a visit to a DIY hypermarket be counted as a 'universal' for today's young people?

22   Wagner (1979), pp. 220–1.

23   A. MacIntyre, *After Virtue: A Study in Moral Theory* (Duckworth, London, 1981), p. 30.

24   J. Dunn, *Western Political Theory in the Face of the Future* (Cambridge University Press, 1979), p. 43.

25   D. Hargreaves, *The Challenge for the Comprehensive School* (Routledge & Kegan Paul, London, 1982), p. 93.

Chapter 6

1   L. McGregor, M. Tate and K. Robinson, *Learning through Drama* (Heinemann, London, 1977), p. 16.

2   In M. Ross, *The Creative Arts* (Heinemann, London, 1978), pp. 63–4.

3   P. Slade, *Child Drama* (University of London Press, 1954), p. 68.

4   See Ross's dispute with Bolton, in M. Ross, 'Postscript to Gavin Bolton', in *The Development of Aesthetic Experience*, ed. M. Ross (Pergamon, Oxford, 1982), pp. 148–52.

5   G. Bolton, ' Drama as Learning, as Art and as Aesthetic Experience', in *Gavin Bolton: Selected Writings*, eds D. Davis and C. Lawrence (Longman, London, 1986), p. 160.

6   G. Bolton, *Drama as Education* (Longman, London, 1984), p. 146.

7   G. Bolton, in Ross (ed.) (1982), p. 146.

8   G. Bolton, 'Weaving theories is not enough', *New Theatre Quarterly*, 2:8 (November 1986), p. 370.

9   See M. Heidegger, *Basic Writings*, ed. D. Krell (Routledge & Kegan Paul, London, 1978), p. 383.

Wherever a present being encounters another present being or even only lingers near it – but also where, as with Hegel, one being mirrors itself in another speculatively – there openness already rules, the free region is in play. Only this openness grants the movement of speculative thinking the passage through what it thinks.

10 Ross (ed.) (1982), p. 148. See also, Bolton's hurt responses to Ross, in G. Bolton, 'Drama in Education: Learning Medium or Arts Process?', in *Bolton at the Barbican*, ed. W. Dobson (National Association for the Teaching of Drama (NATD)/Longman, London, 1983). Also, Bolton (1984), ch. 7.
11 Ross (1978), p. 50.
12 M. Bell, 'In search of a middle ground or drama as a learning arts process', *2D*, 6:1 (Autumn, 1986), p. 30.
13 Ross (ed.) (1982), p. 152.
14 N. Morgan and J. Saxton, 'Who's that tripping over my bridge?', *The NADIE Journal*, 13:1 (September 1988), p. 6.
15 For example, see G. Bolton, 'Theatre Form in Drama Teaching' and 'Drama in Education – a Reappraisal', in Davis and Lawrence (eds) (1986), pp. 164–80, 268. See also 'The Relationship between Theatre and Drama', in N. Morgan and J. Saxton, *Teaching Drama: A Mind of Many Wonders* (Hutchinson, London, 1987), chap. 1.
16 The Cambridge School was founded by F. R. Leavis (who had been a pupil of I. A. Richards) and Q. D. Roth, in the 1920s. *Scrutiny* was the influential journal of the Cambridge School. For a 'deconstruction' of this movement, see the Marxist critic, Terry Eagleton, in T. Eagleton, *Literary Theory* (Basil Blackwell, Oxford, 1983), chap. 1.
17 Eagleton (1983), p. 31.
18 G. Bolton, 'Teacher-in-Role and Teacher Power', in *Positive Images: 1985 Conference Report* (Joint Committee (NATD, NATFHE Drama, NAYT, NADECT, NADA), 1986), p. 39.
19 B-J. Wagner, *Dorothy Heathcote: Drama as a Learning Medium* (Hutchinson, London, 1979), pp. 203–6.
20 R. Williams, *Culture and Society, 1780–1950* (Penguin Books, Harmondsworth, 1961), p. 106.
21 Bolton (1984), p. 147.
22 Eagleton (1983), pp. 26–7. How often do we ask pupils how they felt about a piece of drama and how often what they thought? The language of feeling pervades our verbal evaluations of children's work.

23 See F. R. Leavis, *Mass Civilization and Minority Culture* (Cambridge University Press, 1930), pp. 4–5.

    Upon them depend the implicit standards that order the finer living of an age, the sense that this is worth more than that, this rather than that is the direction in which to go, that the centre is here rather than there.

24 Recent issues of the journal of the National Association for the Teaching of English (NATE), *English in Education*, are the locus for this discussion. See also, *The English Magazine*, published by the ILEA English Centre.

25 Slade (1954), p. 108.

26 Ibid., p. 162.

27 C. Stanislavski, *My Life in Arts*, tr. J. J. Robbins (Eyre Methuen, London, 1980), p. 466.

28 Ibid., pp. 466–7.

29 T. Eagleton, *Marxism and Literary Criticism* (Eyre Methuen, London, 1976), pp. 30–1.

30 *Lehrstück* ('didactic play') was a term used to describe a form of radical music theatre in the 1920s designed to instruct the performers rather than entertain an audience. Brecht was the most famous exponent of these plays, which are sometimes seen as being the precursors of today's theatre-in-education programmes. *Agitprop* (agitation-propaganda) has become a form of theatre used to extol revolutionary change. Originally, the Department of Agitation and Propaganda was set up in 1920 by the Central Committee of the Soviet Communist Party to supervise the propaganda campaign in the media.

31 R. Williams, *Modern Tragedy* (Verso, London, 1979), pp. 111–12.

32 B. Brecht, *Brecht on Theatre: The Development of an Aesthetic*, ed. J. Willett (Eyre Methuen, London, 1978), p. 110.

33 D. Heathcote, *Drama as Context* (National Association for the Teaching of English, Aberdeen University Press, 1980), p. 48.

34 Eagleton (1976), p. 31.

35 Williams (1979), p. 69.

36 E. Fischer, *The Necessity of Art*, tr. A. Bostock (Penguin Books, Harmondsworth, 1963), p. 78. Drama-in-education has succumbed easily to forms of symbolism. For example, see G. Bolton, 'The Process of Symbolisation in Improvised Drama', in Davis and Lawrence (eds) (1986), pp. 145–8.

37 Fischer (1963), pp. 95–6.

Chapter 7

1   G. Bolton, 'A Statement Outlining the Contemporary View Held of
    Drama in Education in Great Britain', in *Gavin Bolton: Selected Writ-
    ings*, eds D. Davis and C. Lawrence (Longman, London, 1986), p. 15.
2   G. Bolton, *Towards a Theory of Drama in Education* (Longman, London,
    1979), p. 31.
3   G. Bolton, 'Teacher-in-Rôle and Teacher Power', in *Positive Images:
    1985 Conference Publication* (Joint Committee (NATD, NATFHE Dra-
    ma, NAYT, NADECT, NADA), 1986), p. 38.
4   Bolton (1979), p. 87.
5   G. Bolton, 'Freedom and Imagination', in Davis and Lawrence (eds)
    (1986), p. 20.
6   G. Bolton, 'Schools Council Drama Teaching Project (10–16)', in
    Davis and Lawrence (eds) (1986), p. 215.
7   G. Bolton, 'The Activity to Dramatic Playing', in Davis and Law-
    rence (eds) (1986), p. 59.
8   Bolton (1986), pp. 38–9.
9   G. Bolton, 'Drama as Learning, as Art and as Aesthetic Experience',
    in Davis and Lawrence (eds) (1986), pp. 158–9.
10 Ministry of Education, *Half our Future* (The Newsom Report)
    (HMSO, London, 1963), p. 157. See also Chapter 1, p. 12.
11 Bolton (1986), p. 39.
12 Here are some from Bolton (1979), pp. 41–2:

    A policeman is a man with a home and a family.
    Some problems seem unresolvable.
    Obstacles can be overcome even without changing the rules – if
        you work hard enough.
    Africans are like us in many ways.
    'Solutions' have consequences.

13 See D. Hornbrook, 'Go play, boy, play: Shakespeare and Educational
    Drama', in *The Shakespeare Myth*, ed. G. Holderness (Manchester
    University Press, 1988), p. 149.
        For a clear example of the way the quest for the universal can
    emasculate a subject, turn to Heathcote's comparison of the drama
    teacher with the dramatic poet in her annotation of Brecht's 'The
    Playwright's Song'. The less than incisive preoccupations of Heath-
    cote's 'artist/teacher' in her search for 'a new outer form for a univer-
    sal inner meaning' are thrown into relief against the harsh aesthetic of

Brecht's political metaphors. See D. Heathcote, 'From the Particular to the Universal', il *Dorothy Heathcote: Collected Writings*, eds L. Johnson and C. O'Neill (Hutchinson, London, 1984), p. 109, and in *Exploring Theatre and Education*, ed. K. Robinson (Heinemann, London, 1980). Nicholas Wright's refutation of her argument, 'From the Universal to the Particular' in this latter collection is also worth reading.

14   For plentiful examples of this happening, see Wagner (1979).

15   G. Bolton, 'Assessment of Practical Drama', in Davis and Lawrence (eds) (1986), p. 220.

16   G. Bolton, 'Drama in the Curriculum', in Davis and Lawrence (eds) (1986), p. 227.

17   M. Polanyi, *Personal Knowledge: Towards a Post-Critical Philosophy* (Routledge & Kegan Paul, London, 1958).

18   For examples, see Bolton (1984), pp. 155–6; G. Bolton, 'Drama and Meaning', in Davis and Lawrence (eds) (1986), pp. 252–3; M. Flemming, 'A sense of context', *Drama Broadsheet*, 2:3 (Summer, 1984), p. 3.

19   G. Bolton. 'Gavin Bolton interviewed by David Davis', *2D*, 4:2 (Spring, 1985), p. 14.

20   M. Polanyi, *The Study of Man* (Routledge & Kegan Paul, London, 1959), p. 22.

21   Polanyi (1958), p. 300.

22   Polanyi (1959), p. 36.

23   Ibid., p. 26.

24   Polanyi (1958), p. 203.

25   Unlike Freud, Polanyi does not see intellectual and moral endeavour as sublimations, but as drives in their own right. He is certainly not prepared to accept that moral conscience might be 'the interiorization of social pressures'. See Polanyi (1958), p. 309fn.

26   Polanyi (1958), p. 203.

27   Ibid., p. 231.

28   Ibid., p. 232.

29   The development of the idea of 'hegemony' is probably Gramsci's most important contribution to Marxist theory. He insists that one class maintains its dominance over another not only by means of politics and economics but also as it projects its own particular way of seeing the world as the natural order, as 'common sense'.

30   W. Dobson, 'The benefits of "marginalization"', *New Theatre Quarterly*, 2:8 (November 1986), pp. 372–3.

31   J. Clark and A. Seeley, 'Soldiers of fortune?', *Drama Broadsheet*, 4:3 (Summer, 1986), p. 8.

32   Dobson (1986), pp. 373–4.

33   Clark and Seeley (1986), pp. 8–9.
34   W. Morris, *News from Nowhere* (1890), in *Three Works by William Morris*, ed. A. Morton (Lawrence & Wishart, London, 1968). Morris's fine picture of an English communist utopia of the future is notable, among other things, for the absence of money, poverty, ill-health and human nastiness in general.

Chapter 8

1   W. Russell, *Educating Rita* (Samuel French, London, 1981), scene 7.
2   M. Young, 'Drama and the Politics of Educational Change', in *Drama in Education: A Curriculum for Change*, ed. J. Norman (National Association for the Teaching of Drama/Kemble Press, 1982), pp. 88–95. The phrase 'really useful knowledge' was coined by the Chartists in the 1830s and 1840s in opposition to what they saw as the dry irrelevancy of state education.
3   For a comprehensive version of this debate about educational knowledge, see *Knowledge and Control*, ed. M. Young (Collier-Macmillan, London, 1971).
4   R. Williams *The Long Revolution* (Penguin, Harmondsworth, 1965), p. 172. A full account of his theory of cultural formation appears in R. Williams, *Marxism and Literature* (Oxford University Press, 1977), especially ch. 8, 'Dominant, Residual and Emergent'.
5   The most famous exposition of the theory of the inevitable triumph of liberalism is probably: H. Butterfield, *The Whig Interpretation of History* (Penguin Books, Harmondsworth, 1973).
6   For an obvious example, see *Education Reform Act 1988* (HMSO, London, 1988). During its progress through parliament this act was known colloquially as the Gerbil (Great Education Reform Bill).
7   R. Addison, 'The arts in education', *National Association for Education in the Arts. Arts Initiatives 1: Integration in the Arts*, 1 (July 1986), p. 1.
8   For examples, see T. Delzenné, 'Why drama hasn't happened', *2D*, 1:3 (Summer, 1982), p. 13.

     Hence society will need, more than ever, positive, caring, imaginative and creative people . . .

     R. Shannon, 'The YOP programme in Hampshire', *Drama Broadsheet*, 2:2 (Spring, 1984), p. 11.

     This statement seems to infer that drama activities are

irrelevant to the 'needs of industry' ... The 'needs' of the individual are not mentioned at all ...

D. Morton, 'Other people's stories: GCSE and drama', *Drama Broadsheet*, 4:3 (Summer, 1986), p. 5.

These basic needs of the *majority* of young people (who truly have the *greatest* needs) must be the baseline for curriculum planning ...

9   B. Wilks, 'Disciples in Need of a Discipline', in *Drama in Education 3: Annual Survey*, eds M. Banham and J. Hodgson (The Pitman Press, Bath, 1975), p. 96.

10 For an account of the questions raised by ideas of empathy and identification, see D. Harding, 'Psychological processes in the reading of fiction', *British Journal of Aesthetics*, II (1962), pp. 133–47.

11 This classic example of the supposed power of improvisation appears on the first page of Brian Way's *Development through Drama* (Longman, London, 1967).

12 See Wagner's summing-up of a Heathcote lesson in Appendix A, 'Lesson 2'.

13 C. Geertz, *Local Knowledge* (Basic Books, New York, 1983), p. 44.

14 Ibid., p. 43.

15 Ibid., pp. 44–5.

16 See examples in B-J. Wagner, *Dorothy Heathcote: Drama as a Learning Medium* (Hutchinson, London, 1979); N. Morgan and J. Saxton, *Teaching Drama: A Mind of Many Wonders* (Hutchinson, London, 1987). It is noticeable that there is a certain formula approach to these images of 'primitive' life. I once saw a boy pointedly ignored by Heathcote when he suggested, *sotto voce*, but in answer to her question, that they should 'honour the dead of the tribe' by eating them.

17 For example, see J. Clark and J. Spindler, *Education for Change in our Society* (National Association for the Teaching of Drama (NATD), 1986), p. 5. In their manifesto, Clark and Spindler press for:

... a system of education that operates from within the community and is not imposed from outside. It needs to be based upon the needs of the immediate community, concerned with that community's needs and future development.

18 Inner London Education Authority, *Race, Sex aand Class: 3. A Policy for Equality: Race* (1983), p. 5.

19   D. Hargreaves, *The Challenge for the Comprehensive School* (Routledge & Kegan Paul, London, 1982), p. 130.
20   G. Lukács, *History and Class Consciousness*, tr. R. Livingstone (Merlin Press, London, 1971), p. 52.

Chapter 9

1   B. Brecht, *Brecht on Theatre: The Development of an Aesthetic*, ed. J. Willett (Eyre Methuen, London, 1978), pp. 146–7.
2   See M. Arnold, *Culture and Anarchy*, ed. J. Dover Wilson (Cambridge University Press, 1971), p. 69.
3   R. Williams, *Marxism and Literature* (Oxford University Press, 1977), p. 154.
4   K. Marx, *Selected Writings*, ed. D. McLellan (Oxford University Press, 1977), p. 389.

      In the social production of their life, men enter into definite relations that are indispensable and independent of their will, relations of production which correspond to a definite stage of development of their material forces. The sum total of these relations of production constitutes the economic structure of society, the real foundation, on which rises a legal and political superstructure and to which correspond definite forms of social consciousness.

5   'Ideology' in this sense should not be mistaken for those simple, prescriptive dogmas so eagerly set up and assaulted by Eysenck, Polanyi and others. This pejorative use of the word has a wide currency, of course, and might be said to be itself ideological.
6   T. Eagleton, *Marxism and Literary Criticism* (Eyre Methuen, London, 1976), p. 5.
7   Ibid., p. 18.
8   Williams (1977), pp. 130–1.
9   J-P. Sartre, *Sketch for a Theory of the Emotions*, tr. P. Mairet (Eyre Methuen, London, 1971), p. 57.
10   Williams (1977), p. 129.
11   For Raymond Williams, to whom I am indebted for this formulation, practical consciousness is 'a kind of feeling and thinking which is indeed social and material, but each in an embryonic phase before it can become fully articulate and defined exchange'. For a much fuller development of this idea, see Williams (1977), pp. 130–1.

12   R. Williams, *Politics and Letters: Interviews with* New Left Review (Verso, London, 1981), p. 159.

13   Williams (1977), p. 132.

14   For all the words that have been written suggesting the contrary, this is not a particularly original view. John Allen, HMI with responsibility for drama for eleven years, whose 1967 report on drama in schools remains one of the most balanced and illuminating accounts of the field, was of the same view:

> My object is simply to suggest, contrary to what some enthusiasts believe, that drama in schools is basically and essentially no different from drama anywhere else.

J. Allen, *Drama in Schools: Its Theory and Practice* (Heinemann, London, 1979), p. 119. See also Department of Education and Science, *Drama: Education Survey 2* (HMSO, London, 1967).

15   Those wishing to pursue further the idea of text as discourse in action might usefully turn to P. Ricoeur, *Hermeneutics and the Human Sciences*, ed. and tr. J. Thompson (Cambridge University Press, 1981), particularly ch. 8, 'The Model of the Text: Meaningful Action Considered as a Text'.

16   This formulation is not dissimilar to music's tripartite arrangement, *composing, performing* and *listening*. Also, it is worth noting that the Arts in Schools Project has proposed a structure for all the arts based upon two essential common elements, making and appraising.

17   With its repudiation of disciplinary content (see Y. Beecham, 'Positive Images', and D. Hornbrook, 'The Process is Rich, the Content is Poor', in *Positive Images* (1986), pp. 32–5, 41–3), drama-in-education's position has tended to be strongly formalist, Bolton, as we have seen, assuring us of the existence of 'inner forms of theatre that children of all ages can sense as significant'. On closer inspection, these 'inner forms' turn out to be predominantly the mechanisms of naturalism. Assumptions of this kind ignore the important truth, recognised both by Hegel and Marx, that artistic form is neither immutable nor the subject of mere random choice, but historically determinant on the content it embodies.

18   For those on the left who still see this as a hopeless surrender to the forces of reaction, may I remind them of these words of Trotsky:

> ... in the matter of language, of skill in choosing the appropriate words and combining them in the appropriate ways, con-

stant, systematic, painstaking work is necessary in order to achieve the highest degree of accuracy, clarity and vividness. The foundation of this work must be the fight against illiteracy, semiliteracy and near-illiteracy. The next stage of this work is the mastering of Russian classical literature. Yes, culture was the main instrument of class oppression. But it also, and only it, can become the instrument of socialist emancipation.

L. Trotsky, 'Culture and Socialism', in *Leon Trotsky on Literature and Art*, ed. P. Siegel (Pathfinder Press, New York, 1970), p. 88.

19   After all, as John Pick argues, the difference between the death of Caesar in Shakespeare's play and a 'killing' in a classroom improvisation is not that one 'comes from the child' and the other is 'literary'.

Both use an imposed, inherited language. Both are *re*-created by the child ... the essential difference lies in the moral universe which the play creates; the balance of praise and blame, guilt and innocence, freedom and fatality. It is the accumulated wisdom of the play which makes it more sophisticated, *better* drama, better because what the child expresses is only half the story.

J. Pick, 'Five fallacies in drama', *Young Drama*, 1:1 (February 1973), p. 9.

20   B. Brecht, *The Mother*, tr. C. Gooch (Eyre Methuen, London, 1978), scene 6.

Chapter 10

1   B. Brecht, 'Portrayal of Past and Present in One', in *Bertolt Brecht: Poems, 1913–1956*, eds J. Willett and R. Manheim (Eyre Methuen, London, 1976), pp. 307–8.

2   For a more detailed account of the dramatisation of Elizabethan life, see J. Briggs, *This Stage-Play World* (Oxford University Press 1983).

3   Readers may remember that during the 1988 United States presidential election campaign, American television ran a dramatic mini-series about a fictional contender in which some of the real candidates took part. Tuning in at the time, it was sometimes impossible to tell whether one was watching real or dramatised interviews.

4   R. Williams, *Drama in a Dramatised Society* (Cambridge University Press, 1975), pp. 15–16.

5   It is perhaps worth noting that the word performance did not gather its theatrical associations, connoting 'playing a part', until the Jacobean period. Before then it had been reserved to describe the carrying out of a task or duty. That both these meanings now happily co-exist in the same word demonstrates again how notions of drama pervade the way we think about human agency.

6   See E. Goffman, 'The Arts of Impression Management', in *The Presentation of Self in Everyday life* (Penguin Books, Harmondsworth, 1969), ch. 6. Incidentally, Gavin Bolton seems now to have joined hands with the ethnomethodologists who advocate this rather impoverished view of drama as behaviour. He puts forward an argument, 'based on an ethnomethodological perspective, that drama is essentially a managed accomplishment'. G. Bolton, 'Drama as Art', in *Drama Broadsheet*, 5:1 (Autumn, 1988).

7   Goffman (1969), p. 24.

8   A. MacIntyre, *After Virtue* (Duckworth, London, 1981), p. 109.

9   For example, see 'Type and Archetype' in E. Bentley, *The Life of the Drama* (Eyre Methuen, London, 1965), ch. 2.

10   MacIntyre (1981), pp. 26–7.

Chapter 11

1   L. Wittgenstein, *Philosophical Investigations*, tr. G. E. M. Anscombe (Basil Blackwell, Oxford, 1958), para. 241, p. 88e.

2   For this reason, Bloom's well known *Taxonomy of Educational Objectives*, in which he divides us into three 'domains', cognitive, affective and locomotor, has remained the ground upon which the battle for the arts has been fought. B. Bloom, *Taxonomy of Educational Objectives* (3 vols) (Longman, London, 1964–7).

3   For notable accounts of theories of logical empiricism, see R. Carnap, *The Unity of Science* (Kegan Paul, London, 1934); C. Hempel, *Aspects of Scientific Explanation* (The Free Press, New York, 1965). A. J. Ayer has been the logical positivist for British critics. *Language, Truth and Logic* (Gollancz, London, 1936) created something of a sensation when in it Ayer claimed that metaphysical propositions are neither true nor false, but nonsense.

4   A. Louch, *Explanation and Human Action* (University of California Press, Berkeley, 1969), p. 233.

5   Readers will remember that for Humpty Dumpty, a word 'means just what I choose it to mean – neither more nor less'. See L. Carroll, *Alice through the Looking Glass*, ch. 6.

6   C. Taylor, *Human Agency and Language: Philosophical Papers 1* (Cambridge University Press, 1985(1)), p. 11.

7   See C. Taylor, *Philosophy and the Human Sciences: Philosophical Papers 2* (Cambridge University Press, 1985(2)), pp. 22–3). Taylor argues that for us to speak intelligibly about 'meaning', our use of the word must satisfy the following criteria: it must be meaning for a subject, an individual or a group; it must be meaning *of* something, a situation or an action, for instance; and, it must be meaning in a field, that is, related to the meanings of other things.

8   See Bolton (1979), p. 41.

9   Similarly, fears of a general indoctrination by individual teachers are largely groundless. Once a teacher is known in the vernacular to be a 'lefty' or a 'racist', in other words, his or her utterances are subsequently mediated through that perception and safely dissipated.

10   Taylor (1985(2)), p. 27.

11   H. Gadamer, *Truth and Method*, tr. W. Glyn-Doepel (Sheed & Ward, London, 1975), p. 258.

12   Geertz (1983), p. 31. For a classic example of this process, see C. Geertz, 'Deep Play: Notes on the Balinese Cockfight', in *The Interpretation of Cultures* (Basic Books, New York, 1973), ch. 15.

13   B. Brecht, 'In Praise of the Revolutionary', tr. S. Gooch, in *The Mother* (Eyre Methuen, London, 1978), scene 6.

14   See J. Habermas, *Theory and Practice* (Heinemann, London, 1974), pp. 11–12. According to Habermas, *ideologiekritik* (literally 'the critique of ideology') addresses itself to:

> ... what lies behind the consensus presented as fact, that supports the dominant tradition of the time, and does so with a view to the relations of power surreptitiously incorporated in the symbolic structures of the systems of speech and action.

See also, readings from the Frankfurt School, in *Critical Sociology*, ed. P. Connerton (Penguin Books, Harmondsworth, 1976).

15   C. Taylor (1985(1)), p. 8. To illustrate this same point (in *Secularization and Moral Change* (Oxford University Press, 1967), pp. 38–42). Alasdair MacIntyre identifies three class-based 'communities' of this kind: 'the Trade Union movement', 'the middle-class businessman' and 'the public school prefect' (for a fine fictional example of the power of the latter, see Joseph Conrad's short story, 'The Secret Sharer'). Also, in a different context, Stuart Hall has argued that politically voters are no longer homogeneously class-based, but have conflicting interests and social identities. They belong, in other words, to a series of 'imaginary communities'.

The profound dilemma facing many young Asian women in this country and their boy-friends is an example of the emotional tension that can be generated by conflicts between rival moral memberships. Owing deep cultural loyalty to a tradition of arranged marriage on the one hand, they may well now also be inescapably members of a European inner-city culture committed to the right of free marital choice.

16   E. Durkheim, *Moral Education* (Free Press, New York, 1961), quoted in D. Hargreaves, *The Challenge for the Comprehensive School* (Routledge & Kegan Paul, London, 1982), p. 108.

17   Hargreaves (1982), p. 151.

18   Ibid., p. 108.

Chapter 12

1   M. Ross, *The Creative Arts* (Heinemann, London, 1978), p. 75.

2   See B. Bernstein, 'On the Classification and Framing of Educational Knowledge', in *Class, Codes and Control: Vol 3. Towards a Theory of Educational Transmissions* (Routledge & Kegan Paul, London, 1977), ch. 5. For Bernstein, 'classification refers to the degree of boundary maintenance' between the contents of the curriculum. Where classification is weak, the teacher can choose from a wide range of content (as in drama-in-education). Frame, on the other hand, refers to 'the range of options available to teacher and taught in the control of what is transmitted and received'. Within dramatic pedagogy (despite contrary claims), frames are strong, reducing the real options of the pupils to control events.

3   Bernstein (1977), p. 90.

4   The idea of gesture is derived from Brecht's gest, which he describes as, 'the realm of attitudes adopted by the characters towards one another'. See B. Brecht, 'A Short Organum for the Theatre', in B. Brecht, *Brecht on Theatre: The Development of an Aesthetic*, ed. J. Willett (Eyre Methuen, London, 1978), para. 61, p. 198.

5   *Mise-en-scène* is a particularly useful term I think (although anglophiles may object). For me it gets over the difficulty of distinguishing between 'performance' and 'presentation' (as in the London and East Anglian Group's Drama GCSE). Once we restore the idea of production, then students can be seen as engaged in literally the 'making of a scene'.

6   It is interesting to note that this idea of editing, or group revising, is also a feature of the National Writing Project. These extracts come

from a statement by the SCDC National Writing Project in Avon, 1987:

> Even young writers need to be aware of the *purpose* of the writing and the eventual *audience* for whom it is intended. They also need to be aware of the range of *formats* which are available to them ... Editing is the stage during which the technical aspects of children's writing are improved. Children edit selected revised pieces of work which may be published.

The comparisons with drama are clear, I think, and show how far creative writing has come since the 1960s.

7   For example, the Northern Examining Association GCSE (1989) offers two syllabuses in Drama, both requiring candidates to 'submit a file of written work containing reviews of three live productions'.

8   The work of the French semiotician, Patrice Pavis, in the field of performance analysis is particularly interesting. See P. Pavis, *Languages of the Stage* (Performing Arts Journal Publications, New York, 1984). Also P. Pavis, 'Theatre analysis: some questions and a questionnaire', *New Theatre Quarterly*, 1:2 (May 1985), pp. 208–12. Susan Bassnett is also making invaluable contributions to this field. See 'Structuralism and after: trends and tendencies in theatre analysis' (2 parts), *New Theatre Quarterly*, 1:1 (February, May 1985), pp. 79–82; and 1:2, pp. 205–7. For theatre semiotics more generally, see K. Elam, *The Semiotics of Theatre and Drama* (Methuen, London, 1980).

9   There has sometimes been a rather superior attitude to the other arts on the part of drama educators. Gavin Bolton, for example, claims that because drama is useful for 'teaching about life', it is justifiably separated from the other arts 'in a way which, of course, other educationalists with a vested interest in the arts do not always wish to acknowledge'. He seems to be blind here, not only to what might reasonably be expected to be his vested interest, but also apparently to the ways in which painting, literature and music also 'teach us about life'. G. Bolton, *Drama as Education* (Longman, London, 1984), p. 161.

On the other hand, for examples of arts collaborations, see: L. McGregor, M. Tate and K. Robinson, *Learning through Drama* (Heinemann, London, 1977); M. Ross, *The Creative Arts* (Heinemann, London, 1978); P. Abbs (ed.), *Living Powers: The Arts in Education* (The Falmer Press, London, 1987). Those pessimistic about drama's chances in this respect in the light of the national curriculum's restriction of 'the arts' to Art and Music should remember that the

national curriculum is concerned to identify content and not delivery
or curriculum organisation.

10   *The Arts in Schools* (Calouste Gulbenkian Foundation, London, 1982),
     p. 143.
11   D. Hargreaves, *The Challenge for the Comprehensive School* (Routledge &
     Kegan Paul, London, 1982), pp. 152–3.
12   B. Brecht, 'On Everyday Theatre', in *Bertolt Brecht: Poems, 1913–1956*,
     eds J. Willett and R. Manheim (Eyre Methuen, London, 1976), pp.
     176–7.

Bibliography

Abbs, P. (ed.), *Living Powers: The Arts in Education* (The Falmer Press, London, 1987).

Abrams, M. H., *The Mirror and the Lamp* (Oxford University Press, 1953).

Allen, J., *Drama in Schools: Its Theory and Practice* (Heinemann, London, 1979).

Amis, K., *What Became of Jane Austen, and Other Questions* (Penguin Books, Harmondsworth, 1981).

Anderson, P., *Arguments within English Marxism* (Verso, London, 1980).

Arnold, M., *Culture and Anarchy*, ed. Dover Wilson, J. (Cambridge University Press, 1971).

The Arts in Schools (Calouste Gulbenkian Foundation, London, 1982)

Ayer, A. J., *Language, Truth and Logic* (Gollancz, London, 1936).

Banham, M. and Hodgson, J. (eds), *Drama in Education 1, 2 and 3: Annual Survey* (The Pitman Press, Bath, 1972, 1973 and 1975).

Benjamin, W., *Illuminations* (Fontana/Collins, Glasgow, 1968).

Bentley, E., *The Life of the Drama* (Eyre Methuen, London, 1965).

Bernstein, B., *Class, Codes and Control: Vol. 3: Towards a Theory of Educational Transmissions* (Routledge & Kegan Paul, London, 1977).

Blake, W., *Songs of Innocence and Experience*, 1794.

Blaug, M., *An Introduction to the Economics of Education* (Penguin Books, Harmondsworth, 1976).

Bloom, B., *Taxonomy of Educational Objectives* (3 vols) (Longman, London, 1964–7).

Boal, A., *Theatre of the Oppressed* (Pluto Press, London, 1979).

Board of Education, *Report of the Consultative Committee on the Primary School* (The Hadow Report) (HMSO, London, 1931).

Bolton, G., *Towards a Theory of Drama in Education* (Longman, London, 1979).

Bolton, G., *Drama as Education* (Longman, London, 1984).

Bowskill, D., *Drama and the Teacher* (The Pitman Press, Bath, 1974).

Brecht, B., *Bertolt Brecht: Poems, 1913–1956*, Willett, J. and Manheim, R. (eds), (Eyre Methuen, London, 1976).

Brecht, B., *The Mother*, tr. Gooch, S. (Eyre Methuen, London, 1978).

Brecht, B., *Brecht on Theatre: The Development of an Aesthetic*, ed. Willett, J. (Eyre Methuen, London, 1978).

Briggs, J., *This Stage-Play World* (Oxford University Press, 1983).

British Film Institute, *Primary Media Education: a Curriculum Statement*, BFI Education, 1989.

Bruner, J. S., *On Knowing: Essays for the Left Hand* (Harvard University Press, 1962).

Bruner, J. S., *Towards a Theory of Instruction* (Harvard University Press, 1966).

Bruner, J. S., *The Relevance of Education* (George Allen & Unwin, London, 1971).

Butterfield, H., *The Whig Interpretation of History* (Penguin Books, Harmondsworth, 1973).

Caldwell Cook, H., *The Play Way* (Heinemann, London, 1917).

Carnap, R., *The Unity of Science* (Kegan Paul, London, 1934).

Carroll, L., *Alice through the Looking Glass*, 1872.

Centre for Contemporary Cultural Studies (CCCS), *Unpopular Education* (Hutchinson, London, 1981).

Chilver, P., *Improvised Drama* (Batsford, London, 1967).

Clark, J. and Spindler, J., *Education for Change in our Society* (National Association for the Teaching of Drama (NATD), 1986).

Connerton, P. (ed.), *Critical Sociology* (Penguin Books, Harmondsworth, 1976).

Cox, C. B. and Dyson, A. E. (eds), *Fight for Education: A Black Paper* (Critical Quarterly Society, 1969).

Cox, C. B. and Dyson, A. E. (eds), *Black Paper 2. The Crisis in Education* (Critical Quarterly Society, 1969).

Davis, D. and Lawrence, C. (eds), *Gavin Bolton: Selected Writings* (Longman, London, 1986).

Department of Education and Science, *Drama: Education Survey 2* (HMSO, London, 1967(1)).

Department of Education and Science, *Children and their Primary Schools* (The Plowden Report) (HMSO, London, 1967(2)).

Department of Education and Science, *A Language for Life* (The Bullock Report) (HMSO, London, 1975).

Department of Education and Science, *Education in Schools* (HMSO, London, 1977(1)).

Department of Education and Science, *Curriculum 11–16* (The Red Book)

(HMSO, London, 1977(2)).

Department of Education and Science and 5 Local Education Authorities, *Curriculum 11–16* (HMSO, London, 1981).

Department of Education and Science, *Training for Jobs* (White Paper) (HMSO, London, 1984).

Department of Education and Science, *Better Schools* (HMSO, London, 1985).

Department of Education and Science, *The National Curriculum 5–16; a Consultation Document* (HMSO, London, 1987(1)).

Department of Education and Science, *Speech by the Minister of State at the Annual Conference of the National Association for Education in the Arts, 28.10.87* (1987(2)).

Department of Education and Science, *National Curriculum: Task Group on Assessment and Testing Report* (The Black Report) (HMSO, London, 1988(1)).

Department of Education and Science, *Local Management of Schools* (Coopers & Lybrand) (HMSO, London, 1988(2)).

Department of Education and Science, *National Curriculum Working Group on English: Terms of Reference* (1988(3)).

Department of Education and Science, *Drama from 5 to 16: Curriculum Matters 17*, HMSO, 1989.

Dobson, W. (ed.), *Bolton at the Barbican* (National Association for the Teaching of Drama (NATD)/Longman, London, 1983).

Dunn, J., *Western Political Theory in the Face of the Future* (Cambridge University Press, 1979).

Durkheim, E., *Moral Education* (Free Press, New York, 1961).

Eagleton, T., *Marxism and Literary Criticism* (Eyre Methuen, London, 1976).

Eagleton, T., *Literary Theory* (Basil Blackwell, Oxford, 1983).

Education Reform Act 1988 (HMSO, London, 1988).

Elam, K., *The Semiotics of Theatre and Drama* (Eyre Methuen, London, 1980).

Ellis, J., *Life Skills Training Manual* (Community Service Volunteers, London, 1983).

Eysenck, H. J., *The Psychology of Politics* (Eyre Methuen, London, 1954).

Fairclough, G., *The Play is Not the Thing* (Basil Blackwell, Oxford, 1972).

Finlay-Johnson, H., *The Dramatic Method of Teaching* (Nisbet (undated)).

Fischer, E., *The Necessity of Art*, tr. A. Bostock (Penguin Books, Harmondsworth, 1963).

Freire, P., *Pedagogy of the Oppressed*, tr. M. Bergman Ramos (Penguin Books, Harmondsworth, 1972).

Gadamer, H. G., *Truth and Method*, tr. W. Glyn-Doepel (Sheed & Ward, London, 1975).

Geertz, C., *The Interpretation of Cultures: Further Essays in Interpretive Anthropology* (Basic Books, New York, 1973).

Geertz, C., *Negara: The Theatre State in Nineteenth Century Bali* (Princeton University Press, 1980).

Geertz, C., *Local Knowledge* (Basic Books, New York, 1983).

Gellner, E., *The Psychoanalytic Movement* (Paladin, London, 1985).

Goffman, E., *The Presentation of Self in Everyday Life* (Penguin Books, Harmondsworth, 1969).

Goodridge, J., *Drama in the Primary School* (Heinemann, London, 1970).

Groos, K., *The Play of Man*, tr. E. L. Baldwin (Heinemann, London, 1901).

Gutiérrez, G., *A Theology of Liberation: History, Politics and Salvation*, tr. and ed. Caridad, I. and Eagleson, J. (SCM Press, London, 1974).

Habermas, J., *Knowledge and Human Interest*, tr. J. Shapiro (Heinemann, London, 1971).

Habermas, J., *Theory and Practice* (Heinemann, London, 1974).

Hall, S. and Jacques, M. (eds), *The Politics of Thatcherism* (Lawrence & Wishart, London, 1983).

Hargreaves, D., *The Challenge for the Comprehensive School* (Routledge & Kegan Paul, London, 1982).

Hartnett, A. and Naish, M. (eds), *Education and Society Today* (The Falmer Press, London, 1986).

Health Education Authority, *High Stress Occupations Working Party Report* (June 1988).

Heathcote D., *Drama as Context* (National Association for the Teaching of English, Aberdeen University Press 1980).

Heidegger, M., *Basic Writings* ed. Krell, D. (Routledge & Kegan Paul, London, 1978).

Hempel, C., *Aspects of Scientific Explanation* (The Free Press, New York, 1965).

Hill, C., Reay, B., and Lamont, W., *The World of the Muggletonians* (Temple Smith, London, 1983).

Hodgson, J. (ed.), *The Uses of Drama* (Eyre Methuen, London, 1972).

Hodgson, J. and Richards, E., *Improvisation* (Eyre Methuen, London, 1966).

Holderness, G. (ed.), *The Shakespeare Myth* (Manchester University Press, 1988).

Hollis, M. and Lukes, S. (eds), *Rationality and Relativism* (Basil Blackwell, Oxford, 1982).

Hozier, A. (ed.), *Augusto Boal: Documents on the Theatre of the Oppressed* (Red Letters, London, 1985),

Hull, C., *Principles of Behaviour* (Appleton-Century-Crofts, New York, 1943).

Husserl, E., *Cartesian Meditations: An Introduction to Phenomenology*, tr. Cairns, D. (Martinus Nijhoff, The Hague, 1960).

Inner London Education Authority, *Race, Sex and Class* (Policy Documents) 1983–5.

Inner London Education Authority, *Improving Secondary Schools* (The Hargreaves Report) (1984).

Inglis, F., *The Management of Ignorance* (Basil Blackwell, Oxford, 1985).

Inglis, F., *Popular Culture and Political Power* (Harvester Press, Brighton, 1988).

Johnson, L. and O'Neill, C. (eds), *Dorothy Heathcote: Collected Writings* (Hutchinson, London, 1984).

Klein, M., Heimann, P., Isaacs, S., and Rivière, J., *Developments in Psychoanalysis* (Hogarth Press, London, 1952).

Kogan, M. (ed.), *The Politics of Education: Edward Boyle and Anthony Crosland in Conversation with Maurice Kogan* (Penguin Books, Harmondsworth, 1971).

Lambert, A. and O'Neill, C., *Drama Structures* (Hutchinson, London, 1982).

Lasch, C., *The Culture of Narcissism: American Life in an Age of Diminishing Expectations* (Sphere Books, London, 1980).

Leavis, F. R., *Mass Civilization and Minority Culture* (Cambridge University Press, 1930).

Louch, A., *Explanation and Human Action* (University of California Press, Berkeley 1969).

Lukács, G., *The Meaning of Contemporary Realism*, tr. Mander, J. and N. (Merlin Press, London, 1962).

Lukács, G., *History and Class Consciousness*, tr. Livingstone R., (Merlin Press, London, 1971).

McGregor, L., Tate, M., and Robinson, K., *Learning through Drama* (Heinemann, London 1977).

MacIntyre, A., *Secularization and Moral Change* (Oxford University Press, 1967).

MacIntyre, A., *After Virtue: A Study in Moral Theory* (Duckworth, London, 1981).

McLellan, D., *Marxism and Religion* (Macmillan, London, 1987).

Marx, K., *Selected Writings*, ed. McLellan, D. (Oxford University Press, 1977).

Marx, K and Engels, F., *The Holy Family*, 1845.

Millar, S., *The Psychology of Play* (Penguin Books, Harmondscorth, 1968).

Ministry of Education, *Half our Furture* (The Newsom Report) (HMSO, London, 1963(1)).

Ministry of Education, *Report of the Committee on Higher Education* (The Robbins Report) (HMSO, London, 1963(2)).

Morgan, N. and Saxton, J., *Teaching Drama: 'A mind of many wonders ...'* (Hutchinson, London, 1987).

Morris, B., *The New Curriculum* (HMSO, London, 1967).

Morris, W., *News from Nowhere (1890)*, in *Three Works by William Morris*, ed. Morton, A. (Lawrence & Wishart, London, 1968).

National Curriculum Council, *English for Ages 5 to 16* (Cox Report), Department of Education and Science, 1989.

National Curriculum Council, *The Arts 5 to 16: a Framework for Development*, Longman, 1990.

Nietzsche, F., *Beyond Good and Evil*, tr. Hollingdale, R. (Penguin Books, Harmondsworth, 1973).

Norman, J. (ed.), *Drama in Education: A Curriculum for Change* (National Association for the Teaching of Drama/Kemble Press, 1982).

Pavis, P., *Languages of the Stage* (Performing Arts Journal Publications, New York, 1984).

Pemberton-Billing, R., and Clegg, J., *Teaching Drama* (University of London Press, 1965).

Polanyi, M., *Personal Knowledge: Towards a Post-Critical Philosophy* (Routledge & Kegan Paul, London, 1958).

Polanyi, M., *The Study of Man* (Routledge & Kegan Paul, London, 1959).

Polanyi, M., *Knowing and Being* (Routledge & Kegan Paul, London, 1969).

Positive Images: 1985 Conference Publication (Joint Committee (NATD, NATFHE Drama, NAYT, NADECT, NADA), 1986).

Ricoeur, P., *Hermeneutics and the Human Sciences*, ed. and tr. Thompson, J. B. (Cambridge University Press, 1981).

Robinson, K. (ed.), *Exploring Theatre and Education* (Heinemann, London, 1980).

Ross, M., *The Creative Arts* (Heinemann, London, 1978).

Ross, M. (ed.), *The Development of Aesthetic Experience* (Pergamon, Oxford, 1982).

Rousseau, J.-J., *Politics and the Arts: The Letter to M. d' Alembert on the Theatre*, tr. Bloom, A. (Free Press, Glencoe, Illinois, 1960).

Rowntree, D., *Assessing Students: How Shall We Know Them?* (Harper & Row, New York, 1977).

Russell, W., *Educating Rita* (Samuel French, London, 1981).

Ryle, G., *Collected Papers, Vol. 2: Collected Essays 1929–68* (Hutchinson, London, 1971).

Sartre, J.-P., *Sketch for a Theory of the Emotions*, tr. Mairet, P. (Eyre Methuen, London, 1971).

Sartre, J.-P., *Kean*, tr. Hauser, F. (Davis-Poynter, London, 1972).

Scher, A. and Verrall, C., *100+ Ideas for Drama* (Heinemann, London, 1975).

Self, D., *A Practical Guide to Drama in the Secondary School* (Ward Lock Educational, London, 1975).

Sennett, R., *The Fall of Public Man* (Cambridge University Press, 1977).

Simon, B., *Intelligence, Psychology and Education: A Marxist Critique* (Lawrence & Wishart, London, 1978).

Skidelsky, R., *English Progressive Schools* (Penguin Books, Harmondsworth, 1969).

Slade, P., *Child Drama* (University of London Press, 1954).

Slade, P. *An Introduction to Child Drama* (Hodder & Stoughton, London, 1958).

Stanislavski, C., *My Life in Art*, tr. Robbins, J. J. (Eyre Methuen, London, 1980).

Stanton, G. P. et al., *Developing Social and Life Skills* (Further Education Curriculum Review and Development Unit, 1980).

Stenhouse, L., *Schools Council Humanities Curriculum Project* (Longman, London, 1969).

Taylor, C., *Human Agency and Language: Philosophical Papers 1* (Cambridge University Press, 1985(1)).

Taylor, C., *Philosophy and the Human Sciences: Philosophical Papers 2* (Cambridge University Press, 1985(2)).

Taylor R., *Educating for Art: Critical Response and Development* (Longman, London, 1986).

Thompson, E. P., *The Poverty of Theory* (Merlin Press, London, 1978).

Trilling, L., *Sincerity and Authenticity* (Harvard University Press, 1971).

Trotsky, L., *Leon Trotsky on Literature and Art*, ed. Siegel, P. (Pathfinder Press, New York, 1970).

Vernon, P. E., *Creativity* (Penguin Books, Harmondsworth, 1970).

Wagner, B-J., *Dorothy Heathcote: Drama as a Learning Medium* (Hutchinson, London, 1979).

Walker, B., *Teaching Creative Drama* (Batsford, London, 1970).

Watkins, B., *Drama and Education* (Batsford, London, 1981).

Way, B., *Development through Drama* (Longman, London, 1967).

Weber, M., *Max Weber: Essays in Sociology*, tr. and eds, Gerth, H. and Wright Mills, C. (Oxford University Press, 1946).

Williams, R., *Culture and Society, 1780–1950* (Penguin Books, Harmondsworth 1961).

Williams, R., *The Long Revolution* (Penguin Books, Harmondsworth, 1965).

Williams, R., *Drama from Ibsen to Brecht* (Penguin Books, Harmondsworth, 1973).

Williams, R., *Drama in a Dramatised Society* (Cambridge University Press, 1975).

Williams, R., *Keywords* (Fontana/Croom Helm, Glasgow, 1976).

Williams, R., *Marxism and Literature* (Oxford University Press, 1977).

Williams, R., *Modern Tragedy* (Verso, London, 1979).

Williams, R., *Politics and Letters: Interviews with* New Left Review (Verso, London, 1981).

Winnicott, D. W., *Playing and Reality* (Tavistock Publications, London, 1971).

Witkin, R. W., *The Intelligence of Feeling* (Heinemann, London, 1974).

Wittgenstein, L., *Philosophical Investigations*, tr. Anscombe, G. E. M. (Basil Blackwell, Oxford, 1958).

Wootton, M. (ed.), *New Directions in Drama Teaching* (Heinemann, London, 1982).

Wright Mills, C., *The Sociological Imagination* (Oxford University Press, 1959).

Young, M. (ed.) *Knowledge and Control* (Collier-Macmillan, London, 1971).

INDEX